Pragmatism, Logic, and Law

American Philosophy Series

Series Editor
John J. Kaag, University of Massachusetts Lowell

Advisory Board
Charlene Haddock Siegfried, Joe Margolis, Marilyn Fischer, Scott Pratt, Douglas Anderson, Erin McKenna, and Mark Johnson

The *American Philosophy Series* at Lexington Books features cutting-edge scholarship in the burgeoning field of American philosophy. Some of the volumes in this series are historically oriented and seek to reframe the American canon's primary figures: James, Peirce, Dewey, and DuBois, among others. But the intellectual history done in this series also aims to reclaim and discover figures (particularly women and minorities) who worked on the outskirts of the American philosophical tradition. Other volumes in this series address contemporary issues—cultural, political, psychological, educational—using the resources of classical American pragmatism and neo-pragmatism. Still others engage in the most current conceptual debates in philosophy, explaining how American philosophy can still make meaningful interventions in contemporary epistemology, metaphysics, and ethical theory.

Recent Titles in the Series:
Endurance Sport and the American Philosophical Tradition, by Douglas R. Hochstetler
Pragmatist and American Philosophical Perspectives on Resilience edited by Kelly A. Parker and Heather E. Keith
Reconstructing the Personal Library of William James: Markings and Marginalia from the Harvard Library Collection by Ermine L. Algaier IV
Rorty, Religion, and Metaphysics by John Owens
Ontology after Philosophical Psychology: The Continuity of Consciousness in William James's Philosophy of Mind, by Michela Bella
Richard Rorty and the Problem of Postmodern Experience: A Reconstruction, by Tobias Timm
The Pragmatism and Prejudice of Oliver Wendell Holmes, Jr., edited by Seth Vannatta
Peirce and Religion: Knowledge, Transformation, and the Reality of God, by Roger A. Ward
William James, Moral Philosophy, and the Ethical Life, edited by Jacob L. Goodson
Epistemic Issues in Pragmatic Perspective, by Nicholas Rescher
Loving Immigrants in America: An Experiential Philosophy of Personal Interaction, by Daniel G. Campos
The Religious Dimension of Experience: Gabriel Marcel and American Philosophy, by David W. Rodick
Richard J. Bernstein and the Expansion of American Philosophy: Thinking the Plural, edited by Marcia Morgan and Megan Craig
Aesthetic Transcendentalism in Emerson, Peirce, and Nineteenth-Century American Landscape Painting, by Nicholas L. Guardiano
Pragmatism, Logic, and Law by Frederic R. Kellogg

Pragmatism, Logic, and Law

Frederic R. Kellogg

LEXINGTON BOOKS

Lanham • Boulder • New York • London

Published by Lexington Books
An imprint of The Rowman & Littlefield Publishing Group, Inc.
4501 Forbes Boulevard, Suite 200, Lanham, Maryland 20706
www.rowman.com

6 Tinworth Street, London SE11 5AL, United Kingdom

British Library Cataloguing in Publication Information Available

Library of Congress Cataloging-in-Publication Data Available

ISBN: 978-1-7936-1697-5 (cloth)
ISBN: 978-1-7936-1699-9 (pbk)
ISBN: 978-1-7936-1698-2 (electronic)

To my friends and colleagues in the Society for the Advancement of American Philosophy

Contents

Introduction

The chapters in this book frame a view of legal pragmatism designed to be consistent with pragmatism writ large, tracing it from origins in late nineteenth-century America to the present, covering various issues, legal cases, personalities, and relevant intellectual movements within and outside law. What is their overriding contribution? I will try to sketch an answer in this brief introduction, and outline the book. My challenge is to inform not just readers interested in *legal* pragmatism but also those concerned with pragmatism in general, still taking shape as an intellectual movement.[1]

While I will address pragmatism's relation to legal liberalism, legal positivism, natural law, critical legal studies (CLS), and post-Rorty "neopragmatism," my overall insight lies in viewing legal pragmatism as an exemplar of pragmatism's general contribution to logical theory. In this regard, it bears two connections to fundamental aspects of the western philosophical tradition: first, it extends Francis Bacon's empiricism into contemporary aspects of scientific and legal experience, and second, it is an explicitly social reconstruction of logical induction. Both notions were articulated by John Dewey in *Logic: The Theory of Inquiry* in 1938, and both emphasize the social or corporate element of human inquiry. What this means is: viewing Baconian empiricism as informed by social as well as individual experience (which includes the problems of conflict and consensus), and seeing beyond the Aristotelian model of induction as *immediate* inference from particulars to generals, a model that assumes a consensual objective viewpoint.[2] Pragmatism explores the *actual*, and *extended*, process of corporate

---

[1] See Joseph Margolis, *Pragmatism Ascendent* (Stanford, CA: Stanford University Press, 2012).

[2] John Dewey, *Logic: The Theory of Inquiry* (New York, NY: Henry Holt & Co., 1938), 185; See also Thomas Nagel, *The View from Nowhere* (New York, NY and Oxford: Oxford University Press, 1986).

inference from particular experience to generalization, in law as in science. This includes the necessary process of resolving disagreement and finding (not assuming or positing) similarity among relevant particulars. How this applies to legal interpretation and decision is the subject of this book.

First, it is distinct from the common-sense application of the term "pragmatic" to particular issues or decisions. Legal pragmatism is too readily associated with that approach, as it is most notably by Richard Posner.[3] His "everyday" pragmatism captures important aspects of the immediate judicial task but fails to consider what the young Oliver Wendell Holmes in 1870 called "successive approximation," the incremental construction of doctrine and the necessity of its constant adjustment in the resolution of conflicts among opposing precedents, considered as models of prior thought and action. This is discussed below in chapters 2 and 3. Posner's aversion to any form of "philosophical" pragmatism would apparently dissociate his approach from the logical considerations emphasized here.

As Philip Wiener wrote in 1949,[4] Charles Darwin had a profound effect on the young Cambridge intellectuals in the latter half of the nineteenth century; it was like removing blinders from their eyes as they looked at the long wake of religious and philosophical texts encountered during their recent attendance at Harvard College. Whether or not one agrees with every detail of Darwin's account of the origin and progress of species and traits, once one accepts his cumulative continuity of nature, continuity and transformation should be applicable to all aspects of human culture and knowledge.

There is little doubt that Holmes adopted this general perspective, but what he did with it is unique and surprisingly missing from the accepted record. It is well known that he avoided the term "pragmatism." In 1916, he wrote to Harold Laski, "I should drop [the term] pragmatism . . . because it diminishes the effect or checks the assent you seek from a reader, if you necessarily put a fighting tag on your thoughts."[5] Despite this remark and his other denials of pragmatist associations, careful students of Holmes's legacy have concluded that his approach has ample traits characteristic of pragmatism.[6] What even

---

[3] Richard Posner, *Law, Pragmatism and Democracy* (Cambridge, MA: Harvard University Press, 2003).

[4] *Evolution and the Founders of Pragmatism* (Cambridge, MA: Harvard University Press, 1949).

[5] Holmes to Laski, September 15, 1916, *Holmes-Laski Letters*, M. D. Howe (ed.) (Cambridge, MA: Harvard University Press, 1953), 21.

[6] In *Pragmatism, Law, and Language* (New York, NY: Routledge, 2014), 252, 255, and 257. Vannatta says he "held that the reality and meaning of values and ideals are found in their functional effects" and "that the norms, principles, standards, and rules, which guide the process of judicial inquiry, are generated by the facts of the case as opposed to being a priori principles and as opposed to being nominalistic fictions, lacking any reality at all." Hence Vanatta suggests calling Holmes a "functional realist." Judge Richard Posner, according to Vanatta the "most prolific scholar of legal pragmatism," separates legal pragmatism from philosophical pragmatism. "A court's decision is correct, according to Holmes, as a result of its 'fit' with the entire set of unarticulated cultural

these scholars have missed, however, is the importance for Holmes of transformative continuity through social interaction in the emergence and often agonistic interplay of ideas in the law. That amounts to a view of law as an exemplar of Dewey's account of the actual and extended process of all social induction from experience to general knowledge.[7]

Instead, Holmes has been held imprisoned by, if not indeed responsible for, a long-standing theoretical problem, one that his sense of logical continuity overrides: the realism-formalism antinomy, or "divide" as it is sometimes called. This is the notion that judges have just one legitimate option in the doubtful case: they must find a deductive rationale (in effect a syllogism) that supports the outcome. "Formalism" is the name for the belief that this is an accurate and imperative description of judging, while "realism" is the flip side of this deductive coin: it is the term applied to an approach (or set of approaches) that recognize that syllogistic logic is unavailable amidst complexity and novelty, so legal scholars should be "realistic" and avoid the pretense that courts can always find an authoritative deductive rationale.

Precisely what they should do then is notoriously controversial.[8] No wonder H. L. A. Hart called it the choice between a "noble dream" and a "nightmare";[9] the noble dream refers to the unrealistic ambition that every case, no matter how novel and complex, is determinable, while the nightmare is that difficult cases can be legally "indeterminate." Alone among legal theorists, Holmes advanced an *inductive* account, an original one as I argue in part I, that removes him entirely from Hart's impossible choice, even while responsibility for supporting (if not initiating) a nightmarish case-specific realism has dogged his legacy for over a century. Scholars have long noted his explicit recognition of the unavailability of syllogistic deduction in uncertain cases, but they have missed his extended view of induction. Not only does it fit Dewey's later conception in *Logic: A Theory of Inquiry*, it illuminates the transformational element that Dewey often struggled to clarify.[10]

---

assumptions that give moral credence, including considerations of social advantages that ensue from the decision."

[7] My terminology of "transformative continuity" and "agonistic interplay of ideas" may appear obscure upon initial reading. I hope to clarify these notions in the following chapters, making their reference visible, in the manner in which Holmes saw legal norms derive from successive particular decisions, modified by a feedback loop of adjustment within the affected community. "Agonistic interplay" refers to the (also extended) manner in which opposing precedents contribute to the ultimate resolution.

[8] See Brian Tamanaha, *Beyond the Formalist-Realist Divide* (Chicago, IL: Chicago University Press, 2014).

[9] H. L. A. Hart, *Essays in Jurisprudence and Philosophy* (Oxford: Oxford University Press, 1983), 123f.

[10] Ralph Sleeper, *The Necessity of Pragmatism: John Dewey's Conception of Philosophy* (New Haven, CT: Yale University Press, 1986), 134; Frederic Kellogg, *Oliver Wendell Holmes Jr and Legal Logic* (Chicago, IL: Chicago University Press, 2018), 193–94.

There are two main sources of this misunderstanding, both involving remarks taken without careful examination of context. In 1881, Holmes published his influential treatise *The Common Law*, opening with his famous line, "[t]he life of the law has not been logic; it has been experience," going on to equate logic with deduction and the syllogism. Fourteen years later Holmes addressed the law students at Boston University with the comment that law is "prediction" of public sanctions enforced by the courts; and he also warned them not to overinterpret "moral" language in legal texts. These remarks have been taken to mean that law is a separate domain from morals, and is equivalent to judicial decisions. The full historical record shows that these remarks fit instead into his understanding of the extended process of induction, one that is not judge-centric but recognizes and addresses (through judicial self-restraint) the social dimension of resolving legal disputes.[11]

This is elucidated in part I below. The extended and social nature of real-world induction, which grounds and validates enforceable norms and rules, is the essential insight that explains pragmatism's advantage over alternative contemporary legal theories. Most can be shown to rely on the classical model of immediate inference, and thence to accept the existence of problematic legal "indeterminacy," although they draw different conclusions from it. This is why the historical context in part I is so important, especially the importance of Baconian empiricism and Holmes's 1866 encounter with J. S. Mill's 1843 *A System of Logic*. That context is important for the chapters that follow in Parts II and III, as it explains how Holmes's inductive logic circumvents the problem of "legal indeterminacy."

In sum, while legal pragmatism has often been associated with a behaviorist or consequentialist legal realism, a principal focus on single decisions is inadequate to illustrate Holmes's extended inductivism, which was concerned from 1870 with the continuum of decisions, and from 1873 with the resolution of opposing relevant precedents in the formation and revision of doctrine. Both formalism and realism are strictly judge-centered, while Holmes's inductivism takes in a much wider context of agency.

The following chapters, some revisions of essays over the past twenty years, draw heavily on Holmes to develop this account of pragmatism in the field of law. Notwithstanding his reluctance, the fighting tag is now firmly in place, and helps to organize an important larger conversation over the future of legal theory. A key part of that conversation here lies in correcting mistaken views that restrain legal pragmatism from its full and appropriate influence in philosophy, as well as in the practical judicial arena.

---

[11] See Kellogg, *Oliver Wendell Holmes Jr*, 1–13. The full dimensions of this are distinct from, and richer than, the narrower discourse models of dispute resolution favored by John Rawls, Richard Rorty, and Jurgen Habermas, a topic that I avoid here as it would occupy a separate volume.

Part I connects the seminal late nineteenth-century interactions among the young intellectuals, who would meet in Cambridge, Massachusetts as (according to Peirce) a "Metaphysical Club," bringing their Darwin-inspired responses to early modern philosophy and both law and science, leading to the idea of continuous inquiry guided by a broad social conception of human experience. Their readings and conversations covered science, philosophy, law and logic. Out of this mixture came Peirce's notions of fallibilism, of truth as the result of infinite inquiry, and of the human quest for belief driven by doubt—and also Holmes's less recognized "successive approximation" (a legal version of fallibilism) and his gradual and convergent "specification" of legal liability in diverse areas (addressing how convergence is possible among opposing precedents).

Chapter 1 focuses on the 1860s, after Holmes had returned from the Union Army and engaged with his peers in the issues of philosophy and science, and chapter 2 moves to the early 1870s when he revised Mill's account of logical induction to apply to the continuity of judicial decisions, not just in particular cases but to the broader problems those cases might involve. While legal "realism" and "formalism" focus on the inquiry confronting lawyers and judges in the particular case, Holmes from the outset saw the case in the context of the still inchoate larger issue, the broader dispute or set of disputes, in which the immediate case may represent a stage in a larger continuum of inquiry.

Holmes's legal continuum of inquiry is more fine-grained than Peirce's fallibilism. Both men were practitioners of roles for which they sought a general understanding, in law and science. Holmes's contribution suggests a more concrete understanding of the operation that Peirce called "fallibilism," which Joseph Margolis associates with his "infinite continuum of inquiry." For Margolis, fallibilism is the nerve of Peirce's entire output, but discussion of it "has been remarkably slack—baffled, really—for all the attention it's received through the 150 years in which Peirce's grand output has been dissected."[12] Holmes casts indirect but germane light.

Holmes used the phrase "successive approximation" to describe the process of articulating a consensual approach to new legal problems. His method, I suggest in chapters 2 and 3, was analogous to scientific experimentalism. Holmes more concretely defines the source of doubt, and how inquiry is driven to correct it. If there is a critical difference, it lies in Holmes's greater concern with dispute and conflict, and his recognition of the element of adjustment of patterns of conduct inherent in the resolution of disputes, perhaps focused by his experience in the Union Army. In law, stable belief often arrives, if at all, through a lens of interaction and dispute.

---

[12] Margolis, *Pragmatism Ascendent*, 62.

Chapter 4 places the Holmesean social continuum of inquiry in a Humean context, identifying and filling a gap in Hume's definition of logical induction. That gap is the element of similarity in the conventional explanation of the inductive process. Similarity is for Hume a critical constitutive element in logic: "When we have found a resemblance among several objects, we apply the same name to all of them, whatever differences we may observe in the degrees of their quantity and quality, and whatever other differences may appear among them."[13] The term "we," with which Hume here refers to the perceiver of a similarity, has by implication already found the resemblance and discriminated away the differences.

Chapters 5 through 8 in Part II contain extended comments on influential bodies of theoretical literature in legal theory, covering legal positivism, natural law (in the relevance of moral principle), neopragmatism, interpretivism, liberalism and CLS. Chapter 5, originally a paper in the program of American Philosophical Association, Eastern Division, elucidates the core model of legal positivism as a synchronic mental picture of law as a system of rules, expressed in propositions. This picture implies a boundary, if only an instantaneous one: the textual limit of all currently accepted authoritative propositions. Because there are always new cases, for which deduction is unavailing, this singular yet conventional image leads to adopting or accepting the notion of "legal indeterminacy." An obvious move, drawing on natural law, which Lon Fuller suggested but Ronald Dworkin deployed in 1977 with deliberate skill,[14] is to claim that moral "principles" can and should be mobilized to ground a decision. This was the target of Hart's dismissal as a "noble dream," appealing again to deduction as the only valid logical method for decision.

The problem (that CLS developed into a full-scale attack on liberal jurisprudence) is that no clear preference for any single general principle will reliably emerge in a controversial case—whether or not a deciding judge's opinion may declare it so. CLS came to prominence in the 1970s among law professors and legal scholars, and challenged basic assumptions of liberalism and liberal legal scholarship. Meanwhile, following Richard Rorty's *Philosophy and the Mirror of Nature* in 1979, the analytical linguistic movement invaded pragmatism, casting off any semblance of social inquiry and resurrecting it with the renaming, "neopragmatism."[15]

Chapters 6 and 7 address these movements. Chapter 6 responds to Rorty's 1990 article on the impact of his neopragmatism on law, "The Banality

---

[13] David Hume, *A Treatise on Human Understanding*, Book 1 Part 1 Sec VII para. 7.

[14] Ronald Dworkin, *Taking Rights Seriously* (Cambridge, MA: Harvard University Press, 1977).

[15] The appearance in 1979 of Richard Rorty's *Philosophy and the Mirror of Nature* revived interest in and changed the fortune of pragmatism. The path that led Rorty toward pragmatism was influenced by philosophers outside the classical pragmatic canon and affiliated with logical positivism and analytic philosophy. Within a decade of this renewed interest, differences in tenor and emphasis brought forth a renaming, "neopragmatism," to describe the new perspective.

of Pragmatism and the Poetry of Justice." Chapter 7 addresses Andrew Altman's analysis of CLS in *Critical Legal Studies: A Liberal Critique*. The focal point of CLS is the concept of the rule of law, and CLS scholars argue that the liberal embrace of the rule of law is actually incompatible with other essential principles of liberal political thinking. Thus they charge that liberalism is logically incoherent and that the liberal commitment to the rule of law is implicated in this incoherence. I outline the pragmatist response, to be discussed at length in chapter 9.

The four chapters in Part III address the notorious problem of contemporary law: the controversial "hard" case. The influential Yale law professor Grant Gilmore, in the 1974 Storrs Lecture, published as *The Ages of American Law*, decried our "age of anxiety," caused by "the conundrum into which Holmes and the legal realists had led American law."[16] Law was simply (as Holmes had apparently said) judicial behavior. "If law was simply what the judges did," asked Philip Bobbitt in his own 2014 Storrs Lecture, "then how could they ever—from a legal point of view—be wrong? But judges often contradicted and reversed each other and themselves—so how could they ever be right?" This is the crisis in American law, deriving from the formalist/realist divide, and still alive today in controversies over judicial appointments and ideological judging.

Chapter 9 is an extended analysis of Holmes's pragmatist position responding to CLS originally published in vol. 65 of the Tulane Law Review as "Legal Scholarship in the Temple of Doom: Pragmatism's Response to Critical Legal Studies." Chapter 10 is a paper written during a MacCormick Fellowship at Edinburgh School of Law, "What Precisely is a 'Hard' Case? Waldron, Dworkin, Critical Legal Studies, and Judicial Recourse to Principle." Chapter 11 was "The Abuse of Principle: Analytical Jurisprudence and the Doubtful Case," a response to Robert Alexy, published in *Archiv fur Rechts-und Sozialphilosophie*.

Part IV addresses the future prospects and influence of legal pragmatism. Much of chapter 11 was published in the *European Journal of Pragmatism and American Philosophy* as "American Philosophy and European Social Theory: Holmes, Durkheim, Scheler, and the Sociology of Legal Knowledge." I explore further implications of the social dimension of legal induction, and discuss its relation to sociology of science and Karl Mannheim's sociology of knowledge.

The persistence of deductivism, as the essential operation in legal decisions, is the cause of a legitimacy crisis in Western law, one that reaches manifestly into the partisan political conflict of opposing ideologies, now extending into the process of nominating judges. In failing to perceive the

---

[16] Philip Bobbitt of Columbia Law School spoke in his 2014 Storrs Lecture of an enduring Storrs Lecture forty years earlier by Grant Gilmore, his professor at Yale.

inductive element of the judicial function, legal theory is blind to the importance of Dewey's theory of democratic inquiry. If there is an overriding issue
that will surely motivate both students and scholars of philosophy during the
next generation and beyond, it is the striking comparison between pragmatic
activism and the complacency and quietism that pervade Richard Rorty's
neopragmatism, and indeed much of analytical philosophy. Francis Bacon's
legacy derives from his mission to end the dominance of axiomatic thinking
in Europe. It was clearly intended for adoption in America by the members of
Peirce's famous Metaphysical Club. Peirce's opening comment, at his third
Lowell Lecture in 1866, exclaimed, regarding logical theory, "Our fate hangs
upon it."[17]

---

[17] C. S. Peirce, *Writings of Charles S. Peirce: A Chronological Edition*, Peirce Edition Project (ed.)
(Bloomington, IN: Indiana University Press, 1981), 1:393.

Part I

ORIGINS OF A LOGICAL RECONSTRUCTION

Chapter 1

The Early History

While still at Harvard in 1857, Chauncey Wright (1830–1875) had become a near-obsessive devotee of "Lord Bacon." Francis Bacon (1561–1626) was the prime figure of English experimental science. If he had one overriding message it was that science, and knowledge in general, should proceed with great caution from "axioms." Bacon wrote in 1620 in his *Novum Organum*:

> There are and can be only two ways of inquiry into and discovery of truth. The one flies from the senses and particulars to axioms of the most general kind, and from these principles and their supposed immutable truth, proceeds to judgement and to the discovery of intermediate axioms. And this is the method that is now in use. The other calls forth axioms from the senses and particulars by a gradual and continuous ascent, to arrive at the most general axioms last of all. This latter is the true but untried way.[1]

This is a broad claim, reaching into every domain of human knowledge. As will be seen, it would resonate for Peirce, James, and Holmes regarding scientific, legal, and philosophical method.

Pragmatism has been closely connected with the group called the Metaphysical Club, of which Charles Peirce records the founding in 1871. The suggestion of such a group came from William James in a letter from Europe to Holmes in 1868. Looking back in 1906, Peirce included himself, Holmes, William James, Chauncey Wright, John Fiske, and N. St. John Green, but in two other accounts he omits Holmes. Much has been written about the club's possible influence on Holmes, or his influence on the club,

---

[1] Francis Bacon, *Novum Organum*, Peter Urbach and John Gibson (trans.) (Chicago, IL: Open Court, 1994), 47–8.

but well before 1871, he wrote to James of having supplanted his focus on philosophy with "law—law—law." We should consider what happened before the club: the meetings and readings of its later members.[2]

Pragmatism is often described as a family of perspectives. If it were considered an extended family, Wright was its first member. An accomplished practitioner of science and mathematics, he grew interested in empirical philosophy from reading Francis Bacon's *Novum Organum* and other works after graduation from Harvard in 1857. Wright was energized by Bacon's mission to oppose uncritical axiomatic deduction, as having tended throughout history to control patterns of belief and discourage empirical investigation. He then became interested in the Scottish philosopher William Hamilton, as well as English followers of Bacon, especially John Stuart Mill and William Whewell. He would become a major influence on James, Peirce, Holmes, and the young Harvard-graduated intellectuals who defined the future of the powerful intellectual force later known as pragmatism. The first step toward distinguishing it from other theories and movements is through its origins in Bacon, the founder of experimental empiricism. Wright brought his focus on Bacon to his interlocutors and to the path that it took in English science. It led directly to two other important figures in pragmatism's formation: Whewell and Mill.[3]

The word "pragmatism" was not used by any of the Cambridge intellectuals until much later. The term has gained scope as it has come to encompass a distinct vision of American thought since the nineteenth century, sometimes including Holmes. We should keep in mind, as Bruce Kuklick and others have written, that concerns other than inventing a new perspective took precedence—the context of religious thought in New England, foundational issues raised by European philosophy, and Darwin's work on evolution, influences that are well known. Less familiar are nineteenth-century reflections on the early modern philosophers, especially Berkeley, Hume, Hegel, and Kant, and writers like Thomas Reid, William Hamilton, Herbert Spencer, and — importantly—Whewell and Mill. Darwin's theory of evolution was shaking claims of certainty and led the Cambridge intellectuals to question philosophical premises for the source and nature of concepts, like abstract space, which

---

[2] The Cambridge (Massachusetts) group's concern grew from commitment to scientific progress, dependent upon a correct inductive method. Mill had famously opposed "intuitionism" as a conservative force against reform and the advancement of knowledge, a view derived from Bacon. Wright brought it to Cambridge along with his interest in science. Holmes grew up in a scientific household, his father having written a famous paper on puerperal fever, an exercise in pure induction. With Wright's encouragement, Holmes read texts from the English debate, later using phrases originating with Bacon and Whewell, like "germs" of ideas and the "true idea of induction."

[3] See Laura J. Snyder, *Reforming Philosophy: A Victorian Debate on Science and Society* (Chicago, IL: Chicago University Press, 2006), 33f.

had played a role in Immanuel Kant's eighteenth-century response to British empiricism.[4]

Bacon's own reformist empiricism guided English scientific progress in the period before the American Civil War, and Holmes and several Cambridge friends followed a renewed debate in England over the ground of knowledge and discovery, contextualized by what is now called "early modern philosophy" (seventeenth- to early nineteenth-century writers from Descartes and Hume to Kant and Hegel), debate engaged in by the scientists Whewell, John Herschel, and Charles Darwin, encompassing a vigorous disagreement over scientific method between Whewell and Mill.

Bacon had recently been the focus of Whewell and Herschel as well as Mill, who records in his *Autobiography* that his 1843 *A System of Logic* was motivated to oppose Whewell's account of the role of ideas in the inductive process. The trail of Wright's interest had moved through Bacon and Hamilton to Mill. He had followed the Mill-Whewell debate, major issues from which are reflected throughout his own writings; and Holmes's early reading list includes Hamilton, Herschel, Whewell, and Mill during the period of regular meetings with Wright.[5]

Only Wright, a solitary Cambridge bachelor, who attended Harvard a decade earlier and welcomed Holmes and others to his rooms in Cambridge to discuss contemporary science and philosophy, received explicit recognition (with the exception of Emerson) in Holmes's later correspondence, as "a philosopher of real merit." Wright is now identified as having occupied an influential role in the formation of pragmatism. He was widely admired for his acuteness and depth of understanding, even by Charles Darwin with whom he corresponded. As a friend of the Peirce family, he had engaged in discussions of science and philosophy with the younger Charles since 1857. In that year, Peirce would record that he talked about philosophy with Wright almost every day.[6]

While at law school after his return from the Civil War, Holmes's diary suggests he had regularly talked with Wright from 1865 to 1867, well before the Metaphysical Club, reading books on science and philosophy that track Wright's interests. Holmes's inductive turn, away from John Austin's analytical jurisprudence, came in 1870, before the Club, although there is later

---

[4] Elizabeth Flower and Murray Murphey, *A History of Philosophy in America* (New York, NY: Capricorn, 1977), 372, 536–53, 568–82; Bruce Kuklick, *The Rise of American Philosophy* (New Haven, CT: Yale University Press, 1977), 12–18, 33–35, 94–95. See Murray Murphey's summary of the intellectual/historical context of pragmatism in *C. I. Lewis: The Last Great Pragmatist* (Albany, NY: State University of New York Press, 2005), 2–12.

[5] Eleanor Little, "The Early Reading of Justice Oliver Wendell Holmes," *Harvard Library Bulletin* 8 (1954): 163.

[6] C. S. Peirce, "Essays toward the Interpretation of Our Thoughts," *1909 MS 620, Charles S. Peirce Papers*, Indiana University.

influence of N. St. John Green. Peirce had already drawn on Whewell's "colligation" for his own insight into abduction.[7]

Through Hamilton, Wright and other American intellectuals sought an accommodation between the "common sense" epistemology of Thomas Reid and the
transcendentalism of Immanuel Kant. Wright would draw from Whewell an
extensive knowledge of the prior history of science, from which Whewell cor-
roborated the enduring value of empiricism in a three-volume *History of the
Inductive Sciences* (1840). Wright became a hub of influence reaching many
younger (and some older) intellectuals, including Holmes and Peirce, the spokes
of the wheel also extending to James and Abbot, variously encouraging them
to engage with European writers including Reid, Kant, Hamilton, Mill, and
Whewell—assuming Professor Bowen had not already reached them at Harvard
with his overlapping interests. Bowen had in 1864 published a treatise on logic
reflecting the influence of these writers on philosophical thought in Cambridge.[8]

Holmes later (on April 16, 1876) wrote to Emerson that "law provides
a way to philosophy . . . and I hope to prove it before I die." What exactly
did he mean, and intend, by this? It has not given rise to a consensus among
Holmes's biographers and other commentators. Holmes was not given to idle
remarks during this period of his life, especially to Emerson. What evidence
do we have of Holmes's philosophizing, and its sources, prior to this letter? He would take on the revision of the major legal encyclopedia *Kent's
Commentaries on American Law* in December 1869 and become coeditor of
the *American Law Review* in 1870. The club had nothing to do with Holmes's
inductive turn, as its first statement came in 1870. However, something
similar was involved: a round-robin of (mainly) one-on-one discussions with
interested friends, including later members of the club.

While the decade 1866–1876 was crucial for the full emergence of Holmes's
perspective, I look to the period 1866–1870, before the Metaphysical Club,
for the origin of the inductive turn, and the connection of his emerging legal
thought with "philosophy," both as that term meant to him and as it may mean
to us today. As his appointed biographer Mark De Wolfe Howe observed,
from the moment Holmes went from Harvard to war, he had become con-
vinced that "the instruments of philosophy are to be found in the methods of
science." Essential for evidence of this are Holmes's two pocket daily diary
books of 1866–1867, his lists of books read, and his early theoretical essay
on law published in August of 1870.[9]

---

[7] See, e.g., Peirce, *Writings*, 1:205–23.
[8] Francis Bowen, *A Treatise on Logic* (Cambridge, MA: Sever & Francis, 1864). Holmes was reading Hamilton in 1866, M. Howe, *Justice Oliver Wendell Holmes: The Shaping Years 1841–1870*
(Cambridge, MA: Harvard University Press, 1957), 203.
[9] Holmes, Daily Diaries, 1866–67, Harvard University Archives. That his reading lists were not
comprehensive is indicated by certain works not listed but mentioned in correspondence as "having

Holmes's diary reveals readings on natural science, logic, and philosophy and conversations involving Peirce, James, Wright, John Chipman Gray, Francis Ellingwood Abbot, and others, following his meeting John Stuart Mill and Alexander Bain on a visit to London in 1866. Planning the voyage appears to have moved him to acquire the 1866 diary book, which then recorded his preparations and details of the trip itself, and was maintained afterward in Boston and Cambridge until December 22, 1867, to be succeeded by a spare (and not quite comprehensive) listing of books read until the end of his life. The later reading diary recorded only occasional personal comments (e.g., on June 17, 1872: "Married [to Fanny Dixwell] sole editor of [American] Law Rev. July no. et seq.").

In the brief period in which Holmes kept the daily pocket diaries we get a glimpse into his life, without which the nature and flow of informal associations, and especially Peirce's early thoughts on logic and his attendance at two of Peirce's 1866 Lowell Lectures on induction and scientific method, would be invisible. There is relatively little evidence of influence on his thought from the post-1871 meetings mentioned by Peirce, but there is much in the diaries from the earlier period. Regarding the two men who would later be identified with the founding of pragmatism, Peirce and William James, Holmes's correspondence was effusive in his respect and affection for James in the immediate postwar years, and the diaries note seeking him out to discuss both science and philosophy. He notes attending at least two of Peirce's remarkable 1866 lectures and receiving from Peirce a bound pamphlet of the latter's papers on logic in 1867.

Wright is mentioned in Holmes's 1867 diary on April 22 in the following cursory notes: "Cambridge to see C. Wright on vis viva [a scientific controversy] he wasn't in so I went to H. James." On September 12 the diary reads: "Read Ch. Wright's article on Herb. Spencer—N. A. Rev. Apr/65," and the next day: "Debauch on Philosophy. Read Abbot's two articles Philosophy of Space & Time & The Conditioned & the Uncond. N. A. Review July & Oct 1864." Less than a month later on October 8: "Had some metaphysics with C. Wright—we agreed esp. on Abbot's view of Space." Then, on October 20, 1867:

Went out and had
a long palaver with
Chauncey Wright
also with Wm James
on philosophy—Kant.

---

been consulted" (e.g., William Thomson, *An Outline of the Necessary Laws of Thought*, mentioned in Holmes to William James, December 15, 1867).

Assessing the diary entries and the list of reading (assuming it to be roughly chronological), we find that sometime in 1865–1866, his second year at Harvard Law School, Holmes turned to philosophy amid law texts, first to histories of philosophy by Ritter and Lewes. He quickly added books on scientific subjects (Youmans on physics and chemistry) and then Herbert Spencer's then-influential *First Principles of a New System of Philosophy*, accompanied by a forceful essay by Wright criticizing Spencer for employing an axiomatic argument to reach his sweeping and later discredited conclusions on evolution.

Wright's outlook has been characterized by twentieth-century commentators as a robust evolutionary naturalism, with a comprehensive opposition to all manner of axiomatic argument from teleological principles, such as the attribution of natural design to the universe. Holmes resigned from Harvard Law School in December 1865 to continue law studies as an apprentice to attorney Robert M. Morse in Boston. He was in and out of Cambridge, visiting James and Wright, and appears to have sharpened his focus on science from Wright's extended comments on scientific method in the essay on Spencer. Immediately below their texts in his reading list he notes Whewell's *History of the Inductive Sciences* and "[John] Herschel's Review of same." Then, Morell's *History of European Philosophy* is followed by William Hamilton's *Metaphysics*, and by Mill's then-devastating *Examination of Sir William Hamilton's Philosophy*. He notes more reading on the history of thought, as well as G. W. F. Hegel, before leaving for Europe in April of 1866.

Holmes returned in late August with undiminished philosophical curiosity. The 1867 note recording agreement with Wright "esp. on Abbot's view of space" (the agreement would most likely have been with Wright's criticism of Abbot) was entered on September 12. The diary suggests perhaps a year or so of visits with Wright, and should indicate, to anyone who looks at Abbot's 1864 article "The Philosophy of Space and Time," the complexity of their discussions, which involved the philosophy of William Hamilton, the nature of fundamental abstractions like time and space, and the influence of Immanuel Kant regarding the nature and source of fundamental conceptions that had preoccupied the early modern philosophers.[10]

James, a student at Harvard since 1861, had returned from a field trip in Brazil to his studies of science when Holmes had mustered out of the army in August 1864 to attend law school, and the two engaged in regular discussions until James's voyage to Europe in April 1866, corresponding by mail thereafter. This correspondence is replete with mutual affection and intellectual respect. (Both are strangely missing, on Holmes's side, from the latter's

---

[10] Kuklick, *Rise of American Philosophy*, 93–103; Flower and Murphey, *History of Philosophy*, 549.

later comments in his lengthy correspondence with the English legal scholar Frederick Pollock.[11]) James had earlier befriended Peirce at Harvard in 1861. The spokes of the wheel connecting all three to Wright were established by the end of 1865.

Holmes's diary notes reflect discussions of epistemological issues emerging from the interaction of British empiricism and German idealism, as well as more recent British commentaries on the history and methods of science by Mill, Whewell, and Herschel. A rough indication of the framework of these discussions, at least with James, might be gleaned from James's 1909 Hibbert Lectures, which begins with a "look back into the sixties," several pages of reflection on the American reception during that period of British and German philosophical ideas. Regarding Holmes's mention of Kant on October 20, the diary also notes that while reading Thomas Reid's *Essays on the Intellectual Powers of Man* he borrowed Kant's *Critique of Pure Reason* on September 29 and finished it on November 13.

The discussions with Wright in late October included abstractions like time, space, and causation, and Kant's complex perspective on the putatively innate categories of human thought. Holmes would write two letters to James in Europe assessing Kant's *Critique* roughly a month later. His letters indicate, if not acceptance, comprehension of difficult issues. James apparently did not respond.[12] Peirce in the latter 1860s was on a trajectory originating with a catalyzing impetus on his thought from Kant's *Critique of Pure Reason*. It led him intensively to reexamine the history of Western logic, analyzing the nature of induction and the varieties of the syllogism, and

---

[11] Holmes in 1908 commented to Pollock of James, "I think pragmatism an amusing humbug—like most of William James's speculations, as distinguished from his admirable and well written Irish perceptions of life." Holmes to Pollock, June 17, 1908, in M. D. Howe (ed.), *Holmes-Pollock Letters*, 1:138–39. When Charles Hartshorne began preparing Peirce's Collected Papers in 1927, he wrote Justice Holmes, at eighty-six the only surviving member of the original Metaphysical Club, and received in reply: "I am afraid that I cannot help you much in the way of recollections of Charles Peirce. I think I remember his father saying to me, 'Charles is a genius,' and I remember the august tone in which, at one of the few meetings at which I was present, Charles prefaced his opinion with 'Other philosophers have thought.' Once in a fertilizing way he challenged some assumption that I made, but alas I forget what. But in those days I was studying law and I soon dropped out of the band, although I should have liked to rejoin it when it was too late. I think I learned more from Chauncey Wright and St. John Green, as I saw Peirce very little." Fisch, "Was there a Metaphysical Club in Cambridge?" *Studies in the Philosophy of Charles Sanders Peirce* (Amherst, MA: U. Massachusetts Press, 1964), 10–11.

[12] James's correspondence does not yet provide comparable evidence of interest in philosophy to that of Holmes, until he had passed through a long depression in early 1870 and began studying Kant, first through the work of Charles Renouvier. Kuklick, *Rise of American Philosophy*, 159–64. Holmes was already discussing Kant in the September 1867 meeting with Wright, and Abbot's view of space. In the letters to James in Germany on Kant's Critique, Holmes's reference to William Thomson (as well as to Henry Mansel in the diary) is evidence of the influence of Hamilton. An extended discussion of logic and philosophy in nineteenth-century New England is found in Flower and Murphey, *History of Philosophy*, 365–87.

(likely with Wright as a medium) intersected with Holmes at crucial points in both of their thinking.

The same issues, relating to early modern epistemology, classical logic and scientific method, pervade Peirce's writings and lectures on logic from 1865–1869 (they represent the greater part of Volumes 1 and 2 of the Chronological Edition) and indicate likely topics of conversation among the young Cambridge intellectuals (as James indeed emphasizes in his 1912 essay "A Look Back Into the Sixties"). Thus, the genealogy and foreground of the Club deserves elaboration. John Shook's essay in *The Real Metaphysical Club* emphasizes the importance of Wright as a hub of influence, whom the others had known in the decade before the formal Club. Shook emphasizes the round-robin aspect of prior informal discussions:

> After 1866, their interactions enlarged and accelerated. Holmes was a regular visitor at the James house, Wright and Fiske were frequent interlocutors, Wright was corresponding with a classmate of Peirce's, Frank Abbot (Harvard 1859), about space and time, and Peirce and Wright were debating over Mill and Kant on a practically daily basis (Wiener 1949, 43). While traveling in Europe, James wrote to Holmes in January 1868 to again confess his longing for deep conversation, and he proposed a plan of action [establishing a philosophical society].[13]

Holmes's own diaries and reading lists for 1865–1868 support and illuminate this. What were the issues already on the table before the Club's early meetings? There is a tendency among scholars to focus on topics identifiable with the actual Club, although they are not well evidenced; Peirce's famous *Popular Science Monthly* essays are neither conclusive nor comprehensive regarding the likely conversations in and around the Club. We know that Wright's path of interest encompassed Mill's debates with Whately over the syllogism, and over the nature of induction and scientific discovery with Whewell, unlike Mill a distinguished scientist, who had wrestled with explaining the source of fresh scientific ideas and theories.

These topics engaged Peirce's attention from 1865 to 1869, as shown by his papers detailing his 1865 Harvard lectures and his 1866 Lowell Lectures. At least two of the Lowell Lectures were attended by Holmes and one by James, and their contents are found in Peirce's papers in volume 1 of the Chronological Edition. Those of 1869, which James says were given without notes, are only summarized in volume 2 (yet Whewell is again favorably

---

[13] Frank X. Ryan, Brian Butler, and James Good, eds., *The Real Metaphysical Club* (Albany, NY: SUNY Press 2019), xiv–xv.

appraised). I suggest that Peirce's logic lectures, especially his comments on induction and the Mill-Whewell debate, are at least as important a source as his two famous *Popular Science Monthly* articles.[14]

Thus, the continuity from earlier English philosophy to the pre-Club Cambridge conversations might well be captured in a probing question posed by the astronomer John Herschel in his 1840 review of Whewell's *History of the Inductive Sciences,* which Holmes read in 1866:

> What is the nature of general and of universal propositions? Are all true universal propositions necessary truths, or is any truth, or all truth, necessary? What is the act or series of acts of the mind in constructing general propositions, and when constructed, in what manner do we rest in them as expressive of truth?[15]

Here the issues of early modern philosophy are reconsidered from the perspective of contemporary science: the relation of induction and deduction, how general propositions and concepts emerge from particular judgments and experiments, how they become and remain entrenched, indeed the nature and stability of fundamental categories of thought.

How might this apply to law? Holmes had read Herschel's review in 1865 and his path in jurisprudence reflects the urgency of similar questions. His 1868 letters to James would presage a rejection of Kant's commitment to unchanging essential categories, and his writing from 1870 advances an original approach to induction.[16]

While Peirce had accepted Kant's notion of transcendent categories of human thought, and would adopt a revisionary approach to them, Holmes was rejecting Kant's basic approach in his correspondence with James in December 1867.[17] In late 1866, after meetings with Mill and Bain in London, Holmes's interest in scientific method and the debates of Western philosophical logic was further stimulated by two lectures by Peirce, on deduction, induction, and scientific method. This background is key to interpreting Holmes's attendance at the lectures and their bearing on his consequential "inductive turn."

[14] Ryan et al., *The Real Metaphysical Club*, 119–45.

[15] John Herschel, "Whewell on the Inductive Sciences," *Review of the History and the Philosophy*, *Quarterly Review* 68 (1841): 177–238.

[16] See chapter 4 infra.

[17] Holmes to James, December 15, 1867: "Hoc nota as to what I conceive a fundamental error of Kant on his own principles (always protesting, as they say in pleading, his whole philosophy is unsound)." The letter continues with several objections to Kant's response to Hume regarding synthetic a priori judgments. Ignas K. Skrupskelis and Elizabeth M. Berkeley, eds., *Correspondence of William James* (Charlottesville, VA: University of Virginia Press), 4:236–40.

PEIRCE'S FOURTH LOWELL LECTURE ON MILL

On October 24, 1866, Holmes attended the first in the series of twelve Lowell Lectures by Charles S. Peirce in Boston, Massachusetts. Peirce's topic for the series was "The Logic of Science, or, Induction and Hypothesis." The first lecture, an examination of types of deductive syllogism, Peirce introduced apologetically as "an exceedingly dry subject which I cannot hope to make entertaining; but the great importance of which to everyone who is to use his mind at all ought to render it interesting . . . Logic is a much abused science. Like Medicine, Law, and in short any branch of knowledge which has important practical bearings, it is . . . no more perfect than any other product of humanity and we have the same right to be dissatisfied with its present state that we have with everything else that we are in a condition to improve. (W1: 358, Peirce's emphasis) Peirce proceeded to a demonstration:

> I have here a bag of balls. I shake them up well; and draw out one. It is red. I draw out another. It is red. I shake them up again and draw out another. It is red, again. Another: red. Another; red. One more: still red.
>
> Now I suppose you have no doubt that almost all the balls in that bag are red. Why? Upon the correct answer to that question much depends. *Our fate hangs upon it* [my italics]. All difficult questions require an understanding of the reason of our faith in experience as a witness to the future and unexperienced [*sic*].

This lecture proceeded from the demonstration to a discussion, one that would continue through November 3, when Holmes returned to the lectures, on the grounds of inductive inference, with many critical references to Mill.[18]

Holmes's daily diary, kept for just two years in the period following his return from the Civil War, reveals that he would attend only the first four of Peirce's lectures, which included diagramming and analyzing various Aristotelean and Theoprastian syllogisms, comments on Zeno, John Locke, Augustus De Morgan, William Hamilton, David Hume, James and [John] Stuart Mill, eventually (in Lecture Three) producing the bag full of colored balls and removing them one by one to demonstrate the experience of induction. His fourth lecture moved from the bag of balls to an extended critique

---

[18] The leading and well-known skeptical objection to induction had famously come in the eighteenth century from David Hume: that the only way to validate inductive inference was through a circular argument—through inductive inference itself. David Hume, "Skeptical Doubts Concerning the Operations of the Understanding," in *An Inquiry concerning Human Understanding*, 1748, secs. 4 and 5. Having devoted most of his time to an examination of the notion of validation through the concept of probability, Peirce announced his intention to devote his next lecture (which Holmes would attend) to "another common answer to our question." Peirce, *Writings*, 1:396.

of J. S. Mill's treatment of the syllogism in *A System of Logic*.[19] That lecture began with Peirce again posing the question of when red balls successively removed from the bag would lead his audience to any inference that other balls in the bag were red; that is, when successive objects encountered in experience would presumably exhibit similar qualities. Here he turned to the other "common answer" (relied upon by Hume and Mill) to the problem of validating induction: the idea that its grounding (in similarity) is supported by a basic aspect of "nature," or the natural world, which appears to be filled with "natural" similarities (like red balls, for example, though of course they have been manufactured by humans and hence may only be presumed similar).

This idea is essential in Mill's *A System of Logic*, and Peirce's fourth lecture was an extended critique of Mill, from his treatment of the syllogism to his thesis that inductive inference could be explained by "natural" uniformities. The matter of concern to Peirce was subtle. As one red ball after another was removed from the bag, Peirce raised questions regarding the process of recognition, by those observing the process, of a common nature in the experience of repeated events, which encompasses both similarity in quality but also in time, or regularity. At what point in human experience is both *similarity*, and its corollary *regularity*, suggested, hypothesized, recognized, established, relied upon? And why? And *how*?[20]

On November 14, after finishing other reading already underway, Holmes borrowed Mill's *Logic* from the Boston Athenaeum and immediately read it through. What was the impact of Peirce's comments, and the reading of Mill's *Logic*? Peirce's extended November 3 commentary on Mill's arguments had addressed Mill's having left the problem of induction yet *unexplained*, in his idea that the inference to generality is automatic and grounded in "natural" similarities. Holmes four years later came to emphasize a view of legal induction that engages the problematic of similarity as it is encountered

---

[19] Holmes first attended Peirce's second lecture on October 27, 1866, in the company of John Chipman Gray. The subject was a survey of various forms of the syllogism; the diary records discussing "logic" with Gray immediately after the lecture. Besides Gray, Chauncey Wright may also have encouraged Holmes to attend (Wright "thought more of [Peirce's] ability than that of any one he knew"). Perhaps James did so as well, as he accompanied Holmes to the fourth lecture on November 3. Soon after, in a letter to his sister Alice on November 14, James wrote that he had gone with Holmes "[t]o C. S. Peirce's Lecture of wh. I cd. not understand a word but rather enjoyed the sensation of listening to for an hour. I then turned in to OW Holmes's [family house in Boston] and wrangled with him for another hour." Holmes had planned to attend the third lecture but wrote in the diary on that date (the thirtieth) that he "[h]ad to cut C. Peirce's lecture on logic to vote at Ward meeting. Soldier's bounty business wh. I am against."

[20] Peirce, *Writings*, 1:404: "Suppose I were to open a book and look at seven pages, and were to find that the first letter upon each of these pages was a vowel. I should not conclude that every page of the book began with a vowel; because that would be even more extraordinary than that the first 7 pages that I lit upon began with vowels."

in the law. Though he never acknowledged the influence of Peirce, two clues might be taken from the two lectures recorded in Holmes's diary.

How does a legal case—before it is decided—compare to a colored ball? Both are particulars appearing in succession before the observer. A comment by Peirce, in the first lecture attended by Holmes, warned against "abusing" the syllogistic form of argument, which utilizes general propositions that often take similarity for granted. According to his notes, Peirce had said: "[T]o say that If the wind is east the barometer rises, is equivalent to saying Every east wind makes the barometer rise. But such a transformation will not enable us to throw arguments into syllogistic form." The example he gave was:

If the wind is east the barometer rises
The wind is east
The barometer rises.

The problem, Peirce noted, is that "we talk here of *occasions* instead of *things* as in ordinary propositions; and the objects which our terms denote are *bounded* by dates not by *positions*." (Peirce's italics) Legal disputes too are occasions bounded by dates, not things bounded by position, and gathering them together in legal analysis or interpretation might also not be (in Peirce's sense) an ordinary (i.e., *thing*-like) proposition.

The second clue, in lecture four, is Peirce's extended commentary on Mill's insistence on thought moving exclusively "from particulars to particulars." Given that nature is not commonly prearranged, like colored balls in a bag, the question arises: Where, then, does the perception of similarity or likeness derive? Mill, claims Peirce, must rely heavily on a direct, somehow *immediate* sense of the existence of "natural" kinds, an implicit assumption of sheer pre-reflective uniformities in the natural world. Peirce expresses several doubts about this assumption, such as "It must be admitted that there are exceptions, to almost any rule. Thus many of the characters which seem to belong to a class universally only belong to part of it. We do not know how far this limitation extends; it seems probable that there really are natural classes and that nearly everything belongs to one. But does this bare circumstance constitute any uniformity?"[21]

---

[21] Peirce, *Writings*, 1:419; his extended commentary on Mill, the second lecture attended by Holmes and James, was on November 3, 1866. It opened with the following reference to the removal of red balls from a bag:

> Gentlemen and Ladies, At the last lecture we asked ourselves an important question. Having taken a bag of balls, we drew seven from it and found them all red; whereupon we judged that nearly all the balls in the bag were red. The question then arose why we know those balls we have not seen to be red? Before entering upon this question, we examined

Taken together, the two lectures illuminate the problem of finding similarity in *occasions*. Holmes's early texts address Mill's thesis in light of Peirce's doubts, examined in the context of the history of the common law. Legal precedents are the record of judgments from prior occasions. They are successions of judgments that, in a unique fashion, have been decided from "particular to particular." As he notes in 1870, the notion of similarity follows as a *practical* matter: "It is only after a series of determinations on the same subject-matter, that it becomes necessary to 'reconcile the cases,'

---

it to ascertain whether it had any meaning and if so what. We found it to mean, does this argument come under the general head of syllogistic arguments such as we have examined hitherto, and if so what is its specific difference from other syllogisms which only explicate knowledge and so not add to it; or does it differ from syllogistic argument, and if so what are the relations of the two modes of inference, and what are the common characters of inference in general? (1:407).

Peirce's Lowell Lectures, titled "The Logic of Science; or, Induction and Hypothesis," began on the evening of Wednesday, October 24, 1866, and continued on Wednesday and Saturday evenings until December 1. Holmes's diary entries suggest that he, John Gray, and James found other occupations on the successive evenings after November 3. Holmes's diary notes no further attendance at the lectures during the weeks following. On the date of the next (fifth) lecture, he notes attending a case in the Superior Court with Shattuck and having "Begun Bowen's Polit. Econ. in horsecar going to Cambridge." He would finish Bowen on Tuesday, November 13, and on Saturday the seventeenth borrowed Mill's System of Logic from the Boston Athenaeum. On November 3, Holmes would have heard Peirce advance his own answer to the question of balls in the bag. "Finally we have seen to use the expression of Plato that syllogism never moves a step beyond its starting point—the conclusion is implicitly stated in the premises—while scientific inference passes not a little but infinitely beyond the premises." Peirce went on to distinguish the three forms of inference, using the syllogistic form. Simplified (Peirce used a number of examples), these are as follows:

Deduction
The balls in the bag are red
These balls come from the bag
These balls are red
Induction
The balls drawn from this bag are red
These balls are red
These balls come from the bag
Hypothesis
These balls are red
The balls in the bag are red
These balls come from the bag

The scientific process employs all three. "Induction is the process by which we find the general characters of classes and establish natural classifications. . . . Hypothesis alone affords us any knowledge of causes or forces, and enables us to see the why of things." 1:428. It is uncertain but explanatory and "ampliative." Hypothesis introduces new ideas; deduction serves to explore its consequences; induction then serves for testing them. Peirce's notes to a proposed 1865 lecture record his view that "Aristotle conceives of no other induction than that which is derived from the major premise of the first figure. Now, there is only one kind of induction which can be thrown into this form; and this is no other than induction by simple enumeration [Peirce's italics]. Bacon therefore was right when he said that Aristotle gave the rules for this form only" (1:265).

as it is called, that is, *by a true induction* [my italics] to state the principle which has until then been obscurely felt. And this statement is often modified more than once by new decisions before the abstracted general rule takes its final shape." The phrase "true idea of induction" originates with Bacon and was repeatedly used by Whewell. Holmes's "true induction" is a *social* induction.

Four years later, Lecture Four may have born indirect legal fruit. The passage from Mill's Logic commenting on Lord Mansfield would resonate in Holmes's first essay on legal *logic*, gain traction in his early essays on legal theory, and lead a decade later to an emphatic concern in the common law with "the paradox of form and substance in the development of the law":

> In form its growth is logical. The official theory is that each new decision follows syllogistically from existing precedents. But just as the clavicle in the cat only tells of the existence of some earlier creature to which a collarbone was useful, precedents survive in the law long after the use they once served is at an end and the reason for them is forgotten. The result of following them must often be failure and confusion from the merely logical point of view. (Holmes 1881, 35)

This marks a full expression of his philosophy as it had developed by 1881. While retaining a pretense of Aristotelian deduction, law embodies an evolving system of classification, continually adapting to normative human demands as new traits are introduced and old ones shrugged off.

Holmes stressed that the process of legal classification appears more analytical than it is, in the sense that consistency always seems to have been discovered, not made.

> The truth is, that law hitherto has been, and it would seem by the necessity of its being is always approaching and never reaching consistency. It is for ever [*sic*] adopting new principles from life at one end, and it always retains old ones from history at the other which have not yet been absorbed or sloughed off. It will become entirely consistent only when it ceases to grow.[22]

Many years later, Holmes compared his jurisprudential theory to anthropology:

> It is perfectly proper to regard and study the law simply as a great anthropological document. It is proper to resort to it to discover what ideals of society have been strong enough to reach that final form of expression, or what have been the

---

[22] O. W. Holmes, *The Common Law* (Boston, MA: Little Brown, 1881), 36.

changes in dominant ideals from century to century. It is proper to study it as an exercise in the morphology and transformation of human ideas.[23]

Here we find what I have called Holmes's legal fallibilism (or, in his words, "successive approximation") elucidated as a mechanism of an evolutionary theory of knowledge. I have traced its roots at least in part to Peirce's 1866 Lowell Lectures, critiquing Mill's view of the syllogism.

Peirce had begun his examination of Mill's doctrine of induction in reference to his experiment with the bag of balls, having removed seven of them at random, all appearing to be the same color. How, he asked, do we infer that the others in the bag are also red? Mill held that "it is essentially an inference from one instance to another." "Suppose, now, that we ask Mr. Mill this question which we have put to ourselves in reference to these balls. What is the Ground of Induction? His answer will be, it is the Uniformity of Nature. It is to the examination of this reply that I propose to devote the remainder of this lecture."[24] Peirce challenged Mill's position for circularity: "to make our warrant for induction (that is his phrase) proved by induction (again his phrase) he falls into that common fallacy called "begging the question.""[25] Peirce's point goes to the essence of Mill's disagreement with Whewell, where Mill deflated the role of hypothesis in the observer's understanding of individual facts. From where, then, does the sense of similarity derive?

Mill's position requires falling back on the notion that observed uniformities are natural, which David Hume had posited as implicit in induction.[26] "Now in opposition to this," notes Peirce in 1866, "I would observe that there are obviously many more relations in nature which are totally irregular than of those which are uniform."[27] This observation was followed by the comment, "Every student of physics knows that a law which is exactly conformed to in nature without interference from other laws is almost if not quite unknown. Every law that is discovered therefore is found to after a few years not to be exact."[28] Peirce's comments on Whewell a year earlier in his Harvard Lectures of 1865 are undeniably sympathetic to "colligation" between scientific facts and ideas, and suggest its influence on his later references to fallibilism and abduction. Yet, as I have suggested, Holmes's immersion in legal research led to a distinct perspective, reflecting the problem of resolution of ongoing disputes in the law.

---

[23] Oliver Wendell Holmes, "Law in Science and Science in Law," in Sheldon Novick (ed.), *The Collected Works of Justice Holmes* (Chicago, IL: Chicago University Press, 1995 [1899]), 3:407.

[24] Peirce, *Writings*, 1:413.

[25] Peirce, *Writings*, 1:414.

[26] Don Garrett, *Hume* (London and New York, NY: Routledge, 2015), 206–7.

[27] Peirce, *Writings*, 1:417.

[28] Peirce, *Writings*, 1:420.

Assuming Whewell's influence on both men, colligation takes on a more pronounced social dimension with Holmes. As noted earlier, legal judgments are not objects with extension, like colored balls in a bag; they are more like the "occasions" of Peirce's Lecture Two. And, the gradual assessment of legal disputes, and their resolution, is rarely limited to a single mind, or even a succession of single minds. Colligation involves an ongoing community of reflecting and responding agents. A single legal decision is by no means the whole story of the resolution of a legal problem. An adequate resolution of doubt must extend to the entire community of affected actors. The final colligation, as in a complicated question like the legality of affirmative action, assisted suicide, or abortion, may take years or even generations, and (as Holmes wrote in 1870) "embodies the work of many minds, and has been tested in form as well as substance by trained critics whose practical interest it is to resist it at every step"[29]

Pragmatic fallibilism, then, is a social phenomenon, denoting the provisional nature of knowledge as it applies to discrete problems as they are progressively understood and defined. Whewell's use of colligation to describe the emergence of laws and concepts in science fits with the social element of pragmatist thought. In Whewell's wake, law and science may come to be seen as branches of the sociology of knowledge. Legal and scientific knowledge can be viewed broadly as forms of community inquiry, focusing on the primacy of cases and exemplars in the process of intersubjective classification, and on the dual role of concepts and theories in both guiding the conduct of professional inquirers and framing and maintaining the coherence and consistency of both expert and general belief.

---

[29] Holmes, "Codes, and the Arrangement of the Law," [1870] *Collected Works* 1:212.

Chapter 2

Induction in Law and Science

Almost everyone knows Lord Mansfield's advice to a man of practical good sense, who, being appointed governor of a colony, has to preside in its courts of justice, without previous judicial practice or legal education. The advice was to give his decision boldly, for it would probably be right, but never to venture on assigning reasons, for they would almost infallibly be wrong.

—John Stuart Mill, *A System of Logic*, 1843

The above passage,[1] from J. S. Mill's influential *A System of Logic*, is part of Mill's contribution in the nineteenth century to a debate (with Joseph Whately) over whether the logical syllogism "is, or is not, a process of inference; a progress from the known to the unknown: a means of coming to a knowledge of something which we did not know before." Mill employs a narrative about William Murray, First Earl of Mansfield, to support his contention that reasoning is inaccurately depicted by the classic syllogistic form. Rather than being informed by generals, "[a]ll inference is from particulars to particulars." The formal syllogism, says Mill, adds nothing to logical thought: "Not one iota is added to the proof by interpolating a general proposition." Mill continues:

Since the individual cases are all the evidence we can possess, evidence which no logical form into which we choose to throw it can make greater than it is; and since that evidence is either sufficient in itself, or, if insufficient for the one purpose, can not be sufficient for the other; I am unable to see why we should be

[1] John Stuart Mill, *A System of Logic Ratiocinative and Inductive* (London: Longmans, Green, Reader & Dyer, 1872), 2:217.

forbidden to take the shortest cut from these sufficient premises to the conclusion, and constrained to travel the "high priori road," by the arbitrary fiat of logicians.[2]

The illustrative example (Mansfield's advice to the colonial governor sitting as local judge) is drawn from law—specifically from judicial practice. This passage relates to my subject, the social dimension of inductive thinking, with regard to the disparate fields of law and science, as viewed in the formative years of pragmatism. Mill's Lord Mansfield story suggests the difficulty of applying syllogistic inference to unique disputes for the individual observer. It also raises a question regarding induction: what is the source of a general inference from accumulated particular judgments? Given Peirce's doubts regarding directly perceived similarities, how does an inquiring mind draw any practical inference? The young Oliver Wendell Holmes, immersed in the records of actual cases, would suggest an explanation.

The syllogism models how the mind operates to justify knowledge of indisputably similar facts; but judges are engaged in resolving disputed facts. They are also part of a community of inquiry, consisting of other judges, lawyers, and indeed the parties affected by the disputes in question. Influenced by peers in Cambridge, perhaps also by his recent experience in the Civil War, Holmes looked to the effects of society on thought, and the question of how a community resolves doubt and reaches conclusions. Max Fisch noted in 1942 that half the membership of the early Metaphysical Club consisted of scientists and half lawyers, and that the two perspectives informed each other. The passage from Mill connects the pragmatist interest in the logic of science with the logic of law, in a common vision of inquiry.

Holmes's principal work, *The Common Law* (1881), notably begins with the famous passage, "The life of the law has not been logic: it has been experience. The felt necessities of the time, the prevalent moral and political theories, intuitions of public policy, avowed or unconscious, even the prejudices which judges share with their fellow-men, have had a good deal more to do than the syllogism in determining the rules by which men should be governed."[3] This community-conscious comment warrants a look at the early period of Holmes's writing to explore his thought about the syllogism. In 1870, we find Holmes, in a formative essay on law, repeating Mill's story of Lord Mansfield's comment, in a text which addresses the relationship of particulars and generals in the law:

It is the merit of the common law that it decides the case first and determines the principle afterwards ... In case of first impression, Lord Mansfield's

---

[2] Mill, *A System of Logic*, 2:214.
[3] Holmes, *The Common Law*, 1.

often-quoted advice to the business man [*sic*] who was suddenly appointed judge, that he should state his conclusions and not give his reasons, as his judgment would probably be right and the reasons certainly wrong, is not without its application to more educated courts. It is only after a series of determinations on the same subject-matter, that it becomes necessary to "reconcile the cases," as it is called, that is, by a true induction to state the principle which has until then been obscurely felt. And this statement is often modified more than once by new decisions before the abstracted general rule takes its final shape. A well settled legal doctrine embodies the work of many minds, and has been tested in form as well as substance by trained critics whose practical interest it is to resist it at every step.[4]

Here, Holmes appears to have absorbed Mill's rejection of the syllogism and his vision of "reasoning from particulars to particulars." But the relation of particulars to generals is different. Holmes adds an element of the emergence of generals from particulars, entirely missing from Mill's account. Whereas Mill had set forth his argument as a rejection of classical logical form, Holmes goes on to address how, in an historical simulation, general rules are attained in a progression from particular judgments to consensually negotiated generals. It would occupy a key place in his thought and career, a vision that he would much later characterize as showing the "morphology of human ideas," or how the common law might be viewed as an historical study in the way society thinks.

What Holmes adds is an addendum to Mill's "Not one iota is added to the proof by interpolating a general proposition."[5] Where Mill simply dismisses that assumption, Holmes seeks a deeper explanation of the relation of particular judgments to general propositions. Focusing on the nature and origin of the general itself, Holmes attributes its emergence to a "series of determinations on the same subject." These are not already given, as they seem in the classic example "all men are mortal," but represent separate judgments in varying circumstances by a community of inquirers, those that form the disparate courts of law.

The topic of interest to Mill was a simple confusion over logical form; the general proposition "all men are mortal" is but a set of unquestionably comparable particulars. But what if the particulars are not patently comparable, as in a set of novel situations or judgments? Then it is certainly not appropriate to "take the shortest cut from premises to conclusion," as Mill puts it. Holmes has highlighted a distinct problem, that of social classification and the emergence of consensus. If the very "general" in question is yet unestablished, a

---

[4] Holmes, "Codes," 212.
[5] Mill, *A System of Logic*, 2:214.

new realm of issues is opened up. Instead of how the individual thinks, it is how society thinks, how new generalized beliefs are formed within the inevitable conflict of perceptions and views.

THE NATURE OF INDUCTION

The debate between Mill and Whewell is nearly forgotten today, even though recently analyzed in detail by Laura Snyder.[6] It was fresh in the minds of the early Metaphysical Club, and it is a necessary resource to put the origins of pragmatism in full perspective. Recovering this perspective now is difficult, especially given the recent transformation of pragmatist philosophy by a dominant analytical attitude, flourishing (even while diverse) with W. V. Quine, Richard Rorty, Robert Brandom, and others. An aid to recovering the earlier perspective is Whewell's own preface to the second edition of his *Philosophy of the Inductive Sciences*:[7]

On the subject of this doctrine of a Fundamental Analysis, which our knowledge always involves, I will venture here to add a remark, which looks beyond the domain of the physical sciences. This doctrine is suited to throw light upon Moral and Political Philosophy, no less than upon Physical. In Morality, in Legislation, in National Polity, we have still to do with the opposition and combination of two Elements; of Facts and Ideas; of History, and an Ideal Standard of Action; of actual character and position, and of the aims which are placed above the Actual. Each of these is in conflict with the other; each modifies and moulds the other. We can never escape the control of the first; we must ever cease to strive to extend the way of the second. In these cases, indeed, the Ideal Element assumes a new form. It includes the Idea of Duty. The opposition, the action and re-action, the harmony at which we must ever aim, and can never reach, are between what is and what ought to be; between the past or present Fact, and the Supreme Idea. The Idea can never be independent of the Fact, but the Fact must ever be drawn towards the Idea. The History of Human Societies, and of each Individual, is by the moral philosopher, regarded in reference to this Antithesis; and thus both Public and Private Morality becomes an actual progress towards Ideal Form; or ceases to be a moral reality. The passage summarizes a thesis regarding the relation of the particular to the general in the historical progress of science, Whewell's "doctrine of a Fundamental Analysis," and claims that it should "throw light upon Moral and Political Philosophy, no less than upon

---

[6] Snyder, *Reforming Philosophy*.
[7] William Whewell, *Philosophy of the Inductive Sciences, Founded Upon Their History* (London: John W. Parker, 1847), x–xi.

Physical." As such it might be seen as a call to joining the two disparate areas of inquiry that the club, and in particular Holmes, would follow.

What was Whewell's thesis? As noted above, it is the idea of a reciprocal and research-centered growth of knowledge created by a tension between the particular and the general: the opposition, interaction, and eventual colligation (combination or negotiation) of the two critical elements, "facts and ideas." These, he says, tend to be seen as in "conflict" with each other, but over time "modify and mould" each other. Moreover, the tension between them is itself transformative; as inquiry progresses, "the Ideal Element assumes a new form." Further, they progress toward a "harmony at which we must ever aim, and can never reach ... The Idea can never be independent of the Fact, but the Fact must ever be drawn towards the Idea."[8]

The epistemic context implied by this is social rather than individual. Whewell implies a process engaging an extended community of inquirers, both physically and chronologically. Moreover, he insists that it is applicable not just to natural science but to moral and political philosophy. Given that Whewell's work was read and discussed in the semi-organized meetings of Metaphysical Club members, and clearly influenced Peirce's notion of abduction and fallibilism, it may also have supported Holmes's 1870 idea of "successive approximation." The precise genealogy of a common perspective among the Cambridge intellectuals is elusive, but my purpose here is to highlight a common thread: understanding the social dimensions of knowledge, and the relation of intersubjective classification to the resolution of doubt and uncertainty.

The epistemic context of social classification is diachronic and transitional, whereas the syllogism is synchronic and deductive. For the latter, doubt is largely a comparative failure of fit. For the former, it is a matter of provisional and responsive adjustment to the arrangement of a changing order. For Mill, the reason why Lord Mansfield's hypothetical decision-maker should "never venture on assigning reasons" is itself inexplicable; but for Holmes, it is to be understood as part of the extended inquiry, leading toward the distinctive future significance of a novel problem. The situation itself is new, a "case of first impression," having critical aspects yet unclassified. The bearing of particular to general for Holmes is not one of logical relation but consensual emergence, integration from repeated experience into a dynamic and always emergent system of order. This attitude implies a distinct approach to uncertainty, as novel experience yet to be integrated within a moving system of classification.

---

[8] Whewell, *Philosophy*, xi.

Prior to the period in which the Metaphysical Club was active, Holmes, in the 1870 essay in which he referred to Mansfield, described the process of common law interpretation as proceeding by "successive approximation." While he did not reiterate this term, the concept behind it reappears throughout his career, woven into his conception of the judicial role in legal interpretation generally, whether strictly engaging common law, or even aspects of statutory and constitutional law. "New cases will arise which will elude the most carefully constructed formula. The common law, proceeding, as we have pointed out, by a series of successive approximations—by a continual reconciliation of cases—is prepared for this, and simply modifies the form of its rule."[9] What might here be called Holmes's "legal fallibilism" is, like Peirce's, a response to new experience: no general formulation can ever be "final." A flexible system of law requires constant retrospective reclassification of disputes. This is assumed by the common law tradition: the day-to-day and case-by-case operation of English and American courts of law. This argument requires holding in abeyance the conventional conception of law as dominated by legislation, with the mechanism of social choice through law deriving from a continuum of inquiry.

In an ambiguous area the common law process begins with particular judgments. It is a process parallel to that of Peirce's community of scientists engaged in the exploration of a common and ongoing, but specific, problem. The "many minds" mentioned in the passage include trained judges, as well as lawyers on opposing sides of a succession of recurring disputes that, when arising at the first instance, are better resolved without prejudgment according to deduction from a preexisting principle. Hence the "business man suddenly appointed judge" should decide the case on its facts but refrain from explanation, and the same indeed goes for "more educated courts." The caution against premature generalization applies to the expert as well as to the layperson. An early decision in an emergent controversy operates akin to a scientific experiment; it opens inquiry by creating a potential precedent for future similar cases.

Like the record of scientific inquiry, that of legal inquiry consists at first of carefully recorded observation of multiple concrete experiences. The "business man" to whom Holmes alludes was acting in this instance more like a jury than a judge, and the role of juries has, since their emergence as deciders of factual questions, been to reach a decision without legal explanation from their findings on the evidence. Multiple evidentiary findings may suggest similarities. After an accumulation of particular decisions discloses a pattern, lawyers and judges initiate the process of generalizing. In law, as

---

[9] Holmes, "Codes," 1:213.

often in science, it is only after sufficient experience establishes a clear pattern that trained observers may begin to "abstract" a "general rule." And, as roughly also in science, this is done by "reconciling the cases," which refers to the distinguishing of relevant from irrelevant detail in the articulation of a common rule or standard.[10] Relevance, of evidence to ultimate conclusion, is an emergent property. As the notion of relevance emerges, so also does the perception—or imposition—of coherence.

This suggests a parallel between scientists and lawyers evaluating and generalizing within an established professional tradition from records of diverse but related data. The data itself, in science and law, would appear radically distinct, but there is a sense in which the two forms of inquiry are comparable. Both are prompted by practical problems or doubts confronting the community at large, reflecting Peirce's doubt-belief model of inquiry. In both, informal and nonprofessional attempts to resolve such problems, once burdened by something akin to superstition, have been replaced by formal and professionalized analysis. The practical understanding underlying legal disputes has, as Holmes suggested in *The Common Law*, supplanted a primitive culture of revenge, even as natural science has supplanted animism and superstition.

In both realms, abstraction and systematic classification have been accompanied by new practices of description and conceptual objectification. Both legal and scientific knowledge might be viewed as forms of community inquiry, focusing on the primacy of cases and exemplars in the process of intersubjective classification, and on the dual role of concepts and theories in guiding the conduct of professional inquirers and framing and maintaining the coherence and consistency of both expert and general belief.

CONFLICT AND THE RESOLUTION OF UNCERTAINTY

If this "fallibilist" account of the emergence of legal doctrine is roughly accurate, it should illuminate the challenge of resolving conflicts among legal rights and duties. Emergent rights are rooted in individual judgments, by jurors and others like the "business man," by comparing injurious with prudent conduct. The grounds on which such judgments are initially made is the familiarity of juries and judges with prevailing standards of conduct in the community at large, with respect to the activity from which an injury has occurred. In some matters there is yet to exist a prevalent standard.

---

[10] Barry Barnes, David Bloor, and John Henry, *Scientific Knowledge: A Sociological Analysis* (Chicago, IL: Chicago University Press, 1996), ix–x.

The particular judgment is part of the process of framing, of a process that Whewell refers to as "moulding."

The chronology, and diachronicity, of this process is important. Standards of conduct are preceded by, and drawn from, patterns of activity. The standards of prudence are inferred from familiarity with the better ways that things are presently being done, with particular concern to ground judgments upon that which is seen to be prudent. Failure to display a certain light on a ship at night, which has become a common practice to decrease the likelihood of collision, becomes, through repeated common law decisions, a ground of strict liability for collision when the light is absent. Thereby practice leads by accumulation of judgments to legal duty. In this simplified account, legal concepts demarcating rights and duties are cognitive products of prevailing patterns of conduct, gathered and evaluated by courts of law.

This suggests an empirical means for resolving conflicts. When legal rights are seen to conflict in the abstract, Holmes's account would not suggest that they can be deductively "balanced" in the abstract. Rather, conflicts are resolved on an experimental, case-by-case basis, as the conflicting rights were themselves previously framed. Holmes described the process of conflict resolution in 1873:

> The growth of the law is very apt to take place in this way: Two widely different cases suggest a general distinction, which is a clear one when stated broadly. But as new cases cluster around the opposite poles, and begin to approach each other, the distinction becomes more difficult to trace; the determinations are made one way or the other on a very slight preponderance of feeling, rather than articulate reason; and at last a mathematical line is arrived at by the contact of contrary decisions, which is so far arbitrary that it might equally well have been drawn a little further to the one side or to the other.[11]

In this description, as in the 1870 text, conflicts among existing rights are not resolved at once, through interpretation and application of an antecedent underlying set of legal principles. Instead they are gradually explored, first by gathering new experience, and then by appropriately timed retrospective examinations of an array of specific prior decisions.

Holmes describes a process whereby new cases are viewed as gradually filling a metaphorical space between the two rules ("cluster[ing] around the opposite poles"). Judges eventually resolve the conflict by recognizing and describing a "line" between the opposing poles or principles. Ultimately the conflict may be resolved by the reasoned analysis of an appellate court.

---

[11] Holmes, "The Theory of Torts," [1873] *Collected Works* 1:327.

Rather than deduction from *a priori* principles, this is a retrospective accounting of the various dimensions of a problem revealed by successive decisions. Despite the emphasis on specific judgments, there is no attempt to avoid the language of objectification; Holmes deploys a metaphor of "line drawing" to emphasize the primary role of particular decisions.

Each new decision is recorded as a point on a metaphorical line defining the boundary between still-evolving separate categories. The image of "clustering" of cases prompts a comparison with scientific research as more recently described by Barry Barnes, David Bloor and John Henry in *Scientific Knowledge: A Sociological Analysis* (1996), noting that, in science also, a "cluster of instances is all that ostensive learning can provide to convey the sense of sameness."[12]

> To describe the growth of scientific knowledge as a movement from one problem to the next on the basis of analogy and direct modeling is to offer a finitist account of the process... A class is its accepted instances at a given point in time: those instances are the existing resources for deciding what else belongs in the class, the available precedents for further acts of classification, the basis for further case-to case development of the classification.[13]

Holmes in 1873 had taken his approach a step further, in applying it to an account of the interaction between conflicting or opposing classes, by his gradual and consensual drawing of a metaphorical line. In one sense the line may be described as "arbitrary," in that it "might equally well have been drawn a little further to the one side or to the other."[14] In another sense, the account describes a process in which conceptual products are negotiated. There is no perfect or ideal shape to law, even as it is repeatedly modified to adapt to new conditions, shaping conduct as it forms and reforms legal concepts.

From these early and other Holmes texts, it appears that the body of law is built up from legal categories and concepts formed by a process of attenuated negotiation. The whole enterprise must be woven together while being adjusted to accommodate shifting standards guiding future conduct. Different cases, situations, parties, judges, lawyers and scholars are all involved in the larger continuum of legal inquiry, as diverse judgments are analyzed and interpreted to forge eventual settlements of multiple controversies. Overall consistency is a dominant goal, but conceptual analysis is only partly an exercise in logical reconciliation. It is also one of negotiating each new

---

[12] Barnes et al., *Scientific Knowledge*, 49.
[13] Barnes et al., *Scientific Knowledge*, 105.
[14] Holmes, "Theory of Torts," 1:327.

adjustment of conduct through the clash of already established patterns of conduct.

Charles Peirce commented in 1869 that Whewell had "shown with great elaboration that in every science two processes have taken place. One, the observation and grouping of facts. The other, controversies which resulted in the establishment of clear conceptions."[15] The law is plainly driven by controversy, and for Holmes an agonistic continuum of inquiry is a social device for the production of knowledge. Legal concepts demarcating rights and duties are cognitive products of opposing patterns of conduct, gathered and evaluated by courts of law. When legal rights are seen to conflict in the abstract, the conflicts are best resolved on an experimental, case-by-case basis, just as the conflicting rights were themselves individually framed. Legal dispute and conflict drive the both sense and reference, meaning and extension, of legal terms and terminology.

Hilary Kornblith, in his 1996 study of inductive inference, wrote, "Naturalistic epistemology has flourished since Quine first championed the cause."[16] This comment, referring to the mid-twentieth century, obscures, if it does not ignore, that the nineteenth-century Bacon-inspired inductivists were previously engaged in the same essential project, to *naturalize* the grounding of knowledge, seeking to understand the "true nature" of induction. John Herschel had asked the question, "What is the act or series of acts of the mind in constructing general propositions?" Holmes implicitly amended it as a matter of acts by "many minds." Mill, as will be discussed next, had asked, "[w]hat really takes place" in the inductive process. It seems perverse that the more recent inquiry has ignored the earlier one, and its explicit recognition of the social dimension of epistemology.[17] If social conflict is part of the domain of logic, the social nature of dispute resolution also bears on the question of epistemology and the validation of logical inference.

SOCIALIZING MILL'S EMPIRICISM

In the imagery of "clusters," Holmes pictured particular decisions as marks on a line between competing analogies, referring to the clusters as opposing "poles." I picture two distinct legal doctrines, in the abstract, which I will call A and B. The opposing "poles" have themselves been the product of prior

---

[15] Peirce, *Writings*, 2:340.

[16] Hilary Kornbluth, *Inductive Inference and its Natural Ground: An Essay in Naturalistic Epistemology* (Cambridge, MA and London: MIT Press, 1996), 1.

[17] Other scholars, in particular Alvin Goldman and Steve Fuller, have addressed social factors influencing the grounds of objectivity; Fuller's account is closest to Holmes. See Steve Fuller, *Social Epistemology* (Bloomington, IN and Indianapolis, IN: Indiana University Press, 2002), 216f.

induction, as described by Holmes in 1870, generated over time from particular cases. Holmes's "poles," then, signify clusters of prior judgments, their conceptual content derived from the factual nature of accumulated cases. This suggests an implicit inductive boundary, such that neither pole could be assumed to extend to cover the new matter. (The term "pole" indicates that the "boundary" is not hard, like a wall, but more like a cautionary navigational mark.) If this seems overly abstract, I have exemplified Holmes's treatment of competing analogies in *Plant v. Woods*, an early case evaluating the legality of labor union picketing in 1900, where the majority chose the analogy of extortion over the right of free association.[18]

Mill had questioned the assumption that correct inferences must be deductive; his radical empiricism viewed abstraction as firmly grounded in particulars. Holmes's conception reflects that notion, in this way: because legal abstraction moves in and through particular judgments, for practical purposes it remains grounded in them. If precedents are cumulative of judgments retrospectively abstracted in "clusters," they are not controlling beyond where their extension is sufficiently entrenched—both believed and acted upon, inside and outside the legal profession. As Holmes remarked in a speech to the New York State Bar Association in 1899, "generalization is empty in so far as it is general. Its value depends on the number of particulars which it calls up to the speaker and the hearer."[19]

Mill's phrasing suggests something like a cumulative "container" theory of meaning, in which a concept consists in generalization only from its past experiential contents. Holmes adopts a more cautious, and forward-looking, characterization in saying that its "value" depends on the "particulars which it calls up to the speaker and the hearer." The "particulars" referred to here are, simplified, the accumulated judgments of prudence in the realm of known experience, "known" in the sense of being formally generalized into a "rule" at the closure of a prior continuum of inquiry. That sort of general, he implies, is not empty, because of its grounding in adjusted practice.

That is Mill's sense of "realism" or "what really takes place"[20] The formation and function of principles exemplify the conceptual element of law, and can be illuminated by the model that Holmes set forth in the early 1870s. Holmes and Mill both used the term "principle" in referring to accepted knowledge, as in the "principles of ethnology" or "principles of admiralty." Yet in *The Common Law* Holmes uses the term in observing, "the law is always approaching, and never reaching, consistency. It is forever adopting

---

[18] The illustrative example of Holmes's dissenting opinions in two union picketing cases is discussed in Kellogg, *Oliver Wendell Holmes Jr*, 80–84.

[19] Holmes, "Law in Science," *Collected Works* 3:419.

[20] Mill, *System of Logic*, 2:196.

new principles from life at one end, and it always retains old ones from history at the other."

He may have recalled that Mill in his *Logic* had also used the term in
explaining the comment on Lord Mansfield's advice to the novice magistrate:

> Lord Mansfield knew that if any reason were assigned it would be necessarily
> an afterthought, the judge being in fact guided by impressions from past experi-
> ence, without the circuitous process of framing general *principles* [my italics]
> from them, and that if he attempted to frame any such he would assuredly fail.
> Lord Mansfield, however, would not have doubted that a man of equal experi-
> ence who had also a mind stored with general propositions derived by legitimate
> induction from that experience would have been greatly preferable as a judge,
> to one, however sagacious! who could not be trusted with the explanation and
> justification of his own judgments.[21]

Whether Mill would join Mansfield in viewing the *second* man, whose
mind is already "stored with general propositions," as preferable to the first, is
unclear, considering Mill's previous insistence that the novice should decide
the case without giving reasons, as they would probably be wrong. Yet, he
resists saying the second man would clearly be *right*. Mill's radical mistrust
of anything resembling "axiomatic" thinking hardly helps to understand how
a new "particular" is affected by the abstract context of prior ideas into which
it arrives.

The resolution of this question depends on the nature and timing of the
new case, and how that governs the finding of its relative similarity to prior
cases. Elsewhere in his *Logic* (Book 4, "Operations Subsidiary to Induction,"
Chapter 2, "On Abstraction, or the Formation of Conceptions"), Mill asks
"what really takes place" in drawing concepts out of facts:

> There are, then, such things as general conceptions, or conceptions by means
> of which we can think generally; and when we form a set of phenomena into a
> class, that is, when we compare them with one another to ascertain in what they
> agree, some general conception is implied in this mental operation. And inas-
> much as such a comparison is a necessary preliminary to induction, it is most
> true that Induction could not go on without general conceptions.[22]

Here he describes the observer gathering "phenomena into a class"
with which to digest new experience. Are they just ingredients or also

---

[21] Mill, *System of Logic*, 1:217–18.
[22] Mill, *System of Logic*, 2:192.

recipes—how do they connect? Mill backs off from the suggestion of any *a priori* connection in the following paragraph:

> But it does not therefore follow that these conceptions must have existed in the mind previously to the comparison. It is not a law of our intellect, that in comparing things with each other and taking note of their agreement we merely recognize as realized in the outward world something that we already had in our minds. The conception originally found its way to us as the result of such a comparison. It was obtained (in metaphysical phrase) by abstraction from individual things. These things may be things which we perceived or thought of on former occasions, but they may also be the things which we are perceiving or thinking of on the very occasion.[23]

This is an extraordinarily spare account of conceptual formation. We don't need anything in our minds than raw ingredients, no conceptual matter at all, whether fully or barely formed, as it derives directly from the process of comparison of the raw data. There is a hint here of Mill's notion of "natural" uniformity, that similarities are simply "there" to be discovered. Mansfield's second man doesn't need to draw on his law school training, if indeed the comparison started from a discrete beginning point. Now comes Mill's account of "what really takes place":

> The facts are not *connected* [Mill's italics], except in a merely metaphorically acceptation of the term. The *ideas* [again Mill's italics] of the facts may become connected, that is, we may be led to think of them together; but this consequence is no more than what may be produced by any casual association. What *really takes place* [my italics], is, I conceive, more philosophically expressed by the common word Comparison, than by the phrases "to connect" or "to super-induce." For, as the general conception is itself obtained by a comparison of particular phenomena, so when obtained, the mode in which we apply it to other phenomena is again by comparison. We compare phenomena with each other to get the conception, and we then compare those and other phenomena with [Mill's italics] the conception.[24]

Mill here says the conception is directly obtained from an early compari-son, and applied to other phenomena by comparing them "with the concep-tion." He gives no explanation of how the conception was first "obtained" in the process of comparison, even while implying a "beginning point" of conceptualization. He proceeds to illustrate this claim with reference to

---

[23] Mill, *System of Logic*, 2:192–93.
[24] Mill, *System of Logic*, 2:196.

Johannes Kepler's discovery that the path of the planet Mars followed an ellipse, a famous topic in his ongoing debate with Whewell. I note that Mill's account of Kepler's direct conclusion, drawn without (what Whewell called) "ampliative inference," has not been readily accepted.[25] Mill explains this position as follows:

> The conception is a conception of something; and that which it is a conception of, is really in the facts, and might, under some supposable circumstances, or by some supposable extension of the faculties which we actually possess, have been detected in them. And not only is this always itself possible, but it actually happens in almost all cases in which the obtaining of the right conception is a matter of any considerable difficulty … The honour, in Kepler's case, was that of the accurate, patient, and toilsome calculations by which he compared the results that followed from his different guesses, with the observations of Tycho Brahe; but the merit was very small of guessing an ellipse; the only wonder is that men had not guessed it before, nor could they have failed to do so if there had not existed an obstinate a priori prejudice that the heavenly bodies must move, if not in a circle, in some combination of circles.[26]

Peirce adopted Whewell's view that Kepler had "amplified" his inferential process with the concept of ellipse, and went on to call the process "abduction" to supply the conceptual element. His fourth Lowell Lecture chided Mill for ignoring the troublesome problem of similarity, which Mill either assumes as presenting itself directly in nature, or bypasses entirely in saying it is directly evident through "comparison." Hilary Putnam observed in 1981 that there is nothing self-explanatory to the finding of similarity: "In fact, everything is similar to everything else in infinitely many respects."[27]

All this presents three problems for exploration: one, the nature of a "conception," two, the finding of "similarity," and, three, identifying whether there is (and if so what it might be) a "beginning point" of inquiry. Examining these problems will clarify where Holmes moves beyond Mill. The best way to address the three problems is to examine Mill's consistent use of the

---

[25] See Snyder, *Reforming Philosophy*, 101–2. N. R. Hanson characterized Mill's position as "ludicrous." Snyder, *Reforming Philosophy*, 103.

[26] Mill, *System of Logic*, 2:193–94.

[27] Hilary Putnam, *Reason, Truth and History* (Cambridge: Cambridge University Press, 1984), 64. Nelson Goodman finds the very notion of similarity elusive: "Similarity, I submit, is insidious. And if the association here with invidious comparison is itself invidious, so much so the better. Similarity, ever ready to solve philosophical problems and overcome obstacles, is a pretender, an imposter, a quack. It has, indeed, its uses, but is more often found where it does not belong, professing powers that it does not possess." Nelson Goodman, "Seven Strictures on Similarity," in *Problems and Prospects* (New York, NY and Indianapolis, IN: Bobbs-Merrill, 1972), 437.

pronoun "we," as in his observation above that "the mode in which *we* apply [a conception] to other phenomena is again by comparison [my italics]."

In 1870, as editor of *Kent's Commentaries on American Law*, Holmes was immersed in the detail of legal cases; how might he have applied Mill's approach to common law legal disputes? Throughout the long history of common law adjudication, opposing sides have constantly contested each other in the process of "comparison" that Mill says "we" must make to "connect" facts in induction. Mill's "we" implies comparison by a single mind; but what, in the common law, is "really tak[ing] place"?

In the passages just quoted, it is Mill's mind that is producing the words, and in seeking the reader's assent he uses the expository "we," an accepted and common practice in logical writing. That usage implies Mill's best guess for the train of thought of an ideal, rational, and objective mind, observing the inductive process—as it takes place within that very same mind. A reader of the passage may find it easy at first blush to accept his point, that objective comparison is necessary in the inductive process; but with Peirce and Putnam in mind, I suggest some questions: what is similarity, how is it found, and does it begin somewhere discrete and identifiable? Is there something identifiably "given" from which comparison and further inquiry commence?

Holmes, with his skepticism of the syllogism and early commitment to induction, could have had such doubts and wondered how comparison "really takes place" in law. He had attended Peirce's two 1866 lectures on induction, noting the difference between comparing "things" bounded by positions to "occasions" bounded by dates, and extensively criticizing Mill's account of similarity as something directly apprehended. For Holmes, comparison must be accomplished over time by "many minds." In 1870 he uses terminology suggesting a beginning point of inquiry (the "case of first impression," a traditional common law notion), but in 1873 the difficult case emerges not by itself, but in a space surrounded by precedents, comprising already "clustered" and articulated comparisons. This is a space, to be sure, of logical reasons, but also of patterns of action; the prior clusters were derived from exhaustive observations of practice in deciding legal cases.

Holmes's 1870 paper suggests that comparison does not take place through immediate apprehension by a single "mind." Nor is it a purely mental operation, given that it arose from judgments regarding conduct, which must themselves have been influenced by prior judgments and prior conduct. Being a comparison of successive occasions, and of judgments regarding those occasions, emergent similarity must take into account a variety of factors influencing social conduct. His 1873 paper reveals the problem of using the expository "we" in examining induction. The difficult or uncertain case arises in a space that is not empty (as Mill suggested) but is already filled with "conceptual matter:" the assessment of prior "clusters." Perhaps a better phrase is "conceptual activity," grounded in statements reflecting an exchange of views among engaged observers. The 1870 essay describes how general terms and concepts arise by cumulative judgments that Holmes described in 1873 as "clusters." In an uncertain case, discrete clusters are deemed similar enough to pull the new case in opposite directions.

Mill's image of comparison, accomplished by a single omniscient "we," obscures the problem of contestation. Holmes roughly outlined a process of convergence in the 1873 paper. As he wrote in 1873: "Two widely different cases suggest a general distinction, which is a clear one when stated broadly. But as new cases cluster around the opposite poles, and begin to approach each other, the distinction becomes more difficult to trace." This tantalizingly succinct outline of poles, clusters and judicial line drawing can be filled in from his own judicial opinions or examples from historical or contemporary experience. Struggling with the problem of the tactics of labor organization, his court in 1895 and 1900 was engaged in the problem of where to draw a perceived line between association and extortion.[28]

Returning to the problem of defining "conception" for Holmes's model of inquiry, as opposed to Mill's, Mill talks in the above passages about how a conception emerges *directly* from the comparison of successive judgments. This reflects his radical empiricist distaste for dependence upon axioms previously formed. Given that background, I infer that he views axioms as fully cognitive, and equates them as such with "conceptions," which, he is determined to insist, only arise from particular experience. That is, in showing how conceptions arise directly from particulars in order to discount their reliance on anything a priori, Mill is nevertheless isolating a purely mental substance of "conceptual matter."

This assumption is then connected with the operation of an ideal universal mind, which is subtly at work through the expository "we," and is blocking out the messy interactive workings of a community of minds. Holmes, on the other hand, describes the process of comparison with the imagery of diverse "clusters" of legal judgments, and from 1873 on he views conceptual development as constantly contested. He gives an account that does not oblige the observer to posit a separate realm of conceptual matter, but rather obliges it to inquire how the conceptual process is accomplished by multiple thinking, talking, and acting humans.

Holmes makes no clear distinction between the particulars of experience and the purely mental element of conception. The reason lies in the cumulative nature of Holmes's model of legal knowledge. The legal principle and the legal precedent influence the law only insofar as they gain consenting belief

---

[28] This is discussed in Kellogg, *Oliver Wendell Holmes Jr*, 80–4.

and conduct amidst a community. Recall his careful phrasing in the 1899 address to the New York lawyers, that "generalization is empty insofar as it is general. Its value depends on the number of particulars which it calls up to the speaker and hearer." Generalizing is an intersubjective activity, a "calling up" of things, involving speakers and hearers, or (right now) a writer and a reader.

Holmes's process of convergence also implies more than a cognitive dimension to the analyzing and reconciling process. There must also be a convergence of *action*. Resolution of the uncertain case requires revising a habitual context, not just an abstract sense of context, because a larger problem may be represented by the specific dispute. What "really takes place" involves an extended comparison of situations and demands a wider perspective before it can be resolved. Defining the "situation," John Dewey, in his own 1938 *Logic*, says, "we never experience nor form judgments about objects or events in isolation, but only in connection with a contextual whole." Moreover, says Dewey, the "object of perception" cannot be "isolated from [its] place or function in promoting and directing a successful course of act[ion]."[29]

Mill in the above passages seized on the importance of "Comparison" (capitalizing C for emphasis) as an underappreciated essence of the inductive process. He rightly identified, as a central aspect of induction, the necessary finding of similarity among objects of inquiry for any degree of inductive inference. But, as Dewey says, more is required for successful inference; induction is purposive, it cannot be isolated from its relevance to prospective human action. The similarity among red balls repeatedly drawn from a bag, leading to an induction that all the balls in the bag are red, assumes a purposive inquiry; even finding the similarity of redness among the withdrawn round objects discounts individual differences of shape, shade, tone, and intensity, presuming them minute or otherwise irrelevant to the question at hand. In that case, a separate issue is whether all the roughly comparable round objects in a bag are closer to a uniform shade of red than any other uniform color. The eventual hypothesis that all the objects in the bag are red is accompanied by another silent hypothesis, that there is such a thing as *redness*, if not also indeed *ballness*. The reason why these hypotheses are not identified as such is that they are already entrenched.[30]

Hilary Kornblith, in his 1996 *Inductive Inference and its Natural Ground: An Essay in Naturalistic Epistemology*, writes "It is precisely because the

---

[29] Dewey, *Logic*, 66–7.

[30] The common notion of redness has become entrenched; as Mary Hesse has observed: "There are some predicates that are better entrenched than others, for instance, 'red' than 'ultra-violet,' 'lead' than 'pi-meson.'" Mary Hesse, *The Structure of Scientific Inference* (London: Macmillan, 1974), 22.

world has the causal structure required for the existence of natural kinds that inductive knowledge is even possible." 1996:35

This argument ignores the hidden hypotheses of similarity, and follows Mill's "uniformity of nature" rather than Holmes's observation that similarities and regularities earn their consensual status through inquiry. Holmes followed a common thread from both Wright and Peirce, that similarity is all-too-commonly presumed among objects of inquiry in explanations of the inductive process. [31]

CONCLUSION

Holmes's approach (dispute-belief rather than doubt-belief) showed that the history and methodology of law can be viewed as a continuous response to new problems of dispute and threatened disorder. Problems are continuously defined and redefined, tentatively settled but then often revisited, in an extended patchwork or web of deductive, inductive, and abductive reasoning. Legal history displays the organic action-based nature of uncertainty and its resolution, deflating (as will be seen in Part II) the notions of hard, inflexible indeterminacy and incommensurability. It recognizes the use of models and analogies (found in legal precedents) to address uncertainty piecemeal, through a creative response to prior belief and theory. Holmes's history of law places all dispute, even violent conflict, within a therapeutic relation to knowledge production. The very nature, the form and character, of social dispute and conflict is malleable, their modes of operation and resolution ultimately subject to human response and choice.

The classical model of induction is a synchronic inference by comparison from an objective point of observation. Holmes's social model of induction recognizes multiple perspectives and is extended in time, engaging adjustment of belief and conduct. When and where dispute is deeply rooted, logical inference is not an individual judge-centered process. *Roe v. Wade* did not end a controversy or solve a problem, nor will the next Supreme Court abortion decision do so. Yet *Roe* should not obscure the long history of convergences among opposing legal precedents. More tractable problems like assisted death have gradually and incrementally moved toward resolution.[32]

As Holmes wrote in 1870, his common law-based model of dispute resolution depends upon the opposition of arguments ("A well settled legal doctrine embodies the work of many minds, and has been tested in form as well as

---

[31] Kornbluth, *Inductive Inference*, 35.
[32] Cass Sunstein, *One Case at a Time: Judicial Minimalism on the Supreme Court* (Cambridge, MA: Harvard University Press, 1999).

substance by trained critics whose practical interest it is to resist it at every step"), but it is manifestly not a strictly *discourse*-based theory of democratic inquiry. Compared to the explicitly discourse-based theory of Jurgen Habermas, it suggests the need for a contingent, rather than programmatic, model of rational ordering, with greater attention to the prospect of failure. Holmes's insights have been ignored in the prevailing contemporary narrative of western legal thought; a version is captured by Habermas in a passage claiming that its latest development is "discursively achieved agreement:"

> From the standpoint of *legal theory*, the modern legal order can draw its legitimacy only from the idea of self-determination; citizens should always be able to understand themselves also as authors of the law to which they are subject as addressees. Social-contract theories have construed the autonomy of citizens in the categories of bourgeois contract law, that is, as the private free choice of parties who conclude a contract. But the Hobbesian problem of founding a social order could not be satisfactorily resolved in terms of the fortuitous confluence of rational choices made by independent actors. This led Kant to equip the parties in the state of nature with genuine moral capacities, as Rawls would later do with parties in the original position. Today, following the linguistic turn, discourse theory provides an interpretation of this deontological understanding of morality. Consequently, a discursive or deliberative model replaces the contract model; the legal community constitutes itself not by way of a social contract but on the basis of a discursively achieved agreement. [33]

This ideal universal model of discursively achieved agreement ignores the fine-grained detail and diverse character of extended disputes, their piecemeal and situational judgments and experimental abductions, competition among opposing analogies, and need for constant situational adjustment of conduct for progress toward resolution.

---

[33] Jurgen Habermas, *Between Facts and Norms: Contributions to a Discourse Theory of Law and Democracy*, William Rehg (trans.) (Cambridge, MA: MIT Press, 1996), 449. Holmes's theory provides a similar contrast to the reflective equilibrium of John Rawls and the deliberative democracy of Richard Rorty.

Chapter 3

Pragmatism and the Problem of Order

On November 11, 1862, Captain Holmes wrote from his regiment in Virginia to his sister Amelia despairing that the Confederacy could be overcome by force. He had been wounded twice, in October of 1861 while his regiment was being thrown by a superior force off Balls Bluff into the Potomac River, and again in September 1862 by a bullet through the neck at Antietam. He would soon be struck again at Fredericksburg, his regiment all but decimated. After witnessing the dead piled five deep at the Battle of the Wilderness, he would decline promotion and resign his commission in August of 1864 and return to Boston to study law at Harvard, soon to be diverted into philosophy by his peers like Peirce and James, Chauncey Wright, and an intense personal curiosity.

Wilfrid Sellars defined the aim of philosophy as understanding "how things, in the broadest possible sense of the term, hang together, in the broadest possible sense of the term."[1] Holmes's despair proved unjustified and the union did somehow hang together—how barely he was acutely aware. Philosophical pragmatism—in its classical form—followed the American Civil War. This was only eighty years after the American Revolution, and sixty years after the War of 1812. Emerging in the wake of three fratricidal wars, it is to be expected that within the origins of pragmatism would be some response, if not a distinctive one, to the problem of human conflict. The flip side of conflict is order; and the problems of moral and intellectual order, if not inseparable, are resistant to separation if we take Sellars seriously. Hume's task in his moral philosophy is analogous to his task in

---

[1] Wilfrid Sellars, "Philosophy and the Scientific Image of Man," in *Frontiers of Science and Philosophy*, Robert Colodny (ed.) (Pittsburgh, PA: University of Pittsburgh Press, 1962).

epistemology: to explain how a common world is created out of private and subjective elements.

Civil war was a catalyst in forming the jurisprudential views of Thomas Hobbes and Oliver Wendell Holmes Jr. Holmes's pragmatism advances a distinct view of order from Hobbes, a dynamic rather than analytical and static conception, which can be seen by comparing their response to perennial conflict, which both made central in all its forms: military, political, moral, and intellectual. The difference is that Hobbes resolved the problem of conflict through authority, while Holmes does so through inquiry and the adjustment of practices.

I propose three dimensions in which to elucidate this: historical, ontological, and practical. By historical I mean Holmes's departure from a Hobbesian analytical model of law, designed to address (and presumably suppress) conflict by state control, with an endogenous model that assimilates conflict in a process of formal but communal inquiry into discrete types of dispute. By ontological I mean Holmes's rejection of the analytical boundary around law, dating to Hobbes and still reflected in the contemporary separation of law and morals, in favor of a holistic fallibilism, which like John Dewey's philosophy encompasses all inquiry—legal, scientific, ethical, aesthetic, philosophical—under one ontological roof. The third or practical dimension refers to Holmes's critique of ideology, best known from the words of his famous dissent in *Lochner v. New York*: "The fourteenth amendment does not enact Mr. Herbert Spencer's Social Statics"; or, more to the point, "general propositions do not decide concrete cases."

If pragmatism has no grand scheme beyond the commitment to deliberative democratic pluralism, does it have some stronger account, as Wilfrid Sellars puts it, of "how things, in the broadest possible sense of the term, hang together, in the broadest possible sense of the term"? In this chapter, I pursue the vision of a distinctly dynamic and transitional concept of order implicit in classical pragmatism, rather than an analytical vision grounded in a fixed cognitive image. Central to this theme is the very different response to human conflict of Holmes from that of Thomas Hobbes.

Holmes, in fundamental ways a successor to Hume (see chapter 4), has not been fully recognized as an original philosopher by legal academics, but a comprehensive reading, in context with his pragmatist contemporaries, adds a distinctive dimension to the making of the moral, and certainly legal, character of that common world. What makes a real community hang together, in the broadest sense of the term? To address this question, we may pick up a line of thought developed by Holmes and continue it in Dewey's extended wake. Dewey's lifelong pragmatic naturalism is a critique of, and an alternative to, the dominant analytical tradition in logic, epistemology, and ontology. I read Holmes as doing the same for jurisprudence: launching a profound naturalist critique of analytical jurisprudence as it reemerged with John Austin in the nineteenth century, following Thomas Hobbes in the seventeenth and continuing today with H. L. A. Hart and Joseph Raz.

Holmes's radical naturalist account highlights critical aspects of Dewey's project, particularly the precarious nature of democratic order, and the lingering presence of authoritarian models of law. It grounds the often overly abstract conversation about pragmatic models of democracy, and while bringing it down to earth, also suggests a pragmatic agenda in other areas of contemporary philosophy. It does this by exploring, as an aspect of pragmatism, the problem of order as one of addressing and reconciling perennial conflict, which both Hobbes and Holmes made central in all its forms: military, political, moral, and intellectual.[2] The difference between them is that Hobbes resolved the problem through authority, while Holmes does so through inquiry and adjustment. How is this related to the origins of pragmatism?

Remarkably, on returning to Cambridge Holmes showed no signs of post-traumatic stress disorder. From 1866 into the 1870s, he was active in round-robin discussions of philosophy with William James, Chauncey Wright, Charles Peirce, and others; after a disappointing stint at Harvard Law School he worked in a Boston law office; he read philosophical and scientific works recommended by Wright, as well as The Lectures on Jurisprudence of John Austin and other legal treatises; he eagerly took over from James B. Thayer the revision of the encyclopedic legal treatise, Kent's Commentaries on American Law, a massive task; and he edited and wrote for the *American Law Review*, eventually tracing a path from which can be devined an original conception of law influenced by Emerson, Wright, Mill, Darwin, Maine, and an immersion in diverse historical and anthropological studies.

His conception was the antithesis of Hobbes's. In this chapter, I examine the mechanism by which Holmes, in the 1870s, came to describe the developing and maintaining of social order. He did not characterize it as such; his subject was law, the common law, and his focus was on cases, rooted in the revision and updating of Kent's *Commentaries*. Yet the nature of this mechanism, eventually applied to constitutional law, holds so much in common with the emergent themes of pragmatism that it is illuminating to abstract from it a cognate response to conflict: a pragmatic theory of order, legal in the immediate sense, moral and conceptual by implication. Once having addressed the three aspects, historical, ontological an practical, I hope the reader will agree with me that what distinguishes the pragmatic approach to jurisprudence is

---

[2] See, e.g., Steven Shapin and Simon Shaffer, *Leviathan and the Air-Pump: Hobbes, Boyle and the Experimental Life* (Princeton, NJ: Princeton University Press, 1985), 15, 99–100. "[S]olutions to the problem of knowledge are embedded within practical solutions to the problem of social order, and [] different practical solutions to the problem of social order encapsulate contrasting practical solutions to the problem of knowledge. *That* is what the Hobbes-Boyle controversies were about." (15)

that law must be analyzed not as a separate entity but as part of the more general problem, or set of problems, of social ordering. Thereafter, we will be in a position to explore pragmatism's approach to conflict as a dynamic theory of order, distinct from the dominant analytical tradition rooted in the linguistic turn and to see its advantages.

Pragmatism is a contested label. Writers of diverse views have adopted it, including Richard Rorty and Robert Brandom. Both have prominently emphasized a social dimension of philosophical inquiry, in distinct versions of what Christopher Voparil refers to as the "ontological priority of the social." Rorty has emphasized radical inclusion in every topic of traditional interest "with an eye to the possibility of changing the course of the conversation." Brandom sees social inclusivity as within the work of "continuing and extending the classical twentieth-century project of philosophical analysis." Both authors reject transcendental appeals to anything outside of transaction within an immediate community. Brandom maintains that this can yield an implicit standard of correctness carrying objective status. For Rorty, philosophy is the pure "conversation of mankind." Like Habermas, their conception is wedded to discursively achieved agreement, with little account of how this supports the ongoing order of society and culture. A basic question, uniquely raised by consideration of Holmes's pragmatism, is how a rational order can be grounded upon inclusive discussion of consequences.[3]

I

It is well known that Hobbes placed conflict at the center of his thinking about law and government. "My mother gave birth to twins: myself, and fear." It is also well known that from the premise of inveterate conflict, he deduced in Euclidian fashion a "social contract" by men in the state of nature to cede certain innate rights to the state to establish and maintain civil society. While hardly the first to conceive of law as an autonomous force maintaining and directing society, Hobbes gave the tradition a modernist and rationalist rebirth, renewed in succeeding centuries by Bentham, John Austin, H. L. A. Hart, and lately Joseph Raz.

It was John Austin's just-published version of analytical jurisprudence that seized Holmes's attention in the 1860s, much as it was Lotze's version of analytical logic that seized Dewey's in 1903.[4] Accepting for the moment the pervasiveness of conflict, is there a more plausible paradigm than Hobbes's

---

[3] Christopher Voparil, "Rorty and Brandom: Pragmatism and the Ontological Priority of the Social," *Pragmatism Today* 2, no. 1 (2011): 133–43.

[4] Sleeper, *Necessity of Pragmatism*, 5, 64–65.

mythical contract for explaining its relationship to law? Exemplifying a historicist naturalism, Holmes's model is taken directly from the law books. His is the recorded one of constant disputes, channeled into law courts and thence organized into legal intelligence. For Holmes, litigation, seen all around us, is a key part of the process of social ordering; and I will suggest that he found within it features that are representative of more general relations between dispute and inquiry, between conflict and theory.

I suggested that the model was original, but it had important precedents. An earlier version of common law based theory was developed in response to Hobbes by Sir Edward Coke (1552–1634) in the *Institutes*, and Sir Matthew Hale (1609–1676) especially in his posthumous *Reflections*, building on Coke. They are the first in the Anglophone tradition to spell out that there is a difference between the form of reasoning implied from the two versions of regulating conflict through law. Law is either exogenous or endogenous.[5] Either you control conflict from outside (leading, as the tradition reveals, to formal analytical thinking) or you assimilate it from within, through a frequently inelegant and messy ad hoc system of negotiation and gradual classification.

Hobbes, who favored Euclidian elegance, was annoyed by common lawyers like Coke and Hale, who resisted his authoritarian model. Late in life he wrote his *Dialogue between a Philosopher and a Student of the Common Law*. Posing as the philosopher, Hobbes asks the student, "Would you have every man to every other man allege for law his own particular reason? There is not amongst men a universal reason agreed upon in any nation, beside the reason of him that hath the sovereign power. Yet though his reason be but the reason of one man, yet it is set up to supply the place of that universal reason, which is expounded to us by our Saviour in the Gospel; and consequently our King is to us the legislator both of statute-law, and of common-law."

Hobbes's attack on Coke was not published until well after his death in 1681; but it was apparently circulated widely enough in manuscript form to come to the attention of Sir Matthew Hale, whose manuscript reply, *Reflections by the Lord Chiefe Justice Hale on Mr. Hobbes his Dialogue of the Lawe*, was unpublished until 1921 when its importance was recognized by the British legal historian Frederick Pollock, by then an old friend and correspondent of Holmes.

---

[5] Common law reason has been described as "within the law." It is rooted in conduct and practice. As Gerald Postema has noted, it was "inseparable from the particular situations brought to the law and resolved by it. It is the reason not of rules and principles, but of cases." It reflects the fact that cases are the byproduct of problematic interaction among humans engaged in social and economic activities, which fall naturally into patterns that might qualify as "custom," from which reason cannot be detached. It is distinct, then, from the meaning given to the term by Hobbes. Gerald J. Postema, *Bentham and the Common Law Tradition* (Oxford: Clarendon Press, 1986), 30.

Hale begins his *Reflections* with an elaborate demonstration that reason is by no means univocal as applied to different subjects of inquiry, such as mathematics, physics and politics, and that it must be permitted to assume a special meaning in the difficult field of law. This is because "the texture of human affairs is not unlike the texture of a diseased body laboring under maladies, it may be of so various natures that such Phisique as may be proper for the cure of one of the maladies may be destructive in relation to the other, and the cure of one disease may be the death of the patient."[6] Though unread by Holmes until much later, it prefigures his own common law habit of thinking from particular situations, closer to raw experience, while resisting easy general answers. By reasserting an endogenous model against Austin's analytical scheme, Holmes was obliged to flesh it out and respond to Austin's more insistent ontological separation of law from morals. Here he would draw on the naturalist, empiricist attitudes of the Scottish Enlightenment that influenced his own education and that of his Harvard-graduated peers like Wright, Peirce, and James.

As noted above, Hale's view was an early challenge to the rationalist approach that Bentham and his disciple John Austin would later elaborate. There was a different response to British rationalism in Scotland in the century after Hale: the moral sense theory of Shaftesbury, Hutcheson, Hume, and Adam Smith. As the legal historian John Cairns writes,

> from the work of Frances Hutcheson . . . rationalist natural law theories in the tradition of Pufendorf had been progressively superseded in Scotland by versions of moral sense theory. A follower of the philosophy of Lord Shaftesbury, Hutcheson attempted to ground ethics in observation and study of the thinking and behavior of human beings. . . . The foundation of moral judgment was not in reason, but in the senses.[7]

Cairns traces the influence of this on Kames, Hume, Smith, and Millar, as well as the influence of Montesquieu on Scottish Enlightenment thinking about law. We may find elements in Holmes of both traditions, that of Coke and Hale as well as of Kames and Smith. He had absorbed Scottish thought as an undergraduate at Harvard through Francis Bowen, who had taught philosophy and political theory to the members of the Metaphysical Club (and even attended some of their meetings). Holmes's postwar diaries show that he too read Hamilton, Bain, and other Scots, as well as Montesquieu, and of course Darwin, a major influence on all the members of the Club.

---

[6] Matthew Hale, *Reflections*, printed in William Holdsworth, *A History of English Law* (London: Methuen, 1956), 503.

[7] John W. Cairns, "Legal Theory," in Alexander Broadie (ed.), *The Cambridge Companion to the Scottish Enlightenment* (Cambridge: Cambridge University Press, 2003), 213.

We might say that Holmes reinterpreted Hale in privileging precedent as the organic body of patterns of decision—or what is beneath, patterns of conduct, eventually translated into legal concepts as they first clashed and then were adjusted and reconciled. He saw common law as pulling moral standards out of conflict resolution, as reworking them and thereby developing and constantly writing and revising the moral component of law. What Holmes does with moral sense theory seems particularly noteworthy. Holmes historicizes Smith's "impartial spectator" in a way that conditionally validates precedent. Holmes's "reasonable and prudent man" was the test for negligence, the standard of care. The prudent person is Holmes's historical spectator. We value precedent because the prudent person has been there all along, in the role of jury and judge, constantly infusing the common law with a historically more plausible—even while still highly idealized—version of Scottish moral sense.

This simplified explanation hides underlying complexity but serves to sketch the lineage. What it fails to show, yet, are the implications for applying conflicting precedents and resolving disputes. Smith's impartial spectator had been a device, a trope, originally devised to emphasize Hutcheson's anti-rationalist ethics. The prudent man is also a device, but it is drawn from legal history (explicitly introduced into English law in 1781 by Sir William Jones) and it speaks with caution, more than a touch of Humean or Burkean skepticism. While Smith's theoretical spectator might say, "Aha! I can look inside myself to do the right thing in any doubtful case," Holmes's prudent man is a consensus builder: "Whoa, I think this looks right for now, to me, in this instance, but first let's check the precedents, allow for future variations, and await a consensus before laying down a rule."

Smith thought the impartial spectator could find the universal in the particular, but Holmes recognized from Kent that this takes time and experience. The prudent judge looks first to precedent, and only finds the universal when the time is ripe. In the passage from his 1870 essay ("It is the merit of the common law that it decides the case first and determines the principle afterwards"), the legal decision is described as coming before the reasoning; the analytical matrix of the law, and its a priori rules of decision, would appear surprisingly irrelevant. This surely appears unsound, until we recognize that Holmes is speaking not of the ordinary case, but of the tough case, the novel situation, often representing a new and at first intractable clash of interests.

The simplified sketch implies—perhaps too much so—that there is no clear rational itinerary from the written law to the specific decision. More importantly, though, it implies a common-law judicial minimalism, deciding "one case at a time." This phrase has most recently been deployed by Cass Sunstein, referring to decisions of the Supreme Court that avoid formulae and withhold sweeping generalization. Sunstein, writing of controversies that are in his phrase "not yet fully theorized," might profitably have cited Holmes for this principle, as Holmes had in 1870 proposed a quite sophisticated model through which common law rules are ideally formulated ("It is only after a series of determinations on the same subject-matter, that it becomes necessary to 'reconcile the cases' . . . A well settled legal doctrine embodies the work of many minds, and has been tested in form as well as substance by trained critics whose practical interest it is to resist it at every step"), the process Holmes called "successive approximation." Legal rules are viewed historically, and Holmes here proposes that they be understood as emerging from classes of activity, or more precisely from classes of disputes within discrete activities.

As new cases arise within a given class, for example, vehicular accidents or communications among people forming contractual arrangements, they are initially decided on their facts, a case at a time. Eventually a body of decided cases can be "reconciled," with the laying down of a general rule, after time has permitted sufficient case-specific analysis, probing the relevant varieties and conditions of accidents or contractual communications. Whereas analytical legal positivism emphasizes language and text, which gives the appearance of fixity, the updated common law model emphasizes patterns of conduct, which may be in the process of adjustment and gradual change. While the positivist model sees legal change as possible primarily through legislation, Holmes saw it as ongoing in areas even already covered by statute; and finality of generalization is ever elusive. The introduction of new forms of travel or communication may require new amendments to the rules of travel or contract, as did the airplane and the telegraph in the previous century. And even new legislation will need to be interpreted and applied on a case-by-case basis.[8]

II

This truncated historical tour brings us short of important developments in the twentieth century, when the analytical tradition was revised by Hart and his disciples at Oxford and elsewhere. The ontological aspect of Holmes's

---

[8] Holmes applied this principle to legislation in "Codes," noting that "New cases will arise which will elude the most carefully constructed formula." Statutes too are the work of many minds, in elected bodies. Diverse circumstances are explored, in legislative committees, often following and drawing upon prior experience through litigation. Yet again unclear circumstances remain, to be addressed in a case-specific manner by the judiciary, if not through legislative amendment. See, e.g., Roscoe Pound, *The Spirit of the Common Law* (Boston, MA: Beacon Press, 1921), 174; Edward H. Levi, *An Introduction to Legal Reasoning* (Chicago, IL: Chicago University Press, 1949), 27–33; Guido Calabresi, *A Common Law for the Age of Statutes* (Cambridge, MA: Harvard University Press, 1982).

position becomes evident when we consider his conception of the difficult case and compare it to that of Hart and the contemporary legal positivists. Recall that Hale's comparison of law to a curative introduced into the "texture of human affairs" separated both his notion of reason and his conceptualization of law from those of Hobbes. His "texture" terminology anticipates Herbert Hart's "open texture" of legal language; but unlike Hart, the texture of interest to Hale is outside the law, a texture of "affairs" or activity, and the element of difficulty would necessarily be located there instead of within the isolated text.

We may compare an example made famous by Hart, the famous bicycle in the park case, and its relation to the notion of an "open texture" in legal language. A local ordinance bans vehicles from a public park. Competent users of English are uncertain or disagree about whether bicycles are vehicles. Hart infers that the rule banning vehicles from the park has a core of determinate meaning and a penumbra of indeterminate meaning, into which the bicycle would fall. For Hart, deciding the bicycle case requires a court to assign to the rule an increment of determinate meaning that it did not previously have.[9] Positivist open texture theory, adopting the conception of metaphorical space in an open-textured entity "law," either renders the project of legal interpretation impossible or the language of judges and lawyers fraudulent.

For the metaphorical space to be truly empty, any gap in a rule must be a gap in the law as a whole, as there would otherwise be someplace else within the law to find an answer. Hence, for such gaps, there is no possibility of deciding a case by interpreting "the law." Picture a circle, with the label "LAW" on the inside, and "MORALS" on the outside. This is the conceptual image of positivist analytical jurisprudence—with law and morals separated by a definable boundary. (I use the idea of a circle for clarity. Perhaps rather than a circle, implying uniformity to varying analytical theories, I should suggest an enclosing line with indeterminate shape.)[10]

The picture is reinforced by language concerning the very question of law's relation to morals, and of analysis of that question. It forces the conversation about law into an epistemic boundary issue, rather than a question of process. It focuses on the issue of how things inherently (or at least presently) are, rather than of how things come to be. This line of inquiry in analytical

---

[9] Hart, *The Concept of Law*, 123–27. This reading is reinforced by Hart's remarks in the Postscript responding to Ronald Dworkin added to the second edition of *The Concept of Law*, 252–53, 272–73.

[10] The picture suggested by Dworkin, in which morals are not posited as outside of the putative boundary has been described as a non-positivist conception, but it retains a fundamental similarity, probing the possibilities of a circle that includes within it an element of the "moral," but nevertheless implying a boundary. The imaginary boundary is still extant, deeply embedded in the conversation, and the attention turns to the explanation of the nature of this distinctive boundary, not questioning whether it exists at all.

jurisprudence is presumed to be a "given," as an ancient, fundamental, and defining question of jurisprudence. A recent comment by the preeminent European legal philosopher Robert Alexy suggests that all of jurisprudence has been and must always be dominated by this question, the question of whether law is separate from morals:

> The central problem in the debate surrounding the concept of law is the relationship of law and morality. Notwithstanding a discussion that reaches back more than two millennia, there remain two basic, competing positions—the positivistic and the nonpositivistic.[11]

Here the "non-positivistic" position is simply the other alternative given by the analytical picture: the option of somehow putting a moral element inside the boundary.

Western jurisprudence is thus overwhelmed by a powerful linguistic bias toward analytical legal theory and method, by a concept of law with a definitive boundary—whether that boundary includes morals or not. If we ignore Hale and accept Alexy's comment, the pragmatic view is then entirely original—a third "basic position." It cannot, however, be so simply mapped, as the pragmatist model of law is part of a model of developing intelligence in the context of all experience.

III

The analytical picture serves to illustrate the practical dimension of Holmes's critique of ideology. Picture again the circle with "law" on the inside, but put aside for the moment the precise location of "morals." If law has a boundary, the question arises, what precisely is inside, and what outside? If a question arises for which legal experts cannot find a clear answer from the materials (statutes, cases, authoritative texts, and so on) that are inside, can they look outside for an answer? And what if "moral principles" are believed to be inside, as Alexy, following Ronald Dworkin, has steadfastly maintained? Can such generals be utilized to decide the difficult case?

Dworkin and Natural Law

Holmes's fallibilism resists the idea of a natural conceptual boundary around law. It sees no difficult case as occupying a place inside or outside a legal

---

[11] Robert Alexy, *The Argument from Injustice: A Reply to Legal Positivism* (Oxford: Oxford University Press, 2002), 3.

boundary. Rather, the hard case presents a degree of novelty or uncertainty. Cases come into the legal process from the chaos of life's complexity. They bring innumerable distinct kinds of uncertainty and difficulty. It is a categorical error to treat all types of legal uncertainty as univocal, of one conceptual kind, an error that seems inevitably to follow from the notion of a boundary, or at any rate from the debate over the ontological separation of law and morals. It is an error that, as Holmes would later complain, may be used to rationalize a judge's predetermining the outcome of an ongoing controversy by circumventing detail and appealing directly to a "moral principle."

From this perspective, two fallacies have followed from the analytical conception, going back at least to John Austin, that law has a distinct conceptual boundary. One is that a particular case, embodying a specific question, can arise outside the boundary, and hence be legally indeterminate. According to the positivist model, law, considered as an adjudicative matrix, either succeeds or fails on its own. When deciding difficult cases this means the positivist must accept the problematic possibility of a radical "legal indeterminacy."

The other fallacy, following from the debate over whether law and morals are separate, is that morals, or moral principles, must be included within the boundary when necessary to resolve the legally indeterminate case. This gives rise to the superficial notion that constitutional rights, as privileged "moral principles," can be available as trumps over statute and precedent whenever their sweepingly general language permits. If a case represents a prevalent controversy on which a judge has strong feelings, and there is a relevant constitutional value such as free expression, annoying facts that may align the case with prior contrary decisions can be ignored, in favor of a rhetorical recitation of the historic importance of the constitutional right.

While this may appear to be a twentieth-century phenomenon, Holmes first encountered a nineteenth-century version of it during his career as a state judge, in the yet unregulated area of labor organization—the tendency to reject picketing as a violation of constitutionally protected freedom of contract.[12] *Lochner*, in 1902, invoked the same right to overrule state welfare regulation, and would be his signal encounter with this phenomenon on the Supreme Court. In both cases, he dissented, and in both his position has been born out by historical developments.

Constitutional rights are important, but they are implemented by raising fundamental questions for society at large, not by dictating, to the individual judge, shortcut answers to new perplexities like union organizing or social welfare legislation. More recent issues in which the temptation exists to avoid complexity are corporate limits on campaign spending, and medically assisted suicide. Why should judges decide such matters on particular

---

[12] *Vegelahn v. Guntner* 167 Mass. 92 (1896) and *Plant v. Woods* 176 Mass. 492 (1900).

grounds, as Holmes counseled, and refrain from reaching into the constitution for a final, irreversible rationale? The simple answer is that law is part of a broad social inquiry, and in the most vexing controversies, inquiry has to run its course before the correct principle, meeting the fully explored contours of a problem, follows in policy as well as language. And, ample room must be given for input from outside the judicial arena.

IV

How do things hang together, amid crisis and serious conflict? Slavery and its aftermath have overwhelmingly been the greatest source of violent dissension in the history of the republic, a clash of deep commitments worked out only through two centuries of gradual and painful adjustment—of habits, practices, beliefs, and even language. The path of that dispute is irreconcilable with a Hobbesian social contract suppressing the operation of conflicting moral views of law. Such a vision could hardly have appealed to Holmes. As a young abolitionist, he was raised on Emerson's call to personal responsibility, and he felt its sting.

For Hobbes, civil war was unmitigated evil to be avoided at all costs, while for Holmes it came to be understood as simply a more explosive manifestation of the constant clash of fundamental interests. We need not condone fratricidal war in recognizing that, in seventeenth-century England and eighteenth as well as nineteenth-century America, it addressed moral deadlocks that political and legal institutions could not break. This insight plausibly led Holmes to the intimate connection of legal cases with their underlying conflicts, and an emphasis less on analytical legal doctrine than the nonlegal dimensions of adjustment. What is missing from Hobbes's view is the constant need for continuous adjustment in any real scheme of social ordering. It is this that I refer to as the dynamic order characteristic of pragmatism, the transactional and transformative aspect of inquiry found in Dewey's work.

The logic of the law is not the a priori dictate of legal reason but rather, paraphrasing Dewey, the product of inquiry. The dimension highlighted in retrospect through Holmes is the element of constant conflict as a catalyzing force. As Ralph Sleeper notes, Peirce's doubt-belief formula directed Dewey's attention to the actual processes of thought. Inherently vague, the idea of doubt has always sought specificity in Dewey's work. For Sleeper the key to Dewey's logic was understanding inference "as a real event of transformational force and power, causally real in the emergence of new features of things 'entering the inferential function.' It takes inference as action, as behavior that causes changes in reality through interaction with things."[13] If the real process of

---

[13] Sleeper, *Necessity of Pragmatism*, 83.

inference begins with doubt, the doubt-belief formula needs to acknowledge that doubt is not merely spectral but must have its own physiology and history.

From Holmes, we gain the insight that legal intelligence is a special case of inference deriving from constant controversies that find their way into the judicial system. Doubt is palpable in the difficult case. The gradual hammering-out of belief through case-specific resolutions is visible in the record of litigation. Flawed and chaotic though it may be, the resolution of conflict by legal problem-solving provides a written record of naturalistic and pragmatic ordering, revealed in its full flawed and chaotic nature. This aspect of knowledge needs to be recognized equally in relation to the dynamic growth of universals and ideals. In an address given to the New York State Bar Association in 1899, Holmes summarized this point in a way that Dewey must have appreciated:

> It is perfectly proper to regard and study the law simply as a great anthropological document. It is proper to resort to it to discover what ideals of society have been strong enough to reach that final form of expression, or what have been the changes in dominant ideals from century to century. It is proper to study it as an exercise in the morphology and transformation of human ideas.[14]

This extraordinary passage demonstrates that Holmes saw law entirely differently from Hobbes. Rather than an autonomous force suppressing conflict as pathological, it is embedded within the social processes assimilating and meliorating conflict as a natural condition. Rather than viewing legal and political theory as a prophylactic program for a discrete governing entity, legal theory is cognate with the rest of knowledge and law is viewed as a written record offering evidence of social norms and ideas as continuously cogenerated. Ideals are products of this view of knowledge as inquiry, and they are constantly developing in response to the changing nature of the human endeavor.

In this original vision, legal philosophy is engaged in a radical departure from the analytical positivist tradition. The Hobbesian model of order can be found throughout assumptions behind the theories of law. As Unger would write in *Knowledge and Politics*, "the eternal hostility of men to one another requires that order and freedom be maintained by government under law." The pragmatic alternative has interesting and illuminating parallels, not so much to other established jurisprudential schools, but rather (as I have suggested elsewhere, 2010) to post-Kuhn studies of science, which have already become a vital research program generating their own account of "the morphology and transformation of human ideas."

---

[14] Holmes, "Science in Law," 3:407.

Chapter 4

Hume, Logical Induction, and Legal Reasoning

Given the overall perspective of Holmes's legal pragmatism outlined in the preceding chapters, we can now address an underlying problem: the nature of legal difficulty or uncertainty, and why it is misleading to identify it as "indeterminacy." In what sense can legal difficulty be viewed as a logical problem? Of course, there are many variants of legal difficulty familiar to the scholar or the practitioner, but what is the role of the classical distinction between deduction and induction?

DEDUCTION AND INDUCTION

In an easy case, the issue is whether I brought my car to a complete stop at a stop sign. There is a clear rule and a clear act, a plain particular covered by a general, decided by deduction. Difficulty increases with the complexity of unanticipated acts that have combined to cause a claim of loss or harm. Where deduction from existing rules is inconclusive, the question approaches becoming an inductive one. How judges decide the difficult or "hard" case is the focus of much controversy, in theory, and also in public conversation—for example regarding abortion, medically assisted death, affirmative action for minority groups, same-gender marriage, or freedom of expression as it relates to other public purposes. It is in the nature of the deductively difficult case that *novel and unanticipated facts* cause it to be uncovered by authoritative law.

This is an aspect of uncertainty distinct from the problem one often envisions as the primary challenge to the deciding judge: semantic unclarity or contradiction *within* the settled law, or vagueness in the meaning or

application of the terms of an applicable rule or standard.[1] The common interpretation of the term "legal logic" is mainly a deductive form of legal reasoning, a meaning familiar to the law student. The body of settled law is massive
and must regularly be applied to the analysis of complex fact situations.
The typical law examination presents complex situations that the student
must analyze, drawing on the body of existing law. Like many actual cases
where deduction may indeed lead to resolution, it tests both the knowledge
of authoritative law and the ability to identify and evaluate its application to
all aspects of a hypothetical problematic situation. But this form of reasoning
does not cover the problem of novelty. It is a dialectic and analogical *inductive* model that performs that function.

The inductive model accepts, but goes beyond, the mainly deductive
model. It concerns, in particular, the *growth* of the law, through the negotiation of disputed meanings and the eventual entrenchment of new similarities
and differences. This is where analogy comes in. To be sure, the opposition
of analogies is *highlighted* by deduction, but argument from their opposition
is part of an inductive process. Properly understood, induction seeks to find,
from experience, the general rule that will resolve not just the case, but the
problem. The problem may be a new one, not yet covered by settled authority.
Is medically assisted death suicide or homicide? The relevant "particulars,"
then, are not just the particular facts of this new case, but the judgments, or
findings, in a *succession* of cases, very like a succession of experiments in
chemistry or physics. Mary Hesse elucidated this at length in the field of
natural science, and it is to natural science that I now briefly turn.[2]

Students in high school physics pour liquid mercury into a clean test tube,
and turn it upside down. A space unexpectedly appears between the tube's
rounded bottom and the heavy liquid through which no air could have passed.
Is this an *empty* space, or is there some substance in that visible area? How,
thought Thomas Hobbes in the seventeenth century, could such a space
paradoxically be "filled with *nothing*"? It took a *succession* of experiments
to find an answer.[3] Where a new matter falls cleanly *outside* or *between*

---

[1] Brian Bix, *Law, Language, and Legal Determinacy* (Oxford: Clarendon Press, 1993); Brian Bix,
"Vagueness and Political Choice in Law," in Geert Keil and Ralf Poscher (eds.), *Vagueness and the
Law, Philosophical and Legal Perspectives* (Oxford: Oxford University Press, 2016).

[2] Hesse, *The Structure of Scientific Inference*, 22.

[3] This is an oversimplification of a famous demonstration originally made by Evangelista Torricelli
in 1644 (where the test tube would have been set within a dish of mercury), and refers to the question raised as to the nature of the "Torricellian space," and whether or not a true vacuum could
exist in nature. The question also arose as to the cause of the suspension of the mercury above the
dish. Hobbes was a "plenist," a view opposed to "vacuism," and opposed Robert Boyle's air-pump
experiments to explore the complex controversy on several grounds, including Hobbes's favoring
a "demonstrative" (and largely deductive) method of inquiry. Shapin and Shaffer, *Leviathan and
the Air-Pump*, 21, 41f.

settled general rules and propositions, *induction* from experience is required to revise, or renew, prevalent belief and conduct. Sufficient experience may take time to gather and evaluate.

The American legal realists offered the controversial, and never fully accepted, claim of indeterminacy regarding decisions in hard cases, where judges, faced with opposing legal authorities, were presumed to choose subjectively, which explained inconsistent rationalization of their decisions. But in novel circumstances, driven by a new problem like medically assisted death, judges may understandably, and quite legitimately, appear unable to agree on a deductive solution, as also have scientists, at least since the eighteenth century, working on successions of experiments to see whether, say, the empty space in the test tube is something we can now (often inexactly) call a "vacuum."

Like scientists, judges don't and shouldn't "choose first and rationalize;" rather, like juries they must surely choose, but not *prematurely* rationalize, as did Thomas Hobbes in opposing (and actually denouncing) Robert Boyle's famous air-pump experiments.[4] What scientists have used is an inductive process, grounded in Francis Bacon's seventeenth-century empiricism, which was reexamined by John Stuart Mill and William Whewell in the 1840s. It was examined and refined again by Charles S. Peirce, William James, and Oliver Wendell Holmes Jr, in the years following the American Civil War. This is addressed at length in a recent study from the University of Chicago Press.[5]

David Hume opened the modern understanding of logical induction by arguing that there was no necessary connection between a series of present facts and that which is inferred from it.[6] No one has succeeded in rejecting this thesis, and contemporary scholars have come to agree that inductive inferences lack the perceived necessity of deduction; hence the response has been, like legal realism, to see skepticism as intrinsic to all inductive inquiry. Skepticism defines an attitude, and its application can readily become a conversation-stopper, an end of inquiry. Yet the question of induction's lack of logical necessity may and should be further investigated, as it has in the study of scientific research, asking how deductive necessity itself is defined and achieved. Bertrand Russell made the following observation in 1914, regarding the relation of induction and deduction:

---

[4] Shapin and Shaffer, *Leviathan and the Air-Pump*, 169f.
[5] Kellogg, *Oliver Wendell Holmes Jr.*
[6] Principles sources are Peter Manicas, *Logic as Philosophy* (New York, NY: Reinhold, 1971); Susan Haack, *Philosophy of Logics* (Cambridge: Cambridge University Press, 1978); Hilary Putnam, *Philosophy of Logic* (New York, NY: Harper & Row, 1971); W. V. Quine, *Philosophy of Logic* (Cambridge, MA: Harvard University Press, 1970); and Bertrand Russell, *Problems of Philosophy* (New York, NY: Henry Holt & Co., 1912).

But induction, important as it is when regarded as a method of investigation, does not seem to remain when its work is done: in the final form of a perfected science, it would seem that everything ought to be deductive. If induction remains at all, which is a difficult question, it will remain merely as one of the principles according to which deductions are effected.[7]

Russell observes here that induction may actually precede and lead to deduction. How? The answer may be sought through exploration of the notion of similarity itself.

In conventional explanations of the inductive process, similarity among objects of inquiry is commonly presumed. The similarity among red balls repeatedly drawn from a bag, leading to an inference that the remaining objects in the bag are red balls, discounts individual differences, presuming them minute or otherwise irrelevant to the inquiry.[8] That is because the question at hand doesn't concern the qualities of redness or ballness, but rather the numerical contents of the bag. The possibility that the color of each ball may have slight differences, or that the shapes of the balls are not precisely identical, is not at issue.

An important question is: What indeed *is* similarity in logic and induction; is it a natural or conventional quality, and how is it perceived and/or derived?[9] The importance of similarity in induction was clearly noted by Hume. No matter how many repetitions of uncontroversially similar events, runs his skeptical claim, we can still have no warrant regarding the occurrence of the next one: that the next object removed from the bag (even after an infinite number of red balls) will also be a red ball, even that the sun will again rise over Boston tomorrow morning. This is because it is the inductive process itself that is called upon to validate any particular induction regarding the bag or the sun.[10]

---

[7] Bertrand Russell, "Logic as the Essence of Philosophy," in *Our Knowledge of the External World* (London: Allen & Unwin 1914), 33.

[8] I use the example of red balls drawn from a bag because it appears in the 1866 lectures by Peirce attended by Holmes, as explored in Kellogg, *Oliver Wendell Holmes Jr* on the origins of Holmes's early inductive turn.

[9] As the philosopher Hilary Putnam observes, "In fact, *everything is similar to everything else in infinitely many respects.* For example, my sensation of a typewriter at this instant and the quarter in my pocket are both similar in the respect that some of their properties (the sensation's occurring right now and the quarter's being in my pocket) are *effects of my past actions* [Putnam's italics]." *Reason, Truth and History*, 64–65. Peirce raised questions regarding how similarity and uniformity are perceived in induction, in an 1866 lecture attended by Holmes. Peirce, *Writings*, 1:415–20. See also Goodman, "Seven Strictures on Similarity," 437; W. V. Quine and J. S. Ullian, *The Web of Belief* (New York, NY: Random House, 1978), 87: "What counts as similarity? Everything is similar to everything in some respect." For a recent approach to "naturalizing" similarity in induction, see Kornblith, *Inductive Inference*.

[10] Hume, "Skeptical Doubts Concerning," sections IV and V.

This uncertainty affects general ideas: Hume wrote, crediting Berkeley, "[A]ll general ideas are nothing but particular ones, annexed to a certain term, which gives them a more extensive significance, and makes them recall upon occasion other individuals, which are similar to them."[11] "Similarity," then, is for Hume a critical constitutive element in logic: "When we have found a resemblance among several objects, we apply the same name to all of them, whatever differences we may observe in the degrees of their quantity and quality, and whatever other differences may appear among them."[12] The term "we," with which Hume here refers to the perceiver of a similarity, has by implication already found the resemblance and discriminated away the differences.

But this approach to similarity implies completion of an unexamined process, as Charles Peirce noted in lectures given in late 1866, attended by his friends James and Holmes. The above passage (from Hume's *Treatise on Human Nature*) hides two critical questions: who indeed is the "we" to whom he refers, and how was the resemblance "found"?

Hum's expository use of "we" is a commonly accepted discursive practice. But its use can leave out the possibility of disagreement over the purpose and consequences of a *disputed* resemblance. The expository "we" deploys an ideal observer of a paradigmatic situation; it obscures whether, in actual life, the general statement of resemblance applies to all possible communities of speakers. It obscures the social dimension of *establishing* similarity. The issue of similarity doesn't arise unless there is a practical uncertainty regarding the resemblance in question. Such practical uncertainty arises constantly in the operation of legal adjudication. It may also be found in science and other branches of human inquiry.

Naming is another crucial constitutive element in logical theory.[13] What if the reach of application by a particular "name" is disputed by opposing interests within the same linguistic community? Parties to legal disputes may seek to gain coverage of a legal term ("liberty," "equality," even "murder") for their own interests, and to exclude other interests. This can be seen in minor disputes, or in major ones like the extension of the constitutional right of free expression to political campaign donations (hence the extension of "liberty"), of murder or homicide to doctor-assisted suicide, or of marriage to same-gender partners (implicating the extension of "equality"). With his famous aphorism "general propositions do not decide concrete cases," Holmes (drawing on influences that will be examined below) resisted responding to such

---

disputes axiomatically, through premature deduction from a general statement or statements about law or rights, rather than inductive exploration, a process informed by experiential feedback into the legal process from society at large. Precisely what induction means in this context is the principal subject of this paper.

For one thing, it implies social resolution of borderline cases. The ancient "Sorites paradox" questions at what point the addition (or subtraction) of an individual grain of sand governs defining a collection of grains as a "heap." "Heap" has thus been accounted an *inherently vague* term, as are many other terms when removed from context. Philosophers of law and language commonly treat semantic vagueness as a natural, in the sense of intrinsic, quality of discourse.[14] This ignores that the *legal* extension of "heap," or any other practically disputed term, can in the process of litigation take on a specific extension: it will be subject to increasingly precise determination through abstraction from particular decisions exploring the context of an emergent or ongoing actual dispute.

Thus, as was noted above regarding analogical reasoning, induction is not immediate; it is often connected with social conflict, with real-world instantiations of dialectical opposition. Its resolution is, moreover, experimental, and engages human creativity in the introduction of analogies and hypotheses; and the enterprise of extending human knowledge is intimately linked to the contentious nature of human conduct. Moreover, the process of legal inquiry is inadequately understood only as an examination of authoritative texts, or of only *judicial* activity and the operation of *legal* institutions alone.

This suggests that a focus on language alone limits and obscures attention to the process of conceptual change; and much contemporary theory is heavily committed to linguistic analysis. One issue that deserves continued emphasis is that the process of resolving uncertainty can be protracted, affecting the *appearance* of uncertainty. It is useful then to consider the implications of *stages* of inquiry. At the initial stage, a comparison of factual situations with existing doctrine may appear at its most uncertain, indeed closest to a description as "indeterminate." At a later stage, relevant factors will have been identified and addressed both within and outside the law, as for example private and public policy in disputes over medically assisted death. It is then that uncertainty and its resolution may yield to description by "general principle," but again, within *and outside* the legal arena.

How did Hume account for induction? "[The] far greatest part of our reasonings, with all our actions and passions, can be derived from nothing

---

[14] See, passim, Timothy A. O. Endicott, *Vagueness in Law* (Oxford: Oxford University Press, 2000); Timothy Williamson, *Vagueness* (London and New York, NY: Routledge, 1994); see also W. V. Quine, *Word and Object* (Cambridge, MA: Harvard University Press, 1960), 125–28.

but custom and habit."[15] Explanation of the operation of habit in Hume is surprisingly limited, especially regarding *conflicting* customs and habits. Some perspective is given in his *History of England*, as in the rise of Puritan manners and their replacement by those of the Restoration. But it is not until 1870–1880 that Holmes, albeit indirectly, suggests a way of seeing the problem of conflicting custom and habit in his exhaustive study of the common law.[16]

Habits in the common law are spelled out in precedents, through the "clustering" of specific decisions, retrospectively classified. Similarity is found in and through the defining and redefining of opposing precedents, coordinate with case-specific choices among conflicting preferences. This is the process of finding-and-imposing similarity, eschewing premature decision by ideology, in the model that Holmes identified in 1873 and eventually applied to all legal interpretation, including constitutional law. We saw that Holmes's main difference from other early pragmatists derived from his experience in the American Civil War. In Holmes's pragmatism, dispute and conflict in both law and social life are not external to philosophy—a malfunction of the legal order or the social system—but part of knowledge production itself, and of the maintenance *vel non* of social order in discrete situations. His interactional and frequently agonistic view of knowledge production carried Peirce's doubt-belief scheme further, as a study of the dependence of networks of legal belief on resolution of specified doubts engendered by specific problems, necessarily realigning patterns of conduct.

Critical to the resolution of conflicting positions is the influence of opposing social standards and the patterns of conduct supporting them. It is not possible for detached individuals, no matter how great their expertise, to resolve a deeply rooted dispute at a single moment, or even a succession of such experts to do so over time, without input from and adjustments within society at large. Knowledge, conduct, language, and conflict are all actively

---

[15] Hume, *Treatise*, Book 1 Part 3 sec. 10 (T118).

[16] Don Garrett writes, "Hume's naturalism and empiricism together require that here be a naturalistic explanation of how sense based concepts develop from experience. His naturalism also requires, however, that there be a naturalistic causal explanation of how normative concepts, whether sense-based or not, acquire normative status." This is the value of Holmes's two early essays in 1870 and 1873, applying Baconian principles to the continuum of inquiry into legal problems, and the process through which general normative concepts emerge from particular experience. Garrett, *Hume*, 170.

> Hume defines 'custom and habit' as the process by which "the repetition of any particular act or operation produces a propensity to renew the same act or operation, without being impelled by any reasoning or process of the understanding." Garrett notes: "[H]abit operates not on volition and bodily motion, but on a new initiating perception to produce an associated idea, and the liveliness of the initiating impression or memory provides the liveliness required to make that idea a belief." Garrett, *Hume*, 179.

interrelated. Inductive inquiry and inference take place (using terms later favored by John Dewey) in a "continuum" over time. It is, moreover, socially "transformative," and its success in practical terms (which I will define as the "convergence" of opposing positions) is never assured.[17]

Prompted by the early readings in his diary and his post-Civil War discussions, especially with James, Peirce, and Chauncey Wright, Holmes came to focus on the method of inductive generalization by judges in the common law tradition: how the elusive property of similarity, which is at the essence of logic in law (and logical induction in general), is found among novel and complex circumstances, and projected into future cases where opposing authorities conflict. In so doing, he reconceived logical induction as a social process, a form of inference that engages adaptive action and implies social transformation. Rather than Hume's famous problem (the impossibility of attributing validation to inductive inference from uncontroversially similar events) his focus turned instead to the logically prior question of *finding* similarity; of how, in legal or everyday inquiry, the objects of induction come to be recognized as similar, such that inductive inference itself (Hume's doubt notwithstanding) becomes even conceivable.

The mechanism of legal induction relies on consensus regarding similarities and differences that the law seeks among various classes of human activity. This approach, focusing on the social process through which legal similarity is found amidst often bitter controversy and eventually entrenched, has been almost entirely missing in accounts by other writers.[18] It implies an original insight, of social inductivism as a general philosophical perspective. It is drawn from John Stuart Mill's psychologistic approach to logical theory, which predated the flourishing of formal logic, wherein the issue of similarity is largely removed from consideration. Holmes's contribution to legal logic consists, in essence, of what might be called a "social-psychologistic" derivation from Mill, a line of logical theory that has yet to be fully recognized and carried forward. It is an early first step toward a sociology of legal knowledge.[19]

---

[17] It is upon the convergence of opposing positions that expository use of "we," implying an objective observer, is cognizable. My use of the term "convergence" is, admittedly, potentially misleading, as the character of opposing sides is inevitably transformed through the process of inquiry, and one side may encounter substantial defeat.

[18] "Entrenchment" in this usage includes general belief and action. This is stronger than linguistic assertion and cognitive acceptance, as in Frederick Schauer's definition in *Playing by the Rules: a Philosophical Examination of Rule-Based Decision-Making in Law and Life* (Oxford: Clarendon Press, 1991), 38f: "Instead of being continuously malleable in the service of changing circumstances, generalizations become entrenched, and the entrenchment of past generalizations impedes the possibility of an infinitely sensitive and adaptable language." (42)

[19] See chapter 11 below.

Part II

PRAGMATISM AND TWENTIETH-CENTURY LEGAL THEORY

Holmes's social inductivism looked beyond the immediate case, and rejected the analytical notion of a conceptual boundary and of a strict ontological separation between law and morals, both implied in the core concept of legal positivism, an analytical model of law that supported the idea of "legal indeterminacy" and the antinomy of formalism and realism, as well as Dworkin's appeal to principle and the radical CLS denial of any neutral governing theory of law. All rely on a primarily deductive, single-case model of immediate inference. The core model of legal positivism is a synchronic picture of law as a system of rules, expressed in propositions. This picture implies a boundary, if only an instantaneous one: the textual limit of all currently accepted authoritative propositions. Because there are always novel cases, for which uncontroversial deduction is unavailing, legal positivism leads to an uncritical acceptance of "legal indeterminacy." An obvious move, which Lon Fuller suggested, and Ronald Dworkin later deployed with deliberate skill, is to claim that moral "principles" can and should be used to ground a difficult decision.

Chapter 5

Positivism and the Myth of Legal Indeterminacy

John Dewey wrote that law is "through and through a social phenomenon" and that all legal theories should be judged as programs for action; he warned against use of the word "law" as a "single general term." Law, he explained, must be viewed as intervening in the complex of other activities, and as itself a social process. Hence (in Dewey's words), "'law' cannot be set up as a separate entity, but can be discussed only in terms of the social conditions in which it arises and of what it concretely does there."[1]

This is a classic statement of law as boundaryless, endogenous, embedded, and, as a social theorist might say, an "open system." I want to compare it with the competing and surprisingly dominant view—generally known as "legal positivism"—which sees law as fundamentally separate, exogenous, autonomous, acting upon society rather than acting within. Both models are in some degree reflected in the methodology of American law; yet the two are at odds. They imply a deep inconsistency in our corporate belief in what law is. What difference does it make which assumption is taken?

A significant one lies in their different approaches to legal interpretation. According to the positivist model of law as a separate and autonomous entity, law, considered as an adjudicative matrix, either succeeds or fails on its own. When it comes to deciding difficult cases this means the positivist must accept the real and problematic possibility of "legal indeterminacy."[2] The

---

[1] John Dewey, *Later Works*, Vol. 14 (Carbondale, IL: Southern Illinois University Press, 1988), 117. An early version of this paper was presented at the 2001 annual meeting of the Eastern Division of the American Philosophical Association. I am grateful to my commentator, Brian Bix, for his helpful comments and suggestions.
[2] See generally Lawrence B. Solum, "On the Indeterminacy Crisis: Critiquing Critical Dogma," 54 *U. Chicago L. Rev.* 462 (1987) and Brian Leiter, "Legal Indeterminacy," 1 *Legal Theory* 481–92 (1995).

issue of the boundary location of law itself becomes intimately involved with the question of legitimacy of judicial decisions. For the alternative model, legal indeterminacy carries a very different meaning, denoting degrees of uncertainty and difficulty.

The term "legal indeterminacy" can be understood conversationally to mean a high degree of difficulty, but this is not its meaning under positivism. The core issue of positivist jurisprudence, lending itself to the technique and style of analytic philosophy, is the definition and boundary of the concept of law. When the law does not appear to have any clear answer to a pertinent question, the positivist paradigm forces the issue whether the answer lies outside the boundary. Hypothetical cases raising boundary issues are critical to the analytical argument associated with positivism and its critics, as in the debates among Lon Fuller, H. L. A. Hart, and Ronald Dworkin.

How are we to adjudicate between two competing conceptions that appear to be mutually exclusive? Or must we adjudicate? The question is profound, and resembles the question that has emerged in philosophy of science at least since Thomas Kuhn's *Structure of Scientific Revolutions*: whether there is a separate and antecedent reality dictating a "correct" or "essential" version, or whether our conceptual understanding is in some strong sense imposed or constructed by humans. One of Ian Hacking's titles characterizes this conflict as between "Representing and Intervening"; does scientific conceptualization represent reality or intervene in it?

We can imagine a Kuhnian "paradigm crisis" in science more readily than in law; a new set of phenomena, demonstrable by experiments replicable by others, gradually undermines general belief. In law, however, belief itself exerts unobservable control over phenomena. For instance, who is to say that a putative right does not exist so long as it is effectively enforced, and widely acted upon? Representation and intervention would appear to be cogenerative. Legal beliefs may control phenomena through commitment to a set of official, professional, and public habits. Habits then provide the perceived empirical foundation for the system of beliefs.

DEWEY AND THE CONCRETE BOUNDARY

Deweyan instrumentalism, like Charles Peirce's pragmaticism, is well known for its emphasis upon subjecting theory (and its conceptual components) to a consequentialist evaluation. In comparing different theories, insofar as there is no programmatic difference, there should be no theoretical difference, regardless of form. A concept with no programmatic relevance should be, if not meaningless, unworthy of serious attention. But if we apply Dewey's consequentialist test to his warning about use of the word "law" as a "single general term," we unearth an issue that Dewey himself had come close to recognizing in "Logical Method and Law:" whether there is any programmatic advantage to be gained in "setting up law as a separate entity."[3]

Separate from what? Take "morals," for instance, the context in which the matter was raised in the debate between H. L. A. Hart and Lon Fuller in the mid-twentieth century. For Dewey the question (call it Q[a]) "whether law and morals are separate" is not a question at all, because it involves "set[ting law] up as a separate entity." So also, by this test, would the question (Q[b]) whether law and morals should be separate, a question that itself may be distinguished into (1) whether law should be believed to be, or (2) made to be, separate from morals. But the last question (Q[b2]) would have programmatic relevance if there were any real prospect of making such a separation. This is an issue obscured by Dewey's warning.

Question Q[b1], whether law and morals should be believed to be separate, lies in an uneasy no-man's-land between positivism and Dewey. It would appear to mix fact and program, empiricism and consequentialism, in implying uncertainty over the underlying issue whether the truth (in this context) is itself given or made. That is, it waffles over whether belief must be sought only in existing operational fact or whether an independent belief might itself generate sufficient operational fact to dig its own empirical foundation. The notion of belief digging a self-sustaining empirical foundation is anathema to natural scientists; but it cannot be ruled out of the question in law.

The Fuller/Hart question (Q[a]) is actually quite close to Q[b1] in implying this same uncertainty. Fuller and Hart could not keep the differing implications distinct, often switching in the middle of their alternating texts from arguments rooted in existing operational fact (like what proper Anglo-American lawyers and judges say and do) to arguments based on prophylactic considerations (like what they ought to do, and whether positivism would or would not expose fascist legal practices). Their failure to quell this uncertainty derived from the fact that the phrase "whether law and morals are separate" hides the lynchpin role of belief that Peirce and Dewey found so crucial.

As noted above, the same uncertainty is found in Dewey's warning against setting law up as a separate entity when using the word as a "single general term." If so doing might generate a belief that results in a practice, and/or a practice that supports a foundation for the belief, then the warning should be

---

[3] There Dewey remarks, "The logic of exposition is different from that of search and inquiry. . . . Exposition implies that a definitive solution has been reached; that the situation is determinate with respect to its legal implications. Its purpose is to set forth grounds for the decision reached so that it will not appear as an arbitrary dictum, and so as to indicate the rule for dealing with similar cases in the future." He appears to recognize here that an autonomous model of law may have benefits in its effect on general belief. John Dewey, "Logical Method and Law," 10 *Cornell Law Review* (1924) 17. 15 MW (1983).

directed elsewhere: to the practices so generated, whether as cart or horse in relation to belief. As for the conclusion Dewey draws to the effect that law "can be discussed only in terms of the social conditions in which it arises and of what it concretely does there," we should note that the only way this proposition can be stated at all is through using the word "law" as a "single general term."

The Deweyan, it seems in retrospect, is stuck with at least the verbal entity "law," and the question of separation is a matter not of whether but how. The Deweyan cannot avoid the fact that theorizing about "law" entails attributing objecthood to it, if only as a thought form. This happens in discussing law even in terms of "the social conditions in which it arises and what it concretely does there." Moreover, insisting otherwise would "block the path of inquiry" (another Deweyan precept: all paths are to be kept open) into the question whether favorable programmatic results might emerge from believing law to be separate, in a concrete sense or in any sense at all.[4]

For noticeable operational results to be forthcoming, it would be necessary for the belief to be reasonably widespread. If this were already the case, belief and separation together would presumably be found embedded in the interaction between law and society: an interaction, that is to say, within the very social conditions that the Deweyan would prefer to privilege. Now we can specify the path of inquiry that Dewey's warning has obscured: not whether law is separate, but to what degree and in what sense it is, might, and indeed should be—judged by the consequences. This brings us back to legal indeterminacy.

IS LEGAL INDETERMINACY A MYTH?

From legal positivism's nineteenth-century roots has emerged, in the post-twentieth-century legacy of H. L. A. Hart, a picture of legal interpretation addressing the metaphorical space between strands of authoritative legal language. Although a rough analogy, it still remains dominant in the discussions of legal philosophers. But it contributes inescapable general qualities to the analysis. Law is seen as a fixed pattern or fabric against which individual cases are compared and either fitted or not. The model naturally leads to attributing the element of uncertainty in legal interpretation (to which the fact of litigation attests) to the relatively static fabric or "body" of law—as opposed to the flow of human problems that bring disputes into the courts.

---

[4] The view advanced by Thomas Hobbes held that the separation of law and morals was necessary to the maintenance of law's authority, an argument still being advanced today, *mutatis mutandis*, by Joseph Raz.

Justice Holmes once wrote, "Great cases, like hard cases, make bad law."[5] In the ideal texture model (one in which the legal texture is clear and unambiguous), "hard" cases (in the sense of indeterminate ones) do not "make" bad law—or make any law. If the texture permits, there will be a right answer, or alternatively the law must be presumed indeterminate and judges must "legislate." The former requires general agreement on a textural vision. The search for the correct vision then becomes a search for consensus on a single right theory or philosophy of law. If this does not succeed, the law must be indeterminate, in a strong, perhaps fundamental, sense—the claim of critical legal studies.[6]

David Lyons (1999) has demonstrated that open texture theory, adopting the conception of metaphorical space in an open-textured entity "law," either renders the project of legal interpretation impossible or the language of judges and lawyers fraudulent. For the metaphorical space to be truly empty, any gap in the rule must be a gap in the law as a whole, as there would otherwise be someplace else within the law to find an answer. Hence, for such gaps there is no possibility of deciding a case by interpreting "the law." Lyons observes that this is inconsistent with what happens in actual legal disputes.

Lyons takes the example used by Hart in his exposition of open texture[7] theory. A local ordinance bans vehicles from a public park. Competent users of English are uncertain or disagree about whether bicycles are vehicles. Hart infers that the rule banning vehicles from the park has a core of determinate meaning and a penumbra of indeterminate meaning, into which the bicycle would fall. Therefore, according to Hart, to decide the case a court must assign to the rule an increment of determinate meaning that it did not previously have.

But, as Lyons observes, this assumes a logical step that is not necessary in actual practice. Assume that a judge decides for the defendant; this would not require incremental meaning for the term "vehicle." The case could simply be decided under the principle that "conduct which is not legally prohibited is legally permitted." Thus, although there might be an appearance of open texture in the language of authoritative legal materials, this does not in practice give rise to gaps in the law, as there is no gap-filling required to decide the matter. A court deciding a paradigmatic "open texture" case need not

---

[5] Holmes, dissenting, in *Northern Securities v. United States*, 193 U.S. 197, 400 (1903). Although "hard" for Holmes here was closer to "draconian," the current meaning is "difficult." While Holmes used the phrase "hard case" in its original sense, as one that "tugs at the heartstrings," it has come to refer to the doubtful or indeterminate case.

[6] Roberto Unger, *The Critical Legal Studies Movement* (Cambridge, MA: Harvard University Press, 1983).

[7] David Lyons, "Open Texture and the Possibility of Legal Interpretation." *Legal Philosophy*, vol. 18, no. 3, 297–309.

become a surrogate legislature by contributing new meaning to the indeterminate term. This is reinforced by the working assumption of lawyers and judges who speak and act in such cases as if they are applying the law. To hold otherwise would imply that judges and lawyers are massively confused or deceitful in purporting to resolve difficult cases according to "the law."

The model of law as texture cannot avoid attributing the precise element of uncertainty to the same ontological entity by which it is to be resolved, thereby rendering its removal impossible by definition. This is the antinomy of Hartian legal positivism.[8]

THE ENDOGENOUS MODEL

In the endogenous or embedded model, uncertainty might arise not from the vagueness of language, but rather from the novelty of the situation itself. The alternative model would view the bicycle situation as principally a case of inadequate city management. Bicycles were certainly in existence when the code provision barring vehicles was adopted, and the uncertainty over the coverage of "vehicle," once noted, should immediately have been cleared up at a special meeting of the city council. Such cases do not generally fill the dockets of the courts of appeal. Those cases may invoke analysis of the extension of terms, but their resistance to resolution more often arises from problematic doubts involving the consequences from applying a given rule to a novel situation.

This can be true of cases involving extension of terms in a settled rule, but it is more typical of cases involving conflicts among apparently settled but conflicting rules. All such novel cases may make bad law because a new precedent must be cut into the settled context from unique conditions. Difficulty in this context is principally associated with anomalous facts. The difficult case that makes bad law would not be one in which a judge is trying to decipher the intent behind a poorly drafted provision, containing facts that clearly ought to have been foreseen. It is a case which no official, whether common law judge or legislator, apparently foresaw.

Some elucidation of the alternative model is necessary. As previously stated, it is drawn from an historical study of the common law, in Holmes's famous remark, "It is the merit of the common law that it decides the case first and determines the principle afterwards." This comment implies a sort

---

[8] W. V. Quine describes an antinomy as a paradox that produces a self-contradiction by accepted ways of reasoning (*The Ways of Paradox and Other Essays*, Cambridge, MA: Harvard University Press, 1976, 5). Timothy Williamson might reply that the problem lies in the epistemic nature of vagueness; see Kellogg, *Oliver Wendell Holmes Jr*, 117f.

of common-law judicial minimalism, deciding "one case at a time."[9] The passage proposes a model through which common law rules are ideally formulated "only after a series of determinations on the same subject-matter." As noted in chapter 2, Holmes called this process "successive approximation." Legal rules are viewed historically, and this passage proposes that they be understood as emerging from classes of activity, or more precisely from classes of private disputes within discrete activities. As new cases arise within a given class, for example communications among people forming contractual arrangements, they are initially decided on their facts, a case at a time. Eventually, a body of decided cases can be "reconciled," with the laying down of a general rule, after time has permitted sufficient case-specific analysis, probing the relevant varieties and conditions of contractual communications. But finality is elusive. The introduction of e-mail may require new amendments, as did the telegraph in the previous century.

Holmes—at least the early Holmes—can be viewed as one of the last of the grand common law theorists. His early writing marries the tradition of Coke, Hale, and Blackstone to the emergence of American pragmatism. His contribution is parallel to Peirce and Dewey: to bring a similarly constructivist approach to the philosophy of law. The issue of legal interpretation suggests that it is of more than merely historical interest. So, reconstructed, common law theory gives a very different location to legal indeterminacy. Hart's positivism places it within the fabric or "body" of law, while Holmes's common law theory puts it outside, assuming it as a more or less constant condition of human interaction and conflict.

This ontological distinction is critical to the definition of pragmatism as a philosophy of law. It is also a defining distinction between pragmatism and the underlying visions of liberal jurisprudence and critical legal studies, as well as the "neopragmatism" of Richard Rorty. The following chapters address these perspectives.

---

[9] See e.g. Sunstein, *One Case at a Time*.

Chapter 6

Pragmatism and Neopragmatism

The most distinctive feature of "neopragmatism" is its own sense of prox-imity to and common purpose with more recent Continental writers of an anti-foundational bent, including some for whom the pragmatic label would not previously have been comfortable, for example, Nietzsche, Heidegger, and Foucault. Accordingly, an important breach opened between followers of Richard Rorty and stalwarts of the "old school" of American pragmatism, in particular over objections by the latter to Rorty's reduction of philoso-phy to mere "conversation"[1] and his attack on John Dewey's metaphysics.[2]

---

[1] See "Symposium on Rorty's Consequences of Pragmatism," *Transactions of the Charles S. Peirce Society* 21 (1985): 1–48. I would like to thank Ralph W. Sleeper, Michael Sullivan, Vincent Colapi-etro, Mark V. Tushnet, Andrew Altman, and Henry S. Richardson and the Editors of *Journal of Speculative Philosophy* for their helpful comments and suggestions on an early draft of this chapter.

[2] See "Dewey's Metaphysics," in R. Rorty (ed.), *Consequences of Pragmatism* (Minneapolis, MN: University of Minnesota Press, 1982), 72–89; elsewhere Rorty claims harmony with Dewey's philosophical intentions:

> "Dewey preferred to skip talk of 'authority,' 'legitimacy' and 'obligation' and to talk instead about 'applied intelligence' and 'democracy.' He hoped we would stop using the juridical vocabulary which Kant made fashionable among philosophers, and start using metaphors drawn from town meetings rather than from tribunals. He wanted the first question of both politics and philosophy to be not, 'What is legitimate?' or, 'What is authoritative?' but, 'What can we get together and agree on?' This is the strand in Dewey's thought which Rawls, especially in his later writings, has picked up and developed. Posner's vision of the function of American judges—his vision of their ability to travel back and forth between the present and the future and to try to fashion a moral unity out of our national history—fits nicely into Dewey's way of thinking. Nor is Posner's vision very different, I suspect, from that of most Americans who take an interest in what the courts, and especially the Supreme Court, are up to—at least those who are grateful for the Court's decision in *Brown v. Board of Education*. For those who believe that the Civil Rights Movement, the movement which *Brown* initiated, was an enormous boost to our national self-respect and a reassuring instance of our continuing capacity for moral progress, the thought that the courts do not just

79

Meanwhile the ramifications of this breach are being discussed by legal philosophers. Historically, developments in American legal theory have roughly paralleled the larger movements of general philosophy, and this seems to be true for neopragmatism. Rorty has written increasingly on legal and political theory, and there are now a substantial number of self-described neopragmatists in legal academia.[3]

What is neopragmatism, and how does it differ from Dewey's pragmatism or Peirce's pragmaticism? And, why is this important? So far, discussion of this problem has turned heavily on the role of epistemology. Rorty has argued, to many persuasively, that Dewey's concern with traditional metaphilosophical questions betrayed a schizoid failure to assimilate the very challenge to traditional epistemic problems and dualisms that he made so effective.

Defenders of Dewey are increasingly anxious over Rorty's project of carrying that challenge to an extreme Dewey clearly did not contemplate: the declaration of an end not only to epistemology but to metaphilosophy in general.[4] Arguments on both sides rely heavily on Dewey's own often-ambiguous language. I suggest that more light can be thrown on this question by examining neopragmatism's entry into legal and political theory, as Richard J. Bernstein has done at an earlier stage of Rorty's writing.[5] The battle over pragmatism's soul is less abstract there, and it is easier to apply its own first principle: tracing the consequences of the conceptual issues.

A genealogy suggests that pragmatism and Continental anti-foundationalism emerge from distinctly different historical origins. The Metaphysical Club, the discussion group in Cambridge, Massachusetts, from which pragmatism is said to have emerged in the early 1870s, consisted in large part of lawyers like N. St. John Green and Oliver Wendell Holmes, Jr. As Max Fisch pointed out 50 years ago, their philosophical interest in the theory of the common law was intertwined with Peirce's analysis of scientific and philosophical inquiry.[6] The main agenda of the Metaphysical Club is seen today as undressing traditional metaphysical problems with a consequentialist test for meaning and belief.[7]

---

apply rules, but make them, is no longer frightening." *Philosophy and Social Hope* (New York, NY: Penguin Books), 111.

[3] See Graham Hubbs and Douglas Lind, eds., *Pragmatism, Law, and Language* (New York, NY and London: Routledge, 2014).

[4] See R. Sleeper, "The Pragmatics of Deconstruction and the End of Metaphysics," in John J. Stuhr (ed.), *Philosophy and the Reconstruction of Culture* (Albany, NY: SUNY Press, 1993), 241.

[5] R. Bernstein, "One Step Forward, Two Steps Backward: Richard Rorty on Liberal Democracy and Philosophy," *Political Theory* 15 (November 1987): 538–63.

[6] M. Fisch, "Justice Holmes, The Prediction Theory of Law, and Pragmatism," *Journal of Philosophy* 39 (1942): 85.

[7] P. Wiener, *Evolution and the Founders of Pragmatism* (Cambridge, MA: Harvard University Press, 1949), 18–30.

But for the lawyers among them this also involved a political mission: articulating a coherent legal theory for a revolutionary democratic republic still less than a century old. Implicit in their discussions was the question, How can the American legal system, founded in revolution against an aristocratic, monarchical order, adopt the common law of England as its legal basis? How could the common law, rooted in British tradition, be understood in a manner consistent with the Declaration of Independence and the United States Constitution? The answer, developed in Holmes's early essays (1870–1880) leading to *The Common Law*,[8] is that the concepts and methods of the common law may be understood as conforming the legal order with a process of rule formation that was, if not democratic in the strict majoritarian sense, nevertheless neither fundamentally autocratic nor surreptitiously counter majoritarian.

Holmes's formulation was that common-law rules are derived by a community-oriented process of "successive approximation" that is strikingly parallel to the process Peirce attributed to the development of scientific laws and general philosophical principles. The function of a community of inquirers was as central to the legal theory of Holmes as to the scientific and philosophical theory of Peirce.[9] The role of juries in legal development was crucial, as their decisions provided the raw data, thousands of case-specific decisions, from which judges eventually abstracted rules. And, jury decisions had the effect of impressing upon the law standards of conduct drawn from outside the legal profession and its body of doctrine.

In deciding where the cost of an injury should lie, juries listened carefully to the explanations of the parties—farmers, tradesmen, ship captains, landlords and tenants—and judges refrained from rule-making until a clear pattern of decisions had established the standards and expectations indigenous to a given practice. This picture had political and philosophical significance. The generalizing element of law, the process of rule-making and the analysis that goes along with it, could be seen not as imposed from above but as subservient to indigenous custom and practice, indeed to the distinctive practices of the new American society. The community of observers that governed Peirce's conception of scientific inquiry translates into a vast community of living actors determining the continuing growth of the common law and making it responsive to emerging social practices.

Moreover, subjective legal theorizing could be reined in by such a model. The creation of legal concepts and classifications would await the deliberate

---

[8] Reprinted in Frederic R. Kellogg, *The Formative Essays of Justice Holmes: The Making of an American Legal Philosophy* (Westport, CT: Greenwood Press, 1984).

[9] Oliver Wendell Holmes, "Codes, and the Arrangement of the Law," *American Law Review* 5 (1870): 1–2, reprinted in Kellogg, supra note 7, 77–78. See also Note, "Holmes, Peirce and Legal Pragmatism," *Yale Law Journal* 84 (1975): 1123.

and fair assessment of the actual consequences of the decisions themselves. Hence, in the legal context we can see the practical importance of the so-called pragmatic maxim, whereby concepts are to be tested by their consequences.[10] If this maxim is not strictly observed in the legal arena, loose abstraction does more than merely cloud or distort theory making; it impinges upon freedom of action, as the abstractions of law in the hands of judges carry coercive power. Let us note how different this is from the Continental roots of neopragmatism. Both have emphasized a critique of the foundationalist tendency of Western philosophy.

But nineteenth century pragmatism came to this view less from a sense of exhaustion of the Enlightenment tradition and more from a democratic reconceptualization of Western scientific and political culture. Pragmatism and neopragmatism both reject any claim of epistemology to a privileged human-centered insight into the source of knowledge. But the original pragmatic version saw itself as providing a corrective insight into the social situation of philosophy, revealing the massive degree of contingency and uncertainty left unaddressed by traditional theory-making, and an equally massive ethical miscarriage that may accompany detached or non-contingent philosophical assertions.

However massive this element is, it is nonetheless a matter of degree of error; neopragmatism sees it as absolute, intrinsic. Unlike neopragmatism, the original pragmatic approach carries a reconstructive tool. Theoretical statements may still be made, even universals postulated, as long as their contingency is adequately recognized and accounted for by a self-evaluative understanding. The message this carries for the debate over epistemology and meta philosophy is clear: The pragmatic version would preserve these disciplines in order to maintain the corrected epistemic perspective, as a means of evaluating the warrantability of theory.

The neopragmatic version, meanwhile, urges abandonment of the epistemic (or "self-evaluative") program, from which it is said to be a short step to relativism and nihilism.[11] The battle over Dewey's alleged metaphysics does not bring this sufficiently to light, I submit, because it is too abstract. It is so general that it is nearly impossible to determine whether and why a disposition to treat, or not to treat, purely epistemological questions as such, makes any difference in terms of practical consequences, the touchstone of pragmatic analysis. This condition derives from the difficulty of explicating a pragmatic program for philosophy at a time of Rorty's rampant criticism and general disillusionment with the main paths of inquiry since the Enlightenment. Any practical bearing of those paths is smothered in the general perception of their failure, and with it is lost the appeal pragmatism

---

[10] C. S. Peirce, *Collected Papers*, Vol. 5 (Cambridge, MA: The Belknap Press, 1978), 258 (5.402).

[11] For Rorty's position with respect to this claim, see, e.g., *Contingency, Irony, and Solidarity*, 75.

originally displayed to its founders as a means of identifying and specifying degrees of uncertainty at every level.

For classical pragmatism, generalizing was tested by consequences and connected to the solution of human problems. In law, this highlights the degree of inclusion; yet not just in law, but in science, and philosophy itself, meaning can be described as but the best consensus of all those confronted with a practical stake in the outcome. Fallibilism originated as a reference to the inherent element of uncertainty and ambiguity in forming and translating that consensus through language. For neopragmatism, evidence of this element seems to indicate an absolute impossibility, while for Peirce and Holmes it is attributed to failures to be adequately consequentialist and inclusive.[12]

Clearly some redescription was in order. Holmes observed that the life of the law has not been logic, it has been experience. In cutting away the presumptively precise and self-determining character of law and replacing it with human exigency, control over the generalizing and rule-making element was detached from its traditional location in the state and rooted in society at large. Holmes's was a revolutionary, putatively classless, society committed to the radical principles of 1776. Hence, it was necessary formally to recognize that everyone had a stake in the outcome of all debate, including philosophical debate, which might affect legal theory and in turn the exercise of sanctions affecting everyone.

Pragmatism thus emerged as the philosophy of democracy, ideally an unbounded democracy of unlimited inquiry, not apologizing for the existing order but rather making actual inquiry, as well as real democratic institutions, always seem inadequate. It is the first philosophy to be based on exigency, fallibility, and representivity. Eliminating the focus on human exigency forces a choice between essentialism and relativism: either we discern the transcendent in sublime detachment from that which impels us, or we do not see it at all. Such a detachment is signified by the tendency of neopragmatists to prefer the term "anti-foundationalism," which implies the impossibility of such discernment.

Classical pragmatism leaves open whether discernments rooted in exigency may lead to general expressions that are, for all recognizable purposes, worthy of consideration as transcendent, although the notion of transcendency is itself subject to a continuing, and evolving, practical test. Moreover, eliminating exigency removes the basis for representivity. Without it, such insights

---

[12] Two observations by Bernstein are worth noting here: that Dewey's notion of the "practical" was not a gross, everyday version that ignored the scientific urge to search for important new problems; and that part of the difficulty of formulating consensus lay in the hypothetical character of generalization, its orientation toward the future and need to encompass yet unknown and hence inherently uncertain and ambiguous developments. See Richard Bernstein, ed., *On Experience, Nature, and Freedom* (Indianapolis, IN: Bobbs-Merrill Co., 1960), xxv, xxviii.

as philosophers may produce need not be evaluated by nonphilosophers nor tested against non- philosophical purposes or needs. Such consensus as may develop need not be expanded beyond a given "school."

Coping with exigency is the original pragmatic criterion of method. Abandoning it forces the fallibilist into nihilism regarding meaning and truth, in which the notion of method has nothing to relate to but a detached and essentialist notion of theory. Rorty's ironism essentially adopts this view. While his criticism of method has been understood to refer to philosophy's traditional obsession with epistemology, his premises oblige him to go further, undermining even such procedural standards as have been given pragmatically transcendent status by legal theory.

In 1990, Rorty authored an article on neopragmatism and legal theory for a symposium at the University of Southern California Law School. In it, he addresses the question "whether the so-called 'new' pragmatists have anything to contribute, anything that we have not already internalized as a result of being taught by people who were raised on Dewey." Rorty writes:

> My own answer to this question is that the new pragmatism differs from the old in just two respects, only one of which is of much interest to people who are not just philosophy professors. The first is that we new pragmatists talk about language instead of experience, or mind, or consciousness, as the old pragmatists did. The second respect is that we have all read Kuhn, Hanson, Toulmin, and Feyerabend, and have thereby become suspicious of the term "scientific method." New pragmatists wish that Dewey, Sidney Hook, and Ernest Nagel had not insisted on using this term as a catchphrase, since we are unable to provide anything distinctive for it to denote.[13]

We know from *Contingency, Irony, and Solidarity* that Rorty's replacement of "experience" with language marks an essential move for him and that, insofar as Rorty is concerned, that move is the critical difference between "new" and "old" pragmatism. Before examining what it means for legal theory, we might recall how Rorty explains this move in the opening chapter, where he praises Donald Davidson for carrying the contingent theory of language to its natural conclusion: "[W]e need to see the distinction between the literal and the metaphorical in the way Davidson sees it: not as a distinction between two sorts of meaning, nor as a distinction between two sorts of interpretation, but as a distinction between familiar and unfamiliar uses of noises and marks."[14]

---

[13] R. Rorty, "The Banality of Pragmatism and the Poetry of Justice," *Southern California Law Review* 63 (1990): 1811–19.

[14] Rorty, *Contingency, Irony, and Solidarity*, 17.

Rorty's emphasis on the utter contingency of language as mere "noises and marks" is connected to a presumption that it is the natural extension of the notion of truth as made, not found. Rorty focuses on the latter as the essential philosophical truth that pragmatism, since its founding, has carried further toward its natural extension since it emerged at the end of the eighteenth century.[15] But considering the nineteenth-century origins of legal pragmatism, we are in a position to ask whether pragmatism was originally concerned, as Rorty has it, only with establishing the notion that truth is made and not found, which is essentially the issue of *whether* truth is made, and not with *how* it is made.

Rorty's simplification collapses into the tautology that pragmatism is no more than part of a process of "making" a truth that itself consists of nothing more than the truth that (by definition) truth is made: a meager outcome for more than a century's worth of effort. In fact, as I have suggested, for the early legal pragmatists the issue of *how* was not only part of the matter, it was the really important part. Rorty's tendency, along with that of so many of the "new" pragmatists, to focus on Kuhn and Feyerabend comes into play here, as these writers have concentrated on aspects of the contingency of scientific theory. And with scientific theory, once those aspects are in sharp focus, the "how" question looks considerably less important than the "whether" question.

That is, once the progress of science is depicted as a series of leaps from one incommensurable paradigm to another, the role of the individual scientific revolutionary tends to overshadow the seemingly reactionary scientific community that seems to do nothing but stand in the way. This is not at all the case in respect to the contingent aspects of legal theory, where the role of the evaluative community is the touchstone of preserving democratic values. And, the Newtons and Einsteins are missing from political theory; in their shoes are a diverse group of grand theorists ranging from Edmund Burke to Karl Marx, few of whom draw unqualified praise from the new anti-foundationalists.

The truth that is made in legal theory, following the pragmatic maxim, can ultimately be translated into a series of prospective rulings by law courts that everyone must do and not do certain things lest they (1) pay money or (2) go to jail. If we care what those rulings are, how they might affect us personally, and where they might be leading our community, we had better care deeply about the "how" question. And the "how" question is, I submit, precisely the question that Rorty rules out in his recent article on legal neopragmatism when he denies that pragmatism has anything distinctive to tell us about legal method.

---

[15] Rorty, *Contingency, Irony, and Solidarity*, 3.

To carry this argument further, Rorty has written that the truth is not "out there," a notion that he calls "the legacy of an age in which the world was seen as the creation of a being who had a language of his own."[16] Instead, "What is true . . . is just that *languages* are made rather than found, and that truth is a property of linguistic entities, of sentences."[17] Language, in turn, is best thought of as Davidson suggests, not as a medium but as a set of metaphors made by "noises and marks." To see the history of language, and thus of the arts, the sciences, and the moral sense, as the history of metaphor is to drop the picture of the human mind, or human languages, becoming better and better suited to the purposes for which God and Nature designed them, for example, able to express more meanings or to represent more and more facts . . . we must follow Mary Hesse in thinking of scientific revolutions as "metaphoric revolutions" of nature rather than insights into the intrinsic nature of nature.[18]

Here it is clearer that what Rorty is saying about contingency is that it exists between separate languages, "final" vocabularies, implying that it is not so readily identified within a language such as that which Rorty and I presumably share. But how do we know when we are within or without? Is my vocabulary so different that it is responsible for our disagreement? Passing this, What happens when we apply his argument to legal theory? Two things happen, according to Rorty's recent writings. First, we relinquish any metatheoretical means of criticizing, correcting, or even controlling legal method as such, the manner in which legal concepts and classifications are arrived at and decisions and rules are made. After all, these are part of some metaphor, incommensurable with any other metaphor that someone speaking a different language might apply to the situation.

But we go further than this; we also amend Holmes's famous dictum, "The life of the law has not been logic; it has been experience," by replacing "experience" with "noises and marks." While experience must be reflected in language, and an accepted expression of the pragmatic approach is that truth is made and not found, language and theory cannot be separated from, nor conflated with, the totality of experience. Rorty has detached this proposition from its earlier context with an exposition of its logical potential. He has done this in the abstract, not unlike grand theorists in the Cartesian tradition. The perception of truth being made and not found is not an absolute, or an abstract truth, or a major premise, or even a proposition that is entitled to any kind of "privilege," even conversational privilege. We need to keep in mind how truth is made, not found. If there is any place where we can see truth plainly

---

[16] Rorty, *Contingency, Irony, and Solidarity*, 5.

[17] Rorty, *Contingency, Irony, and Solidarity*, 7 (emphasis in original, footnote omitted).

[18] Rorty, *Contingency, Irony, and Solidarity*, 16.

being made and not found, it's in legal theory. And even before that discovery, while people were still under the illusion that legal truths were found, the "how" question was important; only it was easier to rationalize the summary execution of those who raised qualms about that question by those who were in charge of the "finding" process.

Ever since it became more obvious that it is a "making" process, summary executions have appeared arbitrary, and "methodological" considerations have gotten in the way, like phenomena referred to in the United States under the topic of "constitutional due process." My point is that neopragmatism ignores that legal method has become not less but more important with the pragmatic emphasis on the "made" quality of truth. So also it ignores the increased importance of seeing law as experience rather than as mere language or metaphor. After all, despite the "noises and marks" that denominate "due process," people even in the twentieth century have ignored key parts of the lesson that Rorty reminds us began to be taught 200 years ago.[19]

Even if heroes of political theory like Karl Marx and Friedrich Nietzsche knew that truth is made and not found, this did not stop Stalin and Hitler from going "back" to practices such as summary execution. We might ask whether Rorty's doctrine of law as metaphor would have stood in the way of that, or stands right now in the way of its happening again. Perhaps it gives dictators an easy out by arguing that those raising qualms about their rationales must be "unfamiliar" with their "vocabulary." It is hard to see how neopragmatism can soften this with Rorty's qualification that utter contingency only exists between "final" vocabularies, implying that tyrants would be obliged to defend against the claim that theirs is, within the language of liberalism, clearly a deviant local practice.

Rorty's main argument is that he wants to force us into "giving up the idea that liberalism could be justified, and Nazi or Marxist enemies of liberalism refuted, by driving the latter up against an argumentative wall."[20] But classical pragmatism did precisely the opposite of driving foundationalists, or theorists of any kind, against an argumentative wall; the wall of certainty was removed, and it held them accountable for the type of experience, the breadth of experience, and the representivity of experience beneath their claims. Rorty is right in his first point, that pragmatism denies a purely metatheoretical check on legal method, if by this is meant a property of language or theory divorced from supporting experience.

But as in Holmes's analysis of common law, method is inextricable from exigency, it is the very process of deciding, and its standards are drawn from the everyday practices of doing the things that are to be decided. Legal theory

---

[19] Rorty, *Contingency, Irony, and Solidarity*, 3.
[20] Rorty, *Contingency, Irony, and Solidarity*, 53.

is part of the practice, in which practice itself is evaluated. "Meta-theory" is an unfortunate term; it should signify simply that the practice is self-evaluative, but it seems to say that theory can evaluate itself in a vacuum. Strictly speaking, argument, *per se*, did not and will not win the day for democratic methods. Nor did classical pragmatism assume this. Both democracy and pragmatic philosophy grew out of a set of historical developments that actually connected 'imperfectly but strategically' sanctions with democratic review and approval.

Classical pragmatism has been intimately connected with democratic experience from the outset, so that its differences with neopragmatism or any other school are unlikely to be resolved by argument, if argument is wholly detached from experience. Our own history of debate over democratic values and institutions should remind us of the difficulty of persuasion by argument alone. Colonial Americans chose democratic revolution in lieu of a British-style aristocracy not from its logical merit but by comparison of different modes of experience. As is so often true of political dialogue, appeals to base human motives were employed to bring home this comparison. Supporters of the crown sought to quell revolutionary zeal by exploiting the colonials' own selfish motives,[21] while advocates of revolution played on envy of those accepting royal advancement.

Eighty years later, Lincoln's adroit arguments against slavery were designed to associate nonexpansion with the basic democratic experience to which the free could relate: "As I would not be a slave, so I would not be a master. This expresses my idea of democracy. Whatever differs from this, to the extent of the difference, is no democracy."[22] But mere argument could not resolve that dispute. Indeed, Rorty himself appeals to experience in defending his position divorcing philosophy and experience. A main thrust of *Contingency, Irony, and Solidarity* is to persuade liberals that he has not abandoned democratic values. Thus, he stretches to demonstrate that "ironist theory can be privatized, and thus prevented from becoming a threat to political liberalism," and to show that a "loathing for cruelty" can be combined, at least in literature, with "a sense of the contingency of selfhood and of history."[23]

To do this, Rorty has to appeal to the most basic experience of all: the idea that we all have an overriding obligation to diminish cruelty, to make human beings equal in respect to their liability to suffering, seems to take for granted that there is something within human beings which deserves respect

---

[21] See Gordon Wood, *Creation of the American Republic* (New York, NY: Norton & Co., 1972), 91–124.

[22] Abraham Lincoln, *Collected Works*, Roy R. Basler (ed.) (New Brunswick, NJ: Rutgers University Press, 1953), 2:532.

[23] Rorty, *Contingency, Irony and Solidarity*, 190.

and protection quite independently of the language they speak. It suggests that a nonlinguistic ability, the ability to feel pain, is what is important, and that differences in vocabulary are much less important.[24]

The question boils down, in Rorty's own words, to whether ideas, language, and pain are related, or alternatively whether "the idea that we all have an overriding obligation to diminish cruelty" does in fact "take for granted" something "which deserves respect and protection quite independently of the language [we] speak." What is signified by Rorty's use of the term "independently" here? He concedes that the "idea" element may indeed be associated with the "ability to feel pain," despite his assertion of intrinsic disconnection between pain and language, and if this consideration is worth relying upon as part of Rorty's case, it is hard to accept that it is independent of the language he speaks, or especially his "philosophy."

In other words, is it implausible to adopt an account of the emergence of democratic philosophy and institutions in which the ideas associated with them were connected with the relevant body of experience, the ability to feel pain, the desire to avoid cruelty and humiliation, as well as other effects of the process of governance, from which language as a means of communication cannot be divorced? In this account the dynamic element, on which the emergence of democracy has ultimately depended, has been the feeling or experiencing, both by afflicted people and for afflicted people, in combination with language and theory, serving to bring home the consequences of competing interpretations of the situation people were in.

Hence, those engaged in interpretive generalizing, and that includes philosophers, cannot avoid their general statements having meaning and consequences as explanation of or prescriptions for comparative modes of experience. To be sure, by the pragmatic standard, language can be misleading and theories can be wrong. Perhaps that will turn out to be the best account of the failures of the Enlightenment. But the remedy is not to attribute this to the innate character of language and fatal entrapments in metaphor. Rather, we might examine the methods used where Enlightenment generalizers went astray. What exigencies did they respond to? Were they sufficiently fallibilistic? How representative were they?

Rorty's interpretation comes from a provisional leap from Kuhn's model of scientific paradigm-shifts to equating the literal and metaphorical across the board, in every field of theory, just because there seems to be no referent "out there" to which the putatively random paradigm-shifts relate. But in legal theory, the shift to a pragmatic paradigm, if we retain its original emphasis on the "how" question, would ground all claims of truth-making in the broadest

---

[24] Rorty, *Contingency, Irony, and Solidarity*, 88.

possible democratic consent: in short, to democratic inquiry.[25] We may not be able to show that democracy derives from something "out there," but does it really qualify as a purely random metaphorical paradigm-shift? Or are we, all of us, prepared to concede to it a long-term superiority, even a "pragmatic" transcendency?

Despite his apologies, Rorty's position implies that sanctions are unimportant to theory unless we can clearly see the relationship between the choice of linguistic arrangements and eternal truth. He might not admit this, because it sounds foundationalist in its own way, but it's true, because sanctions are a major part of what we let into the analysis by using the term that Rorty banishes from pragmatism, "experience." Classical pragmatism was founded on the discovery that sanctions are important, the more so because we cannot clearly see the relationship between what Rorty calls linguistic arrangements and eternal truth. That is the fallibilism aspect of pragmatism; exigency and representivity demand that we methodically seek a less painful and more responsive community, and that we consider the pleas, claims, and insights of everyone.

The linguistic turn has not proved to be as clean a break from so-called Enlightenment foundationalism as it pretends. It tells us that language is utterly contingent, presumably in utterly contingent language. It tells us that we must doubt all metaphilosophical propositions, but that the absence of any relation between philosophy and eternal truth is utterly untouched by doubt. This is not fallibilism at all, but rather another Cartesian coup de philosophe. Rorty's neopragmatism is, by his own account, only a metaphor, so why choose it over "old" pragmatism? Old pragmatism doesn't see itself as a mere metaphor; it says, Choose me if you care about concrete things such as political methods and sanctions.

Pragmatism now faces a challenge. It has to win over skeptics on both sides of the Atlantic who wonder just where its strong fallibilism will lead. It must enlarge the dialogue with vocabularies that are truly different, like those of Eastern philosophy, preparing the way for greater representivity. But suppose over the long run we were to confess inability to identify any clear relation between philosophy and eternal truth, a proposition that classical pragmatism doesn't prejudge. Yet we remain concerned with nothing more than how the discussion might affect things like political methods and sanctions. Should we still be self-evaluative about how we do legal theory? Should we still be self-evaluative about how we do philosophy? Of course, Rorty should answer yes. His disavowal of method, translated into practical terms, is part of that very process.

---

[25] Dewey, *Logic*, 487f; see Robert B. Westbrook, *John Dewey and American Democracy* (Ithaca, NY: Cornell University Press, 1991).

Chapter 7

Liberalism and Critical Legal Theory

In *Critical Legal Studies: A Liberal Critique*,[1] Andrew Altman takes the CLS challenge to liberal jurisprudence seriously and laments the surprising paucity of dialogue between CLS writers and contemporary defenders of liberalism like John Rawls and Ronald Dworkin. By honing it against its sharpest critics, Altman helps us assess the quandary of current liberal legal theory.

Critical Legal Studies began in the mid-1970s. Its early exponents largely congregated on the Harvard Law School faculty, a situation that would later lead to much-publicized battles over faculty appointments and other policies. While they may have lost most of those battles, CLS scholars soon put complacent liberals everywhere on the defensive by adroit demonstrations that much of liberal doctrine is fraught with inconsistency. Meanwhile, major defenders of liberal orthodoxy like Ronald Dworkin curtly dismissed CLS arguments as "spectacular and embarrassing failures."[2]

While attacking vigorously in the trenches, CLS has chosen to ignore the liberal grand theorists, showing a passing disregard for the likes of both Dworkin and Rawls. Rawls, concludes Elizabeth Mensch, "somewhat whimsically, has simply resurrected seventeenth-century social contract theory in an effort-to universalize liberal thought," while Dworkin "simply vacillates between an implicit reliance on natural law theory and reliance on the inherent legitimacy of the liberal tradition."[3] Altman is not easily thrown off the trail by this disdainful non-dialogue. Having absorbed vast quantities of both liberal and CLS literature, he matches opposing arguments and strategies point for point.

---

[1] Princeton, NJ: Princeton University Press, 1990.
[2] Ronald Dworkin, *Law's Empire* (Cambridge, MA: Belknap Press, 1986), 274.
[3] Elizabeth Mensch, "The History of Mainstream Legal Thought," in D. Kairys (ed.) *The Politics of Law* (Basic Books, 1982), 18–19.

The nub of the issue lies, Altman claims, in the CLS challenge to "a principle central to liberal legal thought—the rule of law." Although CLS writings diverge on important matters, "the central contention of CLS is that the rule of raw is a myth." Against this, Altman evaluates the philosophical background of the rule of law, rooted in Plato and Aristotle, developed by Locke and Bentham, and recently defined by H.L.A. Hart, John Rawls, and Ronald Dworkin.[4]

There are three main prongs to the CLS attack. The first claims that the rule of law is not possible in a society espousing a liberal concept of individual freedom. The implied pluralism of fundamentally incompatible moral and political views infects modes of order as well as conflict. Thus, the existence of presumptively pure legal reasoning, autonomous from political and ethical choice, is impossible.[5]

The second prong hinges on the claim that the legal doctrines of contemporary liberal societies are riddled with contradictions. Every legal principle is opposed by another, in every factual context. Judges covertly rely on moral and political considerations in deciding which of the incompatible legal norms they will base their decisions upon. As one CLS writer puts it: "[T] raditional legal theory requires a large amount of determinacy as a fundamental premise of the rule of law. Our legal system, however, has never satisfied this goal."[6] These first two prongs support the CLS thesis that the very idea of the rule of law serves to perpetuate illegitimate relations of power. Exposing the falsehood of that idea is part of the CLS strategy designed to undermine those relationships.[7]

The third prong attacks the notion that law is even capable of constraining the exercise of social and political power. Law is an artifact, a human creation; to regard it as an independent force controlling those who have created and sustained it is akin to fetishism or superstition while liberal jurisprudence has come to accept the assumption that law, and indeed the notion of "society," are human artifacts rather than expressions of an underlying natural order, "no one," says the CLS theorist Roberto Unger, "has ever taken the idea of society as an artifact to the hilt."[8]

Amidst such misgivings about law and conventional liberal doctrine, one might expect a strain of concern over the degree of involvement of courts

---

[4] Altman, *Critical Legal Studies*, 2–26.
[5] See generally Duncan Kennedy, "Legal Education as Training for Hierarchy," in *The Politics of Law*, Vol. 47, D. Kairys (ed.) (Basic Books, 1982); Karl E. Klare, "The Law School Curriculum in the 1980s: What's Left?" 32 *J. Legal Educ.* 340 (1982).
[6] Joseph W. Singer, "The Player and the Cards; Nihilism and Legal Theory," 94 *Yale L.J.* 13 (1984).
[7] See, e.g., Mensch, "The History of Mainstream," 5–6.
[8] Roberto Mangabeira Unger, *Social Theory: Its Situation and Its Task* (Cambridge: Cambridge University Press, 1987), 1.

and lawyers in American life. However, CLS is generally too committed to legal activism, by law journal if not by lawsuit, and seeks to expand the freedom of lawyers to make political arguments. CLS takes the position that the prevailing rationales for judicial restraint are simply part of the body of opposing principles that serve the interests of those in power. They should be abandoned to enfranchise the legal arguments of the powerless. Meanwhile, conservative scholars have been surprisingly silent on the breach between liberalism and CLS, and have failed to exploit the discredit it may cast on legal activism generally.

Altman is careful to point out that CLS writers do not utterly reject liberal values. Unger affirms that individual freedoms should be cherished and preserved. But there are other aspects of human life for which liberal theory does not adequately account, such as community and solidarity. For Mark Tushnet, another leading CLS thinker, it is the civic republican tradition that liberalism fails to appreciate: "[J]ust as the republican tradition correctly emphasizes our mutual dependence, the liberal tradition correctly emphasizes our individuality and the threats we pose to one another."[9] By de-mystifying law, CLS theorists seek to expose and correct the perceived exclusion, or disempowerment, of many segments of modern society; indeed, Unger describes his overall vision as one of "empowered democracy."[10]

Altman discerns important conflicts within CLS, chief among them the division between moderate and radical theorists (pp. 18-21). Radicals generally subscribe to a "deconstructionist" view of the meanings of legal terms, holding that there is no objective structure, that legal terms have no stable or fixed meanings but are "empty vessels", into which lawyers and judges may pour any meanings that suit their purposes. Tushnet, a radical, puts it thus:

> The materials of legal doctrine are almost measureless, and the acceptable techniques of legal reasoning-distinguishing on the basis of the facts, analogizing to other areas of the law where cognate problems arise, and the like—are so flexible that they allow us to assemble diverse precedents into whatever patterns we chose.[11]

Altman claims that this approach rests on flawed and indefensible premises regarding language and social reality.

---

[9] M. Tushnet, *Red, White, and Blue: A Critical Analysis of Constitutional Law* (Cambridge, MA: Harvard University Press, 1988), 23.

[10] See generally Roberto Mangabeira Unger, *False Necessity: Anti-Necessitarian Social Theory in the Service of Radical Democracy* (Cambridge: Cambridge University Press, 1987).

[11] Tushnet, *Red, White, and Blue*, 191–92.

He associates CLS radicalism with the "rule skepticism" of the earlier Legal Realists, the view of Jerome Frank and Karl Llewellyn that rules and precedents were "merely words" without binding force. Altman concedes that rule skepticism, taken to its extreme, would make the rule of law impossible: "People would always govern; the law never could. Our faith in the law as a protection against overweening power would be groundless."[12] As Tushnet concludes: "[I]f the Realists were right, nothing stood between us and the abyss in which the strong dominated the weak, for the law, which liberals thought was our guardian, provided only the illusion of protection."[13]

This view rests on the existentialist position that there are no social institutions or rules that have the power to control individual choice, action, and thought. The social future is entirely open, entirely free from the control of the social past. CLS radicals are forced into two contentions to support this claim: (1) that our common belief in social "structure" capable of controlling individual behavior is a self-deception to relieve us of the anxiety from recognizing the openness of the future, and (2) that not just legal rules, but all rules and norms of any kind, are devoid of any inherent constraining power.

What warrants the CLS belief that the "idea" of the rule of law can maintain illegitimate relations of power? Altman argues that radical rule-skepticism defeats the possibility of individuals controlling other individuals: "Nothing makes it impossible for slaves to revolt, for workers to rebel, for the oppressed to rise up."[14] CLS would respond that it is nothing more nor less than the threat of actual constraint by those holding the weapons of enforcement. The issue of whether rules are more than words then must turn on whether threats of constraint must be felt at every instance of obedience to them.

Altman concedes that there is no evidence of a hidden "force" binding society to its laws and rules, but this does not show that rules *qua* rules cannot exert any constraint at all. "The fact that such rules can be trashed at any moment does not show that they exert no control, only that the control is not total." The real mechanism he suggests to be at work is aversion to criticism:

> To the extent that the feared agent of criticism is just anybody in the population, the experience is one of constraint by rules rather than by specific individuals. That is, insofar as I do X in order to avoid the criticism of no particular person but just anybody who might find out about it, I have an experience of constraint by rules.[15]

---

[12] Altman, *Critical Legal Studies*, 153.
[13] Mark Tushnet, "Critical Legal Studies and Constitutional Law: An Essay in Deconstruction," *Stanford Law Review* 26 (1984): 625.
[14] Altman, *Critical Legal Studies,* 178.
[15] Altman, *Critical Legal Studies,* 180.

We might expect that CLS radicals would respond to this argument by claiming that such fear is part of the tyranny of illegitimate power relationships that CLS seeks to expose.

It may be too glib to suggest that the issue between the radical wing of CLS and legal liberalism thus boils down to whether rules exist by fear of arrest or of bad publicity. However, both camps assume that rules are wholly practical constructs, differing only as to whether they can be justified as such. And both camps assume a far more significant role for lawyers than, for example, Learned Hand, who in 1944 said something very similar to Tushnet's comment on Realism: "Liberty lies in the hearts of men and women; when it dies there, no constitution, no law, no court can even do much to help it. while it lies there it needs no constitution, no court, no law to save it."[16]

Altman's treatment of the moderate strand of CLS is more revealing of the originality of CLS writers, and ultimately of the current arguments for liberal jurisprudence. The moderate position holds that legal terms do have a settled core of meaning, but that the interpretations required to decide cases are inescapably tied to individual moral and political beliefs (p. 19). Our law does have an objective structure, but it derives from a particular, temporal, and inadequate ethical perspective. Unger, the leading "moderate," has said:

> The nation, at the Lycurgan moment of its history, had opted for a particular type of society: a commitment to a democratic republic and to a market system as a necessary part of that republic. The people might have chosen some other type of social organization. But in choosing this one, in choosing it for example over an aristocratic and corporatist polity on the old-European model, they also chose the legally defined institutional structure that went along with it.[17]

In stating the case for liberalism, Altman interprets the Lycurgan choice as somewhat less contingent and capricious. He reduces the rule of law's essence to two requirements: fair notice and the legal accountability of established authority to a pre-existing system of authoritative norms, thereby providing protection of the broadest individual freedoms possible (pp. 23–24). This requires a differentiation between law and politics. The political realm is one in which competing conceptions of the good and right are accommodated through the democratic process, while the realm of law is restricted to interpreting and applying those accommodations (pp. 26–27).

The CLS challenge to that distinction brings this important qualification to Altman: "Virtually every contemporary thinker of note who defends this

---

[16] Learned Hand, "The Spirit of Liberty," in *The Spirit of Liberty: Papers and Addresses of Learned Hand?*, Vol. 144 (New York, NY: Vintage Books, 1959), 193.

[17] Unger, *The Critical Legal Studies Movement*, 5.

version of the rule of law will concede that in practice it is impossible to insulate the legal process completely from the judgments about the relative merits of the views that compete in the political arena" (p. 27). This concession should invite renewed interest in the arguments for judicial restraint advanced by Thayer, Holmes, Hand, and Frankfurter; but Altman does not take that course, as the "rule of law" he defends tends to rely heavily on the firm hand of lawyers and judges.

Altman arrives at this concession by responding to Unger's attack on the "antinomies" of liberalism. Unger has argued from the outset that fatal contradictions lie at the heart of liberal political and legal theory, destroying the possibility of the liberal rule of law: due to the insistence on the subjectivity of values (that is, the lack of any warrant beyond individual choice for one particular value scheme over any other), there can be no neutral process either for interpretation of the law or, indeed, for legislation itself.[18] How can social order be created and maintained if there are no objective values around which it can be built? How can such an order avoid the subjugation of some people to the. subjective choices of others? In Unger's words:

> First, procedure is inseparable from outcome: every method makes certain legislative choices more likely than others . . . . Second, each lawmaking system itself embodies certain values; it incorporates a view of how power ought to be distributed in the society and of how conflicts should be resolved.[19]

Altman responds to this by challenging Unger for failing to distinguish between two kinds of "values," by conflating the "right" and the "good" in one general term. Liberals may insist on the subjectivity of certain important values, but those involve conceptions of the *good*, not the *right*. The good has been held by liberals to be subjective in the sense that no conception of it licenses those who embrace it to coerce those who dissent; but liberalism does not deny the notion of objectivity, or the propriety of coercion, when it comes to matters of justice and moral obligation.[20]

Altman, to his credit, is careful not to rest on this flat response. The very boundary between the right and the good are often in dispute, as in such controversies as abortion rights and the role of the government in promoting social welfare. Liberalism demands legal neutrality, but Altman concedes that "in a context where the very line between the right and the good is at issue, the question whether public power is being exercised in a neutral way will

---

[18] Roberto M. Unger, *Knowledge and Politics* (New York, NY: Macmillan, 1975), 76, 88–100.

[19] Roberto M. Unger, *Law in Modern Society: Toward a Criticism of Social Theory* (New York, NY: The Free Press, 1976), 180.

[20] Altman, *Critical Legal Studies,* 66.

have no noncontroversial answer." If legal neutrality is not possible, liberalism is caught after all in the antinomy of rules and values. In the course of responding to this problem, Altman demonstrates why liberalism lends itself to an activist tradition in jurisprudence. CLS contends that the full interpretation of legal rules will require reliance on some assessment of the contending conceptions of the good and the right whose competition in the political arena helped to generate the rules. This is necessary if only to rank the multiple purposes of a single rule, or the contending purposes of different rules implicated in a given case. Because of this reliance, the normative controversies of the political arena cannot be bracketed from the process of legal interpretation.[21]

Altman does not question the assertion that lawyers should rank the purposes of different rules. Rather, he looks to the leading models of liberal theory to provide an answer. These models, Altman responds, "portray legal reasoning as involving some reliance on moral and political judgments."

> For example, in the model that I defended, there is a dominant convention that prescribes decisions whose grounds have the best fit with the settled law, and when that convention breaks down, there is a convention that prescribes decisions whose grounds fit with some substantial proportion of the settled law. In the latter case, there are likely to be competing grounds for the decision, all of which fit the settled law well enough, so judges will often appeal, implicitly or explicitly, to their own moral or political convictions in selecting among those potential grounds of decision.[22]

This is Altman's paradigm of liberal jurisprudence, one sharing aspects of Rawls, Hart, Sartorius, and Dworkin. Altman defends this position vigorously, and he is punctilious in responding to opposing points of every major CLS author. His adaptation of the early philosophical writings of Willard Quine to respond to the Foucaultian origins of CLS arguments for indeterminacy of legal language is typical of his range, originality, and circumspection. Altman does not shy away from complexity, and his fairness and cogency in evaluating CLS positions should assure him a wide and continuing audience.

Missing from this dialogue—and it is no fault of Altman's—is any hint of an alternative theory rejecting the implicit role lawyers as the principal interpreters of the moral, ethical, and political questions that creep into the interstices of judicial business. It is implicit in Altman's paradigm that the liberal lawyer, after carefully consulting the list of "conventions" to determine how the "law" should resolve a moral question, eventually exercises subjective judgment anyway. CLS clears away the lingo and simply assumes that

---

[21] Altman, *Critical Legal Studies,* 69, 80.
[22] Altman, *Critical Legal Studies,* 89.

lawyers are engaged in politics. For that candor we should be grateful. Both camps are committed to keeping the legal profession in power.

There may be no use in complaining about this, as there are no theorists left in the Thayer-Holmes-Hand-Frankfurter school. For them the law was a discipline, not a self-sufficient entity as liberalism supposes. Their strict notion of jurisdiction kept it from becoming an open-ended forum. The constitutional theory of the last of them, Felix Frankfurter, is now discredited,[23] and the liberal position now seems, to a considerable degree, to have been vindicated by twentieth-century struggles over civil rights and liberties. There is a widespread perception that judicial intervention, and hence interpretation, in a broad range of constitutional issues, is imperative at the first instance in which they are raised.

We might keep in mind for a future time—one in which judicial prophecies are not so widely accepted—that Learned Hand voiced doubts similar to CLS and the Legal Realists about the power of constitutional litigation to save society from its own excesses. But he did so to express the vulnerability, not the impossibility, of a society under law: the danger of relying too much on the legal process. Frankfurter would have preferred to let controversies over civil liberties flare and fester without judicial intervention as long as necessary for resolution in the court of public opinion. And Holmes, confronted with a much more severe crisis over public acceptance of Supreme Court decisions than current commentators can recollect, wholly rejected appealing to one's own moral and political convictions to choose among competing grounds for decision:

> It cannot be helped, it is as it should be, that the law is behind the times . . . As the law embodies beliefs that have . . . translated themselves into action, while there is doubt, while opposite convictions still keep a battle front against each other, the time for law has not come; the notion destined to prevail is not yet entitled to the field. It is a misfortune if a judge reads his conscious or unconscious sympathy with one side or the other prematurely into the law, and forgets that what seems to him to be first principles are believed by half his fellow men to be wrong.[24]

Both liberalism and CLS make far too much of so-called legal *indeterminacy*; it has become for both camps the touchstone of their entire contrasting theories of law. They overlook that the root of indeterminacy lies not in law but life, and that there are means other than litigation or even legislation for resolving it. Altman's timely and scholarly book makes clear that this consideration has little importance in either CLS or liberal legal theory.

---

[23] See generally Frederic R. Kellogg, "Legal Scholarship in the Temple of Doom, Pragmatism's Response to Critical Legal Studies," *Tulane Law Review* 65 (1990): 15; revised as chapter 9 below.

[24] Holmes, Dinner Address to the Harvard Law School Ass'n of N.Y. (February 15, 1913), reprinted in *The Occasional Speeches of Justice Oliver Wendell Holmes*, M. Howe (ed.) (1962), 168.

Part III

THE CRISIS OF CONTEMPORARY LAW

Legal theory, at least in the United States, has a legitimacy crisis, originating in what Grant Gilmore characterized in 1977 as the "Age of Anxiety." Analytical and conceptualist legal theorists are trapped in the assumptions that law has a concrete boundary, and that deduction from a legitimizing proposition must be identified if decisions by law are to be possible. If and when the law "runs out," judges must either legislate or resort to general principles.

Pragmatism offers a way out of the crisis through a theory of democratic inquiry.

Chapter 8

Principles, Politics, and Legal Interpretation

INTRODUCTION

Critical legal scholarship adopted many of the arguments and points of view prominent in the writings of current pragmatic philosophers like Richard Rorty.[1] While Rorty's thought converges with some important aspects of pragmatic philosophy, other aspects of his work are influenced by writers for whom the pragmatic label does not easily fit.[2] Moreover, Rorty himself would insist that there is no orthodox perspective on legal theory to be derived from his view of pragmatism.[3] We may find a sharp divergence between positions

---

[1] See, e.g., Joseph Singer, "The Player and the Cards: Nihilism and Legal Theory," *Yale Law Journal* 94(13) (1971): 1, 7. John Stick in "Can Nihilism Be Pragmatic?" argues that Singer's use of Rorty's work as a blueprint for his own criticism of legal theory misinterprets Rorty and distorts traditional legal theory. Stick maintains that Rorty's pragmatic philosophy is consistent with a broad range of accounts of legal reasoning, including those found in the works of Ronald Dworkin, John Rawls, and other leading contemporary liberal legal theorists, and that Singer exemplifies a CLS tendency to characterize traditional legal theory as far more deductive and axiomatic than it really is on close examination. *Harvard Law Review* 100 (1986): 332, 345–52.
  Stick's account of pragmatism differs from that developed here, which holds that legal pragmatism is not rooted in the fundamental liberal commitment to the "rule of law," as advanced by Dworkin and others. Stick, on the other hand, claims that "Dworkin's theory is compatible with pragmatism, as are the theories of most liberals." *Id.* at 385.

[2] *E.g.*, Ludwig Wittgenstein, Martin Heidegger, Friedrich Nietzsche, Jacques Derrida, and Michel Foucault. *Compare M. Okrent, Heidegger's Pragmatism: Understanding, Being, and the Critique of Metaphysics* (Ithaca, NY: Cornell University Press, 1988).

[3] Rorty, *Consequences of Pragmatism*, 4, 27. Rorty seems to have adopted a broadly inclusive view of legal pragmatism, like Stick's. *See* Stick, *supra* note I. Welcoming Roberto Unger, Ronald Dworkin, and Richard Posner as legal pragmatists, Rorty comments, "The very ease by which these three men are accommodated under this rubric illustrates the banality of pragmatism." Richard Rorty, "The Banality of Pragmatism and the Poetry of Justice," *S. California Law Review* 63 (1990). The articles in this recent symposium issue in which Rorty's article appears take a generally expansive view of legal pragmatism. None suggest a sharp distinction between pragmatism and liberalism or attempt to account for Holmes's judicial restraint.

taken in Critical Legal Studies (CLS) and those found in the work of Oliver Wendell Holmes, Jr. Holmes's views can be associated with the pragmatic writings of Charles S. Peirce, and have at least an equal claim to identification with pragmatic methodology.[4]

Perhaps the most outstanding contrast between Holmes and CLS is that between Holmes's juridical conception of judicial restraint and the CLS opposition to limiting the scope of legal argument to traditional legal doctrine. The CLS position follows from its denial of the distinction between law and politics, discussed below. This CLS contention also leads to the notion that jurisprudence cannot be separated from sociology, economics, and other disciplines concerned with human affairs. Despite its difference with mainstream legal theory over many fundamental points, CLS and the mainstream agree that no such clear separation can be drawn. Pragmatism, meanwhile, insists on our awareness of the intimate connection between thought and practice. Thus, it would invite the question whether we accept the current broad conception of jurisprudence because the regime of law has become so pervasive, or whether the broad reach of law simply follows our expansive conception of it.

What is the proper scope of jurisprudence? Certainly, we can argue that it should be as broad as we like. Law in our era seems to pervade every salient aspect of social life. It has had the capacity for adaptation by those in power

---

[4] *See* Frederic R. Kellogg, *The Formative Essays of Justice Holmes: The Making of an American Legal Philosophy* (Westport, CT: Greenwood Press, 1984) (characterizing Holmes as the founder of legal pragmatism); Thomas C. Grey, "Holmes and Legal Pragmatism," *Stanford Law Review* 41 (1989): 787; Catherine Wells Hantzis, "Legal Innovation Within the Wider Intellectual Tradition: The Pragmatism of Oliver Wendell Holmes, Jr.," *Northwestern University Law Review* 82 (1988): 541; *cf.* R. Summers, *Instrumentalism and American Legal Theory* (1982); all characterize Holmes as a pragmatist. *But see* H. Pohlman, *Justice Oliver Wendell Holmes and Utilitarian Jurisprudence* (1984) (characterizing Holmes as legal utilitarian); LaPiana, "Victorian from Beacon Hill: Oliver Wendell Holmes's Early Legal Scholarship," *Columbia Law Review* 90 (1990): 809, 811–12 (characterizing Holmes as legal empiricist). Grey's account associates Holmes with the relativist strain of recent American "neo-pragmatism," and draws heavily from European antifoundationalism. Thomas C. Grey, "Holmes and Legal Pragmatism," 790 n.16. Thus Grey says that Holmes's contextualism would support critical legal studies: "The point is that if theory is necessarily situated within and closely dependent upon practice, then current theory loses its claim to finality. The application of this idea to law has been one of the central themes of the Critical Legal Studies movement." *Id.* at 814. Grey's account is difficult to square with Holmes's pronounced judicial restraint, a tradition that has been generally attacked by CLS writers. Grey can only account for Holmes's restraint by the unsupported assertion that "Holmes' conservatism has no necessary connection with the basic pragmatist tenets that he so well-articulated." *Id.* at 813. In other words, the version of pragmatism that Grey advances as Holmes's overall theoretical persuasion was somehow separated from a central aspect of his judicial product. The inference can only be that Holmes's jurisprudence was fundamentally flawed or biased. Grey goes so far as to propose that Holmes's deference to legislative judgment derived from his sense of "his own deficiencies as a 'man of affairs.'" *Id.* at 849. Grey suggests that this may be explained in part by Grey's own commitment to a liberal theory of jurisprudence in which constitutional adjudication may be guided by general principles; a position that Holmes clearly rejected. *See, e.g.*, Thomas C. Grey, "The Constitution as Scripture," *Stanford Law Review* 37 I (1984): 5.

as a blanket capable even of controlling the philosophical discourse. Attempts to limit the discussion are drawn into the controversy over who is limiting it and for what purposes. Meanwhile, resistance to limits protects the outer perimeters of law's empire from attack.

Peirce's maxim for pragmatic philosophy enjoins that premises are to be tested by their practical consequences.[5] What are the consequences of unlimited discussion in jurisprudence? The premise that jurisprudence must be unlimited in scope contributes to accepting that law, if not litigation, has a rightful place in any aspect of human affairs. This result is considerably advanced by the main premise of CLS, that there is no practical dividing line between law and politics. Thereafter, unless the law is abandoned altogether, the consequence is to subscribe to unlimited jurisdiction for courts and lawyers. The question CLS needs to confront clearly is whether this is desirable and whether there is an alternative.

Of all CLS writers, perhaps Allan Hutchinson comes closest to doing so:

> Nowhere is antipathy for popular participation more evident than in the modern entrenchment of law and courts at the heart of American politics. No longer acting as a Tocquevillian check on legislative enthusiasms, the judges have taken over the major responsibility for the nation's policymaking. Moreover, instead of chastising courts for their imperial presumption, commentators celebrate them as the preferred forum for democratic deliberation. The cool detachment of philosophical reflection is thought more conducive to democratic wisdom than the heated contestability of popular debate. As such, legal philosophy has been trafficked as the opium of the democratic masses. In a telling metaphor, a leading theorist of judicial legitimacy lionizes judges as princes of law's empire and philosophers (like himself) as its seers and prophets. This is a debasement of the democratic ideal, not its apotheosis. Attempts to pass rule by judicial aristocracy off as a philosophical act of noblesse oblige exacerbates rather than ameliorates the affront.[6]

Hutchinson aligns himself with CLS and, in the paper from which the foregoing passage is taken, challenges Rorty for not being radical enough in his views on law and justice.[7] Rorty has led a revival of interest in pragmatism with sharply critical observations about foundationalist tendencies in modern philosophy, which CLS has enlisted in support of its attacks on

---

[5] Peirce, "How to Make Our Ideas Clear," *Writings*, 3:257.

[6] Allan Hutchinson, "The Three 'Rs': Reading/Rorty/Radically," *Harvard Law Review* 103 (1989): 555, 573–83.

[7] Hutchinson observes that Rorty "champions the work of John Rawls." *Id.* at 564 citing Rorty, "Thugs and Theorists: A Reply to Bernstein," *Political Theory* 15 (1987): 564.

liberal jurisprudence. But Rorty's failure to adopt an equally critical political philosophy is not, suggests Hutchinson, critical enough to qualify as legal pragmatism.[8]

Hutchinson is willing to join the CLS chorus decrying the legal priesthood, but he abstains from breaking with CLS for preferring, as a forum for democratic deliberation, philosophical reflection by legal scholars. CLS cannot escape the charge that it wants to replace the existing legal establishment with another one. It is one thing to sack the temple; it is another to don the stolen robes. Is there no alternative to submission to a political judiciary?

In the passage just quoted, Hutchinson echoes sentiments that were prominent in the writings of James Bradley Thayer, Oliver Wendell Holmes, Learned Hand, and Felix Frankfurter. All four urged that to permit broad constitutional jurisdiction under the Bill of Rights would remove responsibility for overseeing the democratic values therein guaranteed from the public to the legal profession.

First, here is Thayer in 1893:

> The view which has thus been presented seems to me highly important. I am not stating a new doctrine, but attempting to restate more exactly and truly an admitted one. If what I have said be sound, it is greatly to be desired that it should be more emphasized by our courts, in its full significance. It has been often remarked that private rights are more respected by the legislatures of some countries which have no written constitution, than by ours. No doubt our doctrine of constitutional law has had a tendency to drive out questions of justice and right, and to fill the mind of legislators with thoughts of mere legality, of what the constitution allows. And moreover, even in the matter of legality, they have felt little responsibility; if we are wrong, they say, the courts will correct it. If what I have been saying is true, the safe and permanent road towards reform is that of impressing upon our people a far stronger sense than they have of the great range of possible harm and evil that our system leaves open, and must leave open, to the legislatures, and of the clear limits of judicial power; so that responsibility may be brought sharply home where it belongs. The checking and cutting down of legislative power, by numerous detailed prohibitions in the constitution, cannot be accomplished without making the government petty and incompetent. This process has already been carried much too far in some of our States. Under no system can the power of courts go far to save a people from ruin; our chief protection lies elsewhere. If this be true, it is of the greatest public importance to put the matter in its true light.[9]

---

[8] Hutchinson maintains that Rorty's alignment with liberal political theory is inexplicable in the context of Rorty's philosophical pragmatism, 571.

[9] James B. Thayer, "The Origin and Scope of the American Doctrine of Constitutional Law," *Harvard Law Review* 7 (1893): 129, 155–56 (footnote omitted).

Frankfurter would have preferred to let controversies over civil liberties flare and fester without judicial intervention as long as necessary for resolution in the court of public opinion. It is well worth recalling his dissenting opinion in *West Va. State Bd. of Educ. v. Barnette*, showing the direct line of influence from Thayer:

> The whole Court is conscious that this case reaches ultimate questions of judicial power and its relation to our scheme of government. It is appropriate, therefore, to recall an utterance as wise as any that I know in analyzing what is really involved when the theory of this Court's function is put to the test of practice. The analysis is that of James Bradley Thayer:
>
> "[T]here has developed a vast and growing increase of judicial interference with legislation. This is a very different state of things from what our fathers contemplated, a century or more ago, in framing the new system. Seldom, indeed, as they imagined, under our system, would this great, novel, tremendous power of the courts be exerted,-would this sacred ark of the covenant be taken from within the veil.
>
> Great and, indeed, inestimable as are the advantages in a popular government of this conservative influence,-the power of the judiciary to disregard unconstitutional legislation, it should be remembered that the exercise of it, even when unavoidable, is always attended with a serious evil, namely, that the correction of legislative mistakes comes from the outside, and the people thus lose the political experience, and the moral education and stimulus that come from fighting the question out in the ordinary way, and correcting their own errors.
>
> Of course patriotism cannot be enforced by the flag salute. But neither can the liberal spirit be enforced by judicial invalidation of illiberal legislation. Our constant preoccupation with the constitutionality of legislation rather than with its wisdom tends to preoccupation of the American mind with a false value. The tendency of focussing attention on constitutionality is to make constitutionality synonymous with wisdom, to regard a law as all right if it is constitutional. Such an attitude is a great enemy of liberalism. Particularly in legislation affecting freedom of thought and freedom of speech much which should offend a free-spirited society is constitutional. Reliance for the most precious interests of civilization, therefore, must be found outside of their vindication in courts of law. Only a persistent positive translation of the faith of a free society into the convictions and habits and actions of a community is the ultimate reliance against unabated temptations to fetter the human spirit.[10]

---

[10] *West Va. State Bd. of Educ. v. Barnette*, 319 U.S. 624, 667–71 (1943) (Frankfurter, J., dissenting) (quoting J. Thayer, *John Marshall* 104–10 (1901)).

He concluded with this:

> The reason why from the beginning even the narrow judicial authority to nullify legislation has been viewed with a jealous eye is that it serves to prevent the full play of the democratic process.[11]

Holmes said this in Missouri in 1904:

> Great constitutional provisions must be administered with caution. Some play must be allowed for the joints of the machine, and it must be remembered that legislatures are ultimate guardians of the liberties and welfare of the people in quite as great a degree as the courts.[12]

Learned Hand had the following observation in his Holmes Lecture in 1958:

> I often wonder whether we do not rest our hopes too much upon constitutions, upon laws and upon courts. These are false hopes; believe me, these are false hopes. Liberty lies in the hearts of men and women; when it dies there, no constitution, no law, no court can save it; no constitution, no law, no court can even do much to help it. While it lies there it needs no constitution, no law, no court to save it.[13]

Hand expanded on this as follows:

> Each one of us must in the end choose for himself how far he would like to leave our collective fate to the wayward vagaries of popular assemblies. No one can fail to recognize the perils to which the last forty years have exposed such governments. We are not indeed forced to choose between absolutism and the kind of democracy that so often prevailed in Greek cities during the sixth to fourth centuries before our era. The Founding Fathers were acutely, perhaps overacutely, aware of the dangers that had followed that sort of rule, though, as you all know, they differed widely as to what curbs to impose. For myself it would be most irksome to be ruled by a bevy of Platonic Guardians, even if I knew how to choose them, which I assuredly do not. If they were in charge, I should miss the stimulus of living in a society where I have, at least theoretically, some part in the direction of public affairs. Of course I know how illusory would be the belief that my vote determined anything; but nevertheless when

---

[11] *West Va. State Bd. of Educ. v. Barnette*, 650.
[12] *Missouri, Kan., & Tex. Ry. v. May*, 194 U.S. 267, 270 (1904).
[13] Learned Hand, "The Spirit of Liberty," in *The Spirit of Liberty: Papers and Addresses of Learned Hand*, Vol. 144 (I. Dilliard ed. 1959).

I go to the polls I have a satisfaction in the sense that we are all engaged in a common venture. If you retort that a sheep in the flock may feel something like it; I reply, following Saint Francis, "My brother, the Sheep."

I have tried to strike a balance between the advantages of our own system and one in which we might enjoy at least the protection of judges against our frailties. To me it seems better to take our chances that such constitutional restraints as already exist may not sufficiently arrest the recklessness of popular assemblies.

Such is the historic train of unconventional observations, to which Hutchinson adds his paper demanding essentially the same result that Hand and Frankfurter sought through radical judicial restraint: less reliance on law and more on democracy.[14] But surely, Hutchinson cannot claim that this result would be the logical consequence of throwing the doors of legal theory wide open and equating law with politics. He can be counted among a relatively few voices within CLS that display less interest than most in courts as a location for political discourse. They are not without influence, especially if we include the more recent writings of Roberto Unger.[15] But what has not been of much interest is whether and how courts and legal discourse, as these have emerged in the late-twentieth-century United States, can be reconstituted (not replaced, as some CLS writers have implied) to enhance, instead of debase, the democratic ideal. In addressing this question I will make two points, which I will also associate with the growth of pragmatism and its application to legal theory. The first point is that the notion of legal indeterminacy, upon which so much of twentieth-century jurisprudence is founded, is a false one. The roots of indeterminacy lie not in law but in social life, and the real issue is how legal institutions respond to it. The second point has to do with how this condition can more accurately be reflected in legal proceedings and discourse, and hence in legal decisions.

LEGAL INDETERMINACY

It is hard to deny that liberalism has been the dominant strain in twentieth-century American jurisprudence. The central question occupying modern

---

[14] Hutchinson, "Reading/Rorty/Radically," 582–85.
[15] *Compare* Unger, *The Critical Legal Studies Movement* 15 ("The implication of our critique of formalism is to turn the dilemma of doctrine upside down. It is to say that, if any conceptual practice similar to what lawyers now call doctrine can be justified, the class of legitimate doctrinal activities must be sharply enlarged.") *with* Unger, *False Necessity*, 452 ("The characteristics of the traditional judiciary – devoted, as it primarily is, to the settling of more or less focused rights and wrongs under the law-make it a less than ideal instrument for far-reaching and systematic intervention in social practice.").

liberal scholars has been the problem of accounting for so-called "legal indeterminacy"—how theory addresses the manner in which judges decide cases
that are not clearly covered by existing legal rules. This was the principal
concern of the debate among liberal theorists as to whether law and morals
are separate, as well as of the CLS challenge to liberal theory itself. It also
happens to have been a central concern of Holmes's early essays which lead
to *The Common Law.*

For Holmes, writing over a century ago, indeterminacy was a presumed
natural condition of the larger social context from which rules were gradually abstracted by the common law.[16] The problem was finding a satisfac-
tory explanation both for the conventions under which this had been done
throughout the centuries and for the role of legal concepts and classification.
For reasons unrelated to this analysis, the modern debate has become intro-
verted, viewing indeterminacy not as external to but as internal to the law,
within the body of legal rules, whose normal function is seen as molding
conduct like a die. Thus, it treats indeterminacy as a symptom of law with
disputed implications for theory. Constitutional law, rather than common law,
has provided the primary context.

Scholars have widely ignored the fact that legal inquiry was an important
subject among the nineteenth-century pragmatists. Max Fisch, in 1942, was
the first to notice that Holmes's analysis of the common law had important
features in common with Peirce's "pragmatic" methodology. He pointed to
the possibility that the discussions among members of the Metaphysical Club
in Cambridge during the 1870s, half of whom were lawyers exploring more
or less the same theoretical issues as Holmes, had influenced Peirce with their
observations about common law methodology.

While we will not find references to foundationalism or perspectivism in
Holmes's writings, or any explicit remarks about "pragmatic" methodology,
we can nevertheless find striking parallels to Peirce. Holmes published a
paper entitled "Possession" in 1878,[17] roughly when *Popular Science Monthly*
published the well-known two-part Peirce paper "Fixation of Belief"[18] and
How to Make Our Ideas Clear.[19] Peirce later described this paper as having been circulated earlier among the group he called the "Metaphysical
Club."[20] Although Peirce records Holmes as an occasional member, there is

---

[16] *See* Holmes, "Codes," 1:212; Holmes, "Theory of Torts," 1:326.
[17] Holmes, "Possession," *Collected Works* 3: 37.
[18] Peirce, "The Fixation of Belief," *Writings,* 3:242.
[19] Peirce, "How to Make Our Ideas Clear," *Writings,* 3:257.
[20] Wiener, *Evolution and the Founders of Pragmatism,* 25.

no evidence that either read the other's paper. Comments by both suggest that their common influence was Chauncey Wright.[21]

In an example of the pragmatic maxim, applied to the concept of force in physics, Peirce writes: "if we know what the effects of force are, we are acquainted with every fact which is implied in saying that a force exists, and there is nothing more to know."[22] His purpose was to attack the notion that there is an entity, a structure, or a metaphysics belonging to the concept of force. Similarly, Holmes's purpose in "Possession" was to demonstrate that there is a tendency toward endowing legal concepts with an inherent content. This commonly takes the form of importing one or another of the prevailing doctrinal systems. Holmes showed how the Kantian bias in favor of free will had infected analyses of possession with the notion that it contained an element of intent to use the object in question for one's own benefit. Such a bias, he noted, could and did quickly assume an authoritative place in legal treatises and opinions.[23]

But Holmes showed that this was a compounded error. If we look at the derivation of the concept of possession as a legal classification, tracing its history as a cause of action, we find that a "self-regarding" intent was not necessary.[24] The earliest possessory actions grew out of the need for a remedy against the stealing of cattle. These actions reflected the facts that cattle were generally not watched by their owners and that others were in the best position to fulfill the requirements of primitive legal proceedings: to follow the trail, to make the seizure, and to initiate a claim with the making of an oath.[25]

We can find an expression of the pragmatic maxim for law in Holmes's 1878 article "Possession," published simultaneously with Peirce's more conspicuous pronouncement. Holmes's maxim, like that of Peirce, is that we must consider only the effects that have practical bearings. In other words, we must consider the consequences that the object of our conception—the legal concept—has for the particular form of legal inquiry. Our conception of these effects is then the whole of our conception of that object. This is the nineteenth-century forerunner of what is now termed "antifoundationalism" among CLS scholars.[26]

It is also the antecedent of the twentieth century challenge to "mechanical jurisprudence," as well as of the more extreme CLS notion that law is a mere

---

[21] Peirce, "Pragmatism in Retrospect: A Last Formulation," in *Philosophical Writings of Peirce,* 270 (J. Buchler ed. 1955); Letter from Holmes to Sir Frederick Pollock (August 30, 1929), *Holmes-Pollock Letters* 2:252 (M. Howe ed. 1941).

[22] Peirce, "How to Make Our Ideas Clear," *Writings,* 3:265.

[23] Holmes, "Possession," *Collected Works* 3:700–02.

[24] Holmes, "Possession," *Collected Works* 3:702–03.

[25] Holmes, "Possession," *Collected Works* 3:688–97.

[26] Holmes, "Possession," *Collected Works* 3:702, 719–20. *See* Grey, "Holmes and Legal Pragmatism," 799 (associating Holmes and pragmatism with antifoundationalism).

"artifact." It directly challenged the idea that the "law," or some logical or decalogical quality inhering in legal concepts such as possession, operates like a die controlling conduct, or like a "force" creating rights or duties. As Holmes says in the 1878 article, "the law does not enable me to use or abuse this book which lies before me. That is a physical power which I have without the aid of the law."[27]

Another parallel to Peirce can be found between the Peircean notion that all inquiry proceeds not by strict induction or deduction but by "abduction," and Holmes's observation that the law proceeds from particular cases to rules by means of what he, in an article published in 1870, called "successive approximation."[28] This demonstrates the essence of early pragmatism's external view of indeterminacy as inhering not in law but in the generality of experience.

The common law begins, just like scientific inquiry, with an external problem—say, the invention of the wheel leads to the invention of the carriage and thence, to the emergence of traffic, traffic accidents, and the problem of resolving claims of people injured in traffic accidents. Traffic cases, although long familiar and settled by rules, were once original matters and initially resulted in little more than a bunch of decisions, tentatively offered as a set of hypotheses as to how like situations should be resolved. As with all emerging areas of controversy, eventually these hypotheses are sifted and tested by a community of engaged observers in a process that Holmes in 1870 famously described in "Codes."

Although some legal realists were influenced by pragmatism, leading realists like Jerome Frank and Karl Llewellyn steered jurisprudential debate in an introspective direction. In their zeal to undermine mechanical (or "formalist") jurisprudence—the notion that rules dictated automatic and nonsubjective legal decisions—realist "rule skeptics" stressed the supposedly "internal" characteristics of codes and precedents that appeared vague and open-ended. This introspective turn had a profound impact on both of the leading liberal schools of Anglo-American jurisprudence, positivism and natural law. The defense by H.L.A. Hart of positivism in *The Concept of Law*[29] included what has been called a "domestication" of the realist indeterminacy thesis.[30]

---

[27] Holmes, "Possession," *Collected Works* 3:702.
[28] Holmes, "Codes," *Collected Works* 1:213. On the parallel to Peirce's theory of reasoning, see Hantzis, "Legal Innovation Within the Wider Intellectual Tradition, 551–57 (interpreting Holmes's statements within the framework of pragmatic philosophy); Kellogg, "Holmes, Pragmatism, and the Deconstruction of Utilitarianism," *Transactions of the Charles S Peirce Soc'y* 23 (1987): 99, 107–09 (demonstrating Holmes's divergence from utilitarianism); Note, "Holmes, Peirce and Legal Pragmatism," *Yale Law Journal* 84 (1975): 1123 (suggesting that Peirce was a more important and direct influence on Holmes than Holmes admitted).
[29] Hart, *The Concept of Law*, 119, 123–25.
[30] Altman, "Legal Realism, Critical Legal Studies, and Dworkin," *Philosophy and Public Affairs* 15 (1986): 205, 207.

Hart conceded to the legal realists that some indeterminacy arose by reason of the ineliminable open texture of natural language. All general terms have a range of clarity, and it is controversial as to whether they apply to particular situations outside that range. He claimed, however, that this indeterminacy is a largely peripheral phenomenon in a system of rules that, on balance, provide a specific outcome to cases.[31] But given the vigorous re-emergence of concern over rule indeterminacy in CLS, Hart seems to have underestimated the strength of the realist claims that all cases implicated a "cluster" of rules and that in any cluster there are competing rules leading to opposing outcomes.[32]

While conceding that "there is no authoritative or uniquely correct formulation of any rule to be extracted from cases," Hart asserted that "there is often very general agreement, when the bearing of a precedent on a later case is in issue, that a given formulation is adequate."[33] For CLS this begged the question, in that even if there *is* general agreement, it does not follow that the *law* determines the outcome. Agreement on both the outcome and on the rough statement of the rule used to justify the outcome may "be the result of some more fundamental political value choice."[34]

This critique, that any such agreement was informed by political values, gained in trenchancy after the scholarly debate in America passed beyond legal realism and became preoccupied with the transatlantic debate over the separation of law and morals.[35] High on Hart's agenda was maintaining the positivist separation of law and morals, which had its roots in the British obsession with providing a strict empirical foundation for legal theory. His position failed to satisfy a large constituency of American scholars who were concerned that the proposition that law and morals were separate would undermine the notion that constitutional courts could appeal to fundamental principles in reviewing duly enacted legislation.[36]

Ronald Dworkin filled this lacuna with his argument that the law consists of more than just legal rules. It is also influenced by ethical principles and ideals, of which rules are an often imperfect expression: "legal obligation [is] imposed by a constellation of principles as well as by an established rule."[37] Yet this position eventually led Dworkin to defend a position which the work of CLS scholars has made highly vulnerable. Starting from the premise that legal obligation is informed by principles as well as rules, Dworkin was naturally forced to address the question of *which* principles are legally binding;

[31] Hart, *The Concept of Law*, 31–32.
[32] Altman, "Legal Realism," 208–09.
[33] Hart, *The Concept of Law*, 131.
[34] Altman, "Legal Realism," 210.
[35] Altman, "Legal Realism," 225–26.
[36] Dworkin, *Taking Rights Seriously,* 58–64.
[37] Dworkin, *Taking Rights Seriously*, 44.

his answer has been: Those that belong to the "soundest theory of the settled law."[38]

CLS scholars accept the notion that legal rules are infused with ethical principles and ideals, but maintain that the incorporation of them into the law cuts precisely against any rescue of the law from the jaws of indeterminacy. They have demonstrated in diverse subject areas that legal doctrine is infused with irreconcilable principles. But before exploring their arguments, we should first ask what the pragmatic position would be on the realist indeterminacy thesis that Hart sought to meet with his "general agreement" argument.

Realist indeterminacy arguments were addressed to the so-called "hard" cases, those controlled by no clearly predominant rule or precedent. Of this type of case, Holmes occasionally remarked, "[H]ard cases make bad law."[39] The meaning of this aphorism is that the very cases that appear to bear out the realist assessment of implicating a "cluster" of rules leading to opposing outcomes are, in fact, perilous ones on which to rely as precedents for the future. Holmes implied two distinct propositions: First, that framing the opinion, whether attempting to reconcile the competing rules or to explain the choice of one over the other, will involve a large degree of subjectivity; second, that the reasoning and outcome may not stand up to further scrutiny in subsequent cases. Seen in retrospect, after a pattern has emerged in a controversial area, decisions in early "hard" cases are often inconsistent with the emergent pattern.

However, "hard" cases are not the ones from which "determinacy" is derived. As Holmes described in "Codes," common-law rules are themselves derived from repeated experience with particular disputes. Far from being legislated by judges, they reflect developments external to the law: the emergence of patterns, and eventually standards, of conduct. Only after becoming implicated in standards established through practical experience, reflected in (and to some extent affected by) multiple fact-based judicial determinations, are rules abstracted from experience by judges. Thereafter, rules may come into conflict; Holmes, in 1873, described this process in "Theory of Torts."

If an analogy like "cluster" is to be used in analyzing the determinacy question, this passage suggests that, for Holmes, it was more accurate to view the cases as clustering around the rules than to view the rules as clustering inside the cases. The effect is to emphasize that, when particular lines of precedent are examined, indeterminacy is an episodic phenomenon, associated with periodic stages of "growth" as new areas are opened up, rather than a chronic and defining characteristic of law.

---

[38] Altman, "Legal Realism," 213 (quoting Dworkin).

[39] *Northern Securities Co. v. United States*, 193 U.S. 197, 400 (1903) (Holmes, J., dissenting) ("Great cases like hard cases make bad law.").

It also suggests that it is not meaningful to debate the question of inde-terminacy in terms of inhering or not inhering in the "law." At least in the common-law context, the true source of indeterminacy is in experience. Expressed another way, *legal indeterminacy* is simply an inevitable func-tion of the process whereby what we define as the legal order is imposed upon particular, uncertainly or inarticulately defined areas of conduct. Legal indeterminacy might be viewed as the residue from, or, more accurately, the impression we get from (and hence the way we describe) the judiciary's periodically concentrated experience with the tentativeness inherent in the enterprise of social ordering.

Accordingly, neither the realists nor Hart were entirely correct when it came to the crux of their difference over legal indeterminacy. The realists were correct insofar as they viewed "hard" cases as *legally* indeterminate, but this perception could not be universalized to demonstrate a fundamental indeterminacy throughout the experience that we describe as "law." Hart was correct insofar as he sought to differentiate the very real, but nevertheless episodic, phenomenon of sheer indeterminacy from circumstances in which broad agreement was possible, but this too could not be universalized to vali-date a positivist concept of law.

Holmes's common-law model assumes that law is given content (1) by the character of urgent controversies that require resolution, and find their way into the courts; (2) by the tendency of repetition to engender both accepted practices and standards of conduct; and (3) by emergent consensus, not domi-nated by any single judge, or even judges as a class, but including juries and many actors outside the legal process who are engaged in the activities which generate both patterns of conduct and controversy: farmers, drivers, ship captains, bailors and bailees, landowners and tenants. Also, although rules are generally stated in the absolute, they are almost never completely final. There may be an exception deriving from experience outside the purview of that giving rise to the existing formulation.

As stated earlier, Ronald Dworkin sought to resolve the problem of rule indeterminacy by arguing that the law consists not only of rules, but also of a "constellation of principles." These principles did not conflict in the same manner as rules because principles, according to Dworkin's account, have differing "weight."[40] The CLS contention, which has made Dworkin's posi-tion particularly vulnerable, is that principles have their weight and scope of application determined, not by some philosophical principle that imposes order and harmony, but by an ideological power struggle in which coherent

---

[40] Dworkin, *Taking Rights Seriously*, 26.

theories become compromised and truncated as they fit themselves into the body of law.[41]

Dworkin claims that judges must decide hard cases according to principle by identifying "the soundest theory of the settled law"; but for CLS this fails to acknowledge that the settled law as a whole, and each field within it, embodies the outcome of ideological conflict. The law is like a "patchwork quilt" of irreconcilably opposed ideologies.[42] Underlying this picture is the idea that "all of those ideological controversies which play a significant part in the public debate of our political culture are replicated in the argument of judicial decision. [T]he spectrum of ideological controversy in politics is reproduced in the law."[43] How does this argument affect the pragmatic perspective?

Holmes's position was clearly antithetical to Dworkin's. The well-known dissent in *Lochner v. New York*[44] establishes Holmes's reluctance to countenance appealing to principles in constitutional cases. There, the majority of the Supreme Court overturned a state statute limiting the permissible hours that bakers could work on the ground that it violated freedom of contract, and thereby constitutional due process.[45] Objecting to the importation of *laissez faire* doctrine into constitutional law as a legal "principle," Holmes explained that "a constitution is made for people of fundamentally differing views."[46]

This contains a response not only to Dworkin but to CLS as well. The settled law may indeed embody the outcome of ideological conflict. However, that does not mean that judges may subvert the democratic process by applying their own notions. When confronted with a properly enacted statute, they must refrain from overruling it on ideological grounds perceived as rooted in one or another of the Constitution's general guarantees. The outcome of ideological conflict is properly embodied in the law by legislation. In cases such as *Lochner v. New York*, the primary obligation of the judge is to apply legislation so as to carry out the legislative purpose and intent.

CLS would be quick to point out that this does not, however, address the role of the judge in the considerable array of cases in which statutory interpretation is not involved. CLS contends that the common law itself is replete with conflicting principles:

> In contract law, for example, there are *two* principles: there is a reliance, solidarity, joint enterprise concept, and there is a hands-off, arms-length,

---

[41] *See* Altman, "Legal Realism," 221–22, 228–34.

[42] Kennedy, "The Political Significance of the Structure of the Law School Curriculum" *Seton Hall Law Review* 14 (1983): 1, 15 (referring to doctrine as a "patchwork").

[43] Altman, "Legal Realism," 222.

[44] *Lochner v. New York*, 198 U.S. 45, 74–77 (1904) (Holmes, J., dissenting).

[45] *Lochner v. New York*, 64 (majority opinion).

[46] *Lochner v. New York*, 75–76 (Holmes, J., dissenting).

expectancy-oriented, "no flexibility and no excuses" orientation. They can be developed very coherently, but only if one accepts that they are inconsistent. There are fifteen or twenty contract doctrines about which there is a conflict. That is the structure of contract doctrine, and it's typical. Doctrine is not consistent or coherent. The outcomes of these conflicts form a patchwork, rather than following straight lines.[47]

Clearly, if true, this contention creates serious problems for Dworkin's reliance on "the soundest theory of the settled law." There simply is no coherent settled theory to be found.

But the presence of inconsistent principles in legal doctrine does not present similar problems for pragmatism. Conflicting and inconsistent principles are, after all, implicit in the way members of a society regard their patterns and standards of conduct. It should not be surprising that conflicts between principles are played out in the law, or that some prevail in some cases and others prevail in other cases. The context in which Holmes wrote the 1873 passage in "Theory of Torts" involved resolving the conflict between two rules governing the height of a structure built by a landowner on property adjacent to neighboring houses. One litigant asserted the right of unregulated use of private property; the other asserted protection of the neighborhood's interest in light and air.[48]

Both rules had derived from antecedents in which their application had given rise to a "right," generally expressed in the absolute. Moreover, the rights contained in each could be said to imply conflicting political or ideological principles. One appealed to an individualist conservatism, the other to a communitarian liberalism. Nevertheless, an accommodation between the two had been reached, even before the era of regulation, by a series of fact-based jury determinations resulting in a general rule governing the height of a structure:

> To leave the question to the jury for ever is to leave the law uncertain. Accordingly, we read in a recent equity case that what was left at large to the jury fifty years ago has now become a mathematical rule; that a building cannot be complained of unless its height exceeds the distance of its base from the base of the ancient windows.[49]

This is admittedly a simple example, but it serves to demonstrate the appropriate role of the common-law judge. Ethical principles and values, as well as

---

[47] Kennedy, "The Political Significance," 15.
[48] Holmes, "Theory of Torts," *Collected Works*, 1:654.
[49] Holmes, "Theory of Torts," *Collected Works*, 654–55.

choices involving policy, are not introduced into rules through the medium of law. Rather, they are implicated both in the development of standards of conduct, which are in turn reflected in the decisions of cases in a given area of liability, and in the development of the consensus from which the rule eventually emerges. They do not exist apart from the situations that are submitted to legal institutions for resolution, thence to be imported into the decision, as both Dworkin and CLS maintain.

PRAGMATISM AND THE CANONS
OF LEGAL ANALYSIS

The common law model that Holmes drew from his early historical research did not have the inherent problems that have given rise to so much public and theoretical debate in this century. It did not have an unrealistic "mechanical" view of the manner in which rules supposedly control the outcome of cases, a view for which the later legal realists criticized the conventional theorists in the early part of the century. Nor did it propose the wholly skeptical view that conflicting rules give rise to radical indeterminacy and thus unmitigated discretion on the part of judges, a view for which Hart and the positivists challenged the realists at mid-century. Furthermore, unlike Hart's reaction against legal realism, Holmes's common-law model was not forced into the notion that "indeterminacy" was somehow resolved by "general agreement" within the legal community whenever it reared its discomfiting presence.

As a condition of life, indeterminacy did not call for immediate explanation or resolution by judges or legal scholars. Even when clearly within the jurisdiction of the common law, a new class of controversy might require a period of narrow case-specific decisions before the time was ripe for the articulation of a governing rule. Moreover, judges should not create rules subjectively, but should abstract them from the less speculative accretion of prior decisions. Thus, Holmes's theory did not require a Dworkinian system of judicially interpreted principles derived from a hypothetical "soundest theory of the settled law." Cases not clearly covered by existing rules were decided not on principle but on narrow factual grounds; principles might eventually find expression in a later court rule, but only by imposition from sources other than the courts. By providing ample room for diversity among principle both within and without the texture of the law, while resisting judicial license to decide according to a subjective choice of one over another, the common-law model did not fall prey to the CLS thesis that law and politics were synonymous.

However, Holmes's common-law model did not gain widespread adherence among contemporary legal theorists. Nineteenth-century legal theory was heavily influenced by utilitarianism, which began as a philosophy of social reform directed in part against the shortcomings of the common law in addressing social ills. Bentham saw legislation as the key to maximizing social utility by the application of incentives and disincentives.[50] The influential lectures of John Austin, a disciple of Bentham, elaborated a system of law consisting of rights and duties with innate content and obligatory influence,[51] the notion Holmes later challenged in his 1878 article, "Possession."[52] While Holmes would have more influence on legal realism and sociological jurisprudence in the early twentieth century, his common law theory of the "growth of the law" was largely ignored.

He found likewise that it did not gain much of a following among his colleagues once he became a judge. While most of the nineteenth century judges with whom he served were unlikely utilitarian reformers, they were open nonetheless to the view that law consisted of authoritative abstract rights, incorporating ethical or political principles that could be judicially applied in new substantive areas despite the opposition of competing considerations or principles.[53] Accordingly, Holmes found that a considerable effort was required to explain his contrary view. Consider the language he used in *Hudson County Water Co. v. McCarter*:

> All rights tend to declare themselves absolute to their logical extreme. Yet all in fact are limited by the neighborhood of principles of policy which are other than those on which the particular right is founded, and which become strong enough to hold their own when a certain point is reached. The limits set to property by other public interests present themselves as a branch of what is called the police power of the State. The boundary at which the conflicting interests balance cannot be determined by any general formula in advance, but points in the line, or helping to establish it, are fixed by decisions that this or that concrete case falls on the nearer or farther side.[54]

---

[50] J. Bentham, *An Introduction to the Principles of Morals and Legislation* 178–79 and nn.1–2 (1948) [1823].

[51] See John Austin, *Lectures in Jurisprudence or the Philosophy or the Philosophy of Positive Law*, 3 edition (London: John Murray, 1873).

[52] Holmes, supra note 22, at 714–17.

[53] There are radically differing accounts of the nature and basis of this, on which no position is taken here. Compare G. E. White, The *American Judicial Tradition* 2 1976 (contending that the principle thrust of nineteenth-century jurisprudence was the "oracular" theory, in which judging was seen not as making but as "finding" law, which was conceived of as a "mystical body of permanent truths") *with* M. Horwitz, *The Transformation of American Law 1780–1860*, at 245–56 (1977) (arguing that the "declaratory" theory of law was eroding by the first part of the nineteenth century and that the character of later nineteenth-century law was "formalism," in which common-law rules were given the appearance of being self-contained, apolitical, and inexorable, but emphasizing that it consisted of doctrines maintaining the new distribution of economic and political power established by mid-century.

[54] *Hudson County Water Co. v. McCarter*, 209 U.S. 349, 355 (1908).

Meanwhile, a development was underway that would create unforeseen difficulties for Holmes in applying his common-law model as a judge and would eventually refocus American jurisprudence: the rapid expansion of constitutional jurisdiction under the "due process" clauses of the fifth and fourteenth amendments.

This was well underway by the time Holmes was appointed to the Supreme Court. In 1889, Professor Charles A. Kent of Michigan University surveyed with alarm the startling growth of appeals to the Supreme Court that sought to overturn state regulatory legislation on due process grounds: "[J]urisdiction exists in all this class of cases," he opined, "and the time may come when that court, with a changed membership and changed tendencies, may set aside State laws deemed most important for the proper administration of justice."[55] Only one year later, the Court decided the watershed case of *Chicago, Milwaukee, & St. Paul Railway v. Minnesota,*[56] overturning a state ratemaking action on fourteenth amendment grounds.

This development disturbed Holmes's common-law theory in a subtle way. At first, Holmes attempted to fit constitutional claims into the model first outlined in the 1873 article,[57] describing the growth of the law as cases clustering around conflicting rules like poles of opposing magnets.[58] *Hudson County Water Co. v. McCarter*[59] is a good example. The case involved a fourteenth amendment due process claim against the state of New Jersey for subordinating private water rights to a public water project. Holmes described the "right" of private property as "limited by the neighborhood of principles of policy," generally described as the police powers of the state.[60]

The problem lay in the fact that constitutional claims were not adjudicated in the same manner as traditional common-law causes of action, wherein judges and juries gradually sifted through numerous cases with case-specific determinations until patterns and rules emerged. Rather than involving marginal issues of private law pressed at the first instance on lay juries, these constitutional claims involved original questions of public policy presented directly to judges.[61] Earlier determinations were not subject to leisurely

---

[55] Address by Professor Charles A. Kent, University of Michigan Celebration Making the Centennial of the Constitution (1889), *printed in* Michigan University, *Constitutional History of the United States as Seen in the Development of American Law* 333 (1889), *quoted in* Paul Freund, *On Law and Justice* 4 (1968).

[56] *Chicago, Milwaukee & St. Paul Ry. v. Minnesota*, 134 U.S. 418 (1890).,

[57] "Theory of Torts," *supra* note 16, at 653–55.

[58] *See generally* Kellogg, "Common Law and Constitutional Theory: The Common Law Origins of Holmes' Constitutional Restraint," 7 *George Mason Law Review* 177 (1984) (suggesting that, by 1905, Holmes had replaced his early model of judicial decision making with a cognate theory of judicial restraint where constitutional questions were concerned).

[59] 209 U.S. 349 (1908).

[60] *Id.* at 355.

[61] *See* Kellogg, *supra* note 72, at 188–201.

reconsideration with differing points of emphasis; they were likely to be final. The sweeping language of the Constitution implied a much more powerful magnet pulling clusters of cases into its orbit, overwhelming the coverage of common-law rules and the jurisdiction of lower courts and even legislatures.

In other words, there would be hardly any area of existing law, as well as federal or state regulation, wherein a cognizable denial of liberty or property without due process could not be argued by a party aggrieved at the outcome. Even if every federal judge understood Holmes's theory and tried to avoid making policy, simply marking what Holmes described in *Hudson County Water Co. v. McCarter* as "points in the line,"[62] the line itself would be skewed by the fundamental nature of the Constitution and the breadth of its language. Due process jurisdiction would grow like topsy, unchecked by any neutral convention of restraint. With such sweeping jurisdiction, subjective values of judges were bound to assert themselves.

Treating constitutional law as simply another branch of common law, the Supreme Court would become a supreme national court of general jurisdiction over all codes, regulations, and decisions. Hence, Holmes's general theory of common law decision-making required a special exception for constitutional law. By the time of *Lochner v. New York,*[63] Holmes had worked out the outlines of a special theory.[64] Although a partial departure, it was rooted in the understanding Holmes had reached in developing his common-law model, particularly in the two elements of pragmatic method that Holmes had developed parallel to Peirce in the 1870s.

The first element of pragmatic method was the meaning-limiting maxim that appeared in the 1878 article *Possession.* Under that maxim, any legal concept, including a constitutional "right," was denied any inherent content and was limited in meaning to its consequences for the particular form of legal inquiry. The embodiment of those consequences was, for Holmes, found in prior precedent. The maxim had revealed the fallacy of importing a Kantian component of "free will" into the concept of "possession," which required an intent to exert dominion for the plaintiff's benefit. Instead, the legal meaning of possession was limited to its application as a traditional cause of action available to bailees as well as owners, requiring only an intent to exclude others.[65]

The maxim also uncovered the fallacy of reading extra-legal doctrine, such as *laissez faire* economic theory, into constitutional due process. The majority of the Supreme Court had done this in *Lochner v. New York,* overturning

---

[62] 209 U.S. at 355.
[63] 198 U.S. 45 (1905).
[64] *See* Kellogg, *supra* note 72, at 177.
[65] Holmes, "Possession," *Collected Works* 3:717.

a state labor restriction on the ground that it limited freedom of contract. Rather, the content of the concept of due process was limited, like possession, to the context in which legal impingements on contract rights had been permitted in previously decided cases. The courts had long upheld restrictions on freedom of contract such as taxes on business transactions, prohibitions of business on Sunday, and all manner of regulation of free enterprise designed to protect the general health and welfare.

From the pragmatic maxim emerged a key feature of Holmes's constitutional restraint. In essence, constitutional standards do not flow from the plain meaning of broad constitutional language but are rooted in the common law. They do not provide jurisdiction for federal courts to review established state common-law precedents as would a supreme national court of common-law appeals. The most explicit statement of this is found in Holmes's dissent in *Muhlker v. New York & Harlem Railroad.*[66] The second element of pragmatic method was the process of rulemaking by "successive approximation,"

---

[66] *Muhlker v. New York & Harlem R.R.*, 197 U.S. 544, 571–77 (1905) (Holmes, J., dissenting). In *Muhlker*, a landowner had acquired title to property abutting a New York City street under a grant that had been construed by state courts to include easements of light, air, and access. He sued for compensation for infringement of those rights by a state-authorized elevated railroad. An award of compensation was appealed to the highest state appellate court, where it was overturned in a complex ruling evaluating the precedents on which the easement had been founded. The case was presented to the United States Supreme Court under the fourteenth amendment, under the *Lochner* theory of abridgement of contract rights. Reversing the New York Court of Appeals, a majority of the Supreme Court could not resist this comment on the facts:

> There is something of a mockery to give one access to property which may be unfit to live on when one gets there. To what situation is the plaintiff brought? Because he can cross the railroad at more places on the street, the State, it is contended, can authorize dirt, cinders, and smoke from 200 trains a day to be poured into the upper windows of his house.

Muhlker, 563–64. The Court held as follows: "When the plaintiff acquired his title those cases were the law of New York, and assured to him that his easements of light and air were secured by contract as expressed in those cases, and could not be taken from him without payment of compensation." *Muhlker*, 570.

In effect, this was to ignore the entire body of admittedly conflicting state common-law precedent, because the highest state court had ultimately found that it led to a result that the Supreme Court found unsympathetic. Holmes directly addressed the contract claim:

> The plaintiff's rights, whether expressed in terms of property or of contract, are all a construction of the courts, deduced by way of consequence from dedication to and trusts for the purposes of a public street. They never were granted to him or his predecessors in express words, or, probably, by any conscious implication.

Muhlker, 572 (Holmes, J., dissenting). Thus, the New York courts might have held from the outset that no easement existed in this particular context-indeed, other jurisdictions had so held-and under that circumstance there could be no argument that any constitutional right had been violated. Holmes noted:

> So much, I presume, would be admitted by everyone. But if that be admitted, I ask myself what has happened to cut down the power of the same courts as against that same Constitution at the

which paralleled Peirce's theory of reasoning.[67] In the common-law context, this process served two important purposes: It permitted sufficient room for external influences to guide legal decisions and inform their moral, ethical, and political content; and it obliged judges to respond to an emergent consensus as to the rule best suited to those affected by the class of controversy. Successive approximation was the mechanism through which democratic values were preserved in the growth of the common law.

In constitutional cases, the degree to which both of these purposes were realizable was drastically threatened by the breadth of the claims and the judge-centered manner of their resolution. This was an additional reason for resisting general constitutional jurisdiction coextensive with constitutional language and for confining it within the web of settled common-law precedent. But it also required the courts to refrain from substituting their own factual assessments for those that had already been made by a legislature. Holmes saw legislation as providing a distinct and comprehensive public alternative to the slow, private, common-law rulemaking process: "The time has gone by when law is only an unconscious embodiment of the common will. It has become a conscious reaction upon itself of organized society knowingly seeking to determine its own destinies."[68] The factual basis for legislative lawmaking was not placed before courts; hence, as he wrote in *Otis v. Parker,* "Considerable latitude must be allowed for differences of view as well as for possible peculiar conditions which this court can know but imperfectly, if at all."[69]

This did not, incidentally, mean that Holmes denied the legitimacy of constitutional review of legislation. The next sentence in *Otis* reads: "Otherwise a constitution, instead of embodying only relatively fundamental rules of right, as generally understood by all English-speaking communities, would become the partisan of a particular set of ethical or economical opinions, which by no means are held *semper ubique et ab omnibus.*"[70] The import of this is that, given that the content or doctrine of the Constitution is cognate

---

present day I know of no constitutional principle to prevent the complete reversal of the elevated railroad cases tomorrow, if it should seem proper to the Court of Appeals.

But I conceive that the [appellant] must go much further than to say that my last proposition is wrong. I think he must say that he has a constitutional right not only that the state courts shall not reverse their earlier decisions upon a matter of property rights, but that they shall not distinguish them unless the distinction is so fortunate as to strike a majority of this court as sound. *Muhlker,* 573–74 (citation omitted).

[67] *See* note 52 *supra.*
[68] Holmes, "Privilege, Malice, and Intent," *Collected Works,* 3:371, 380.
[69] *Otis v. Parker,* 187 U.S. 606, 608–09 (1903).
[70] *Otis v. Parker,* 609.

with the common law, when fundamental common-law "rules of right" are violated, the Constitution may be invoked.

It might appear that this is open to the CLS criticism that judges still have a license to engage in politics. The common law is replete with sufficient opposing "fundamental rules of right" to warrant ruling either way in a close case. Holmes appears to have been aware of this issue, having addressed it obliquely (although not in a constitutional law context) in an article written in 1894,[71] in his dissents in *Vegelahn v. Guntner* (1896)[72] and *Plant v. Woods* (1900),[73] in an address published as an article in 1899,[74] and ultimately in a speech discussing the Supreme Court's constitutional jurisdiction in 1913.[75] The outcome of his analysis does not lead directly into the jaws of the CLS critique, although his resolution of the problem may require a high degree of intellectual subtlety and integrity on the part of a judge.

The answer seems to be based on the principle that, while the common law process of successive approximation has largely been supplanted in modern society by popularly enacted legislation, there nevertheless remains a role for the courts. Legislatures are the main interpreters of ethical, moral, and political values, and, unlike legislatures, judges cannot "apply" these directly–by which Holmes meant that they cannot think directly from the values to the outcome. The only way in which judges may apply the fundamental rights expressed in the Constitution is through specific and factual analogies with prior settled precedent.

Before examining what that means, it is important to establish what it does not mean. Judicial lawmaking is fundamentally retrospective; a good judicial abstraction is one that summarizes coherently and adequately, but not comprehensively. A large component of legislation is prospective. In the latter, there is a great deal of present uncertainty as to future results. As the above passages from *Otis* suggest, courts are physically removed from the legislative analysis and thus not properly qualified to evaluate it.

A good many of the early due process claims sought to get judges to do precisely what this thesis forbade. Judges applied to legislation sweeping and absolute principles allegedly drawn from the law and the Constitution, which, insofar as they could be found in precedent, were in fact inherently truncated in their prior application by the process that Holmes described in 1873 in "Theory of Torts." Legislators choose among competing ethical or political

---

[71] Holmes, "Privilege, Malice, and Intent," *Collected Works*, 3:371.

[72] *Vegelahn v. Guntner*, 167 Mass. 92, 107–09, 44 N.E. 1077, 1079–82 (1896).

[73] *Plant v. Woods*, 176 Mass. 492, 504–05, 57 N.E. IOI I, 1015–16 (1900) (Holmes, J., dissenting).

[74] Holmes, "Law in Science and Science in Law," *Collected Works*, 3:406.

[75] Speech by O. W. Holmes, Dinner of the Harvard Law School Ass'n of N. Y. (February 15, 1913), in *The Occasional Speeches of Justice Oliver Wendell Holmes*, 168 (M. Howe comp. 1962) [hereinafter Holmes Speech]. CW 3:507.

principles, as only legislators are competent to do. Only legislators can look ahead; judicial law can only look backward.[76]

This position may appear vulnerable to the CLS criticism that there are ample competing analogies from which to draw in arguing for opposing outcomes, and that therefore Holmes does not actually reduce the "political" role of judges. This is the basic criticism that CLS has leveled against liberal jurisprudence in both constitutional and common-law contexts. Tushnet writes,

> The materials of legal doctrine are almost measureless, and the acceptable techniques of legal reasoning-distinguishing on the basis of the facts, analogizing to other areas of law where cognate problems arise, and the like-are so flexible that they allow us to assemble diverse precedents into whatever pattern we choose.[77]

It is fairly clear from the Holmes writings cited above that he was aware of the problem. His response, particularly in light of his dissents in the *Vegelahn* and *Plant* cases, which upheld injunctions against picketing in labor disputes, would be twofold. First, the analogies used to justify a decision in an original case must be specific and factual. It is not appropriate to "analogize to other *areas* of law," nor especially to "assemble diverse precedents into *patterns*."[78] Rather, the court should refer to specific lines of decision, and to the facts on which they are based.

This accomplishes two things. First, it serves to limit the impact of the new decision, which may be quite important if (as in the *Vegelahn* and *Plant* cases) it may have considerable public policy implications. Second, it forces more candid, and hence more careful, judicial reasoning of a nature considerably more open to reconsideration by a subsequent decision or by legislation. In both the *Vegelahn* and *Plant* cases, the issue was whether it was

---

[76] *See* Hand, *The Bill of Rights*, 66–67:

> This distinction in the case of legislation demands an analysis of its component factors. These are an estimate of the relevant existing facts and a forecast of the changes that the proposed measure will bring about. In addition, it involves an appraisal of the values that the change will produce, as to which there are no postulates specific enough to serve as guides on concrete occasions. In the end, all that can be asked on review by a court is that the appraisals and the choice shall be impartial. The statute may be far from the best solution of the conflicts with which it deals; but if it is the result of an honest effort to embody that compromise or adjustment that will secure the widest acceptance and most avoid resentment, it is "Due Process of Law" and conforms to the First Amendment. In theory, any statute is always open to challenge upon the ground that it was not in truth the result of an impartial effort, but from the outset it was seen that any such inquiry was almost always practically impossible, and moreover it would be to the last degree "political."

[77] Tushnet, *Red, White, and Blue*, 191–92.
[78] Tushnet, *Red, White and Blue*, 191–92 (emphasis added).

legal for workers to conduct organized opposition to an employer's terms of employment. In *Vegelahn*, striking furniture workers presented demands for a nine-hour day and wage increases, and established a picket line. There were incidents of violence, including obstruction of factory entrances and verbal harassment of potential customers and nonstriking workers.[79]

Holmes was an Associate Justice of the Supreme Judicial Court of Massachusetts, sitting as a trial judge to hear the employer's request for an injunction. After first issuing a comprehensive preliminary injunction, he later modified it to enjoin the physical interference and intimidation by threats of violence, but to permit the strikers to maintain two pickets to notify patrons of the strike and to urge them not to enter the premises.[80]

When the case reached the full Supreme Judicial Court of Massachusetts, Holmes's modification was overruled by the majority on the ground that any organized opposition constituted an interference with freedom of contract, which was presumed to be protected by the constitutions of both Massachusetts and the United States. Holmes dissented in this decision on grounds similar to his later dissent in *Lochner v. New York*: that "in numberless instances" the law already permitted other kinds of "intentional inflict[ion] of temporal [economic] damage," and if organization and combination by employers and businesses were permissible for purposes which included gaining economic advantage at the expense of others, then the abstract principle of interference with contract rights was plainly not a sufficient legal ground.[81]

Four years later, the case of *Plant v. Woods* raised a closely related issue before the Supreme Judicial Court of Massachusetts. *Plant* involved an employer's challenge to the legality of a union's efforts to induce its employees to join that union and quit a competing one.[82] This time, the majority again authorized an injunction, and Holmes again dissented, but not on the same grounds as in *Vegelahn*.[83] The majority refrained from invoking a sweeping general principle and came very close to crediting Holmes for this fact. The majority opinion refers to the analysis of general principles in the law set forth in Holmes's 1894 article:

> See, on this, an instructive article in 8 Harv. Law. Rev. 1, where the subject is considered at some length. It is manifest that not much progress is made by such general statements as those quoted above from Allen v. Flood, whatever may be their meaning.[84]

---

[79] *Vegelahn,* 167 Mass. at 93–94.
[80] *Vegelahn,* 167 Mass. at 95–96.
[81] *Plant,* 105–09, 44 N.E. at 1080–82 (Holmes, dissenting).
[82] *Plant,* 494, 57 N.E. at 1012.
[83] *Plant,* 504, 57 N.E. at 1015 (Holmes, dissenting).
[84] *Plant,* 500, 57 N.E. at 1014 (majority opinion).

The majority thereupon decided *Plant* according to an analogy with unlawful extortion: "obtain[ing] a sum of money from [someone], which he is under no legal obligation to pay."[85]

"[M]uch to my satisfaction, if I may say so," wrote Holmes in his dissent, "the court has seen fit to adopt the mode of approaching the question which I believe to be the correct one, and *to open an issue which otherwise I might have thought closed.*"[86] While Holmes disagreed with the analogy to extortion, his satisfaction lay in the larger victory of opening the issue. He could now point out that the crux of the matter would thereafter lie in the demonstration of unlawful motive by the workers. Therefore, future cases would be governed by a far more limited proposition. As Holmes wrote in the 1894 article, "The danger is that such considerations should have their weight in an inarticulate form as unconscious prejudice or half-conscious inclination."[87]

It must be remembered that *Vegelahn* and *Plant* were on the cutting edge of the field of labor law and, after a major struggle, would eventually lead to comprehensive federal regulation. Judicial intervention alone should not have been expected to resolve the multifaceted interests and complex considerations involved. "To measure [such considerations] justly," Holmes observed in his article, "needs not only the highest powers of a judge and a training which the practice of law does not insure, but also a freedom from prepossessions which is very hard to attain. It seems to me desirable that the work should be done with express recognition of its nature."[88]

Judicial decision by factual analogy did not assure that cases like *Vegelahn* and *Plant* would be decided fairly, but it did operate more faithfully to the purposes of what Holmes had in 1870 called "successive approximation." Use of the extortion analogy in *Plant* limited the precedent to cases involving similar activity, instead of granting carte blanche for enjoining all union interference with employment relationships. It invited the introduction of evidence in future cases to counteract the majority's presumption that the motive was to extort money,[89] rather than what Holmes termed the "more remote" purpose of "strengthen[ing] the defendants' society."[90] It permitted the maximum degree of legislative freedom to regulate the activity by not creating a judicially pronounced cloud of unconstitutionality. Mainly, it came far closer to doing the work with express recognition of its nature.[91]

---

[85] *Plant*, 501, 57 N.E. at 1014.
[86] *Plant*, 504, 57 N.E. at 1016 (Holmes, dissenting) (emphasis added).
[87] Holmes, "Privilege, Malice, and Intent," *Collected Works*, 3:380.
[88] Holmes, "Privilege, Malice, and Intent," *Collected Works*, 3:380.
[89] *Plant*, 176 Mass. at 501, 57 N.E. at 1014 (majority opinion).
[90] *Plant*, 176 Mass. at 505, 57 N.E. at 1016 (Holmes, dissenting).
[91] See Holmes, "Privilege, Malice, and Intent," *Collected Works*, 3:380.

Nevertheless, Holmes does not appear to have been entirely satisfied with this manner of resolving controversial cases. Between the *Plant* dissent, written while he sat on the Massachusetts Supreme Judicial Court, and his encounter with the much greater constitutional caseload of the Supreme Court, he gave an address to the New York State Bar Association in 1899, describing some of his underlying concerns about the law. The picture of law that emerged still maintained the earlier notion of an "approach toward exactness [in which] we constantly tend to work out definite lines or equators to mark distinctions which we first notice as a difference of poles."[92] But more pronounced is a newer theme of law as a medium for the resolution of urgent conflicts in a far less leisurely manner than in the gradual growth of common-law rules out of particular jury determinations. In this new climate, the courts could not avoid being called upon to choose among opposing social interests, battling each other for advantage.[93]

No matter how strict the rules of advocacy, Holmes perceived that advocates of "social desires" would find some way to insert their claims into the judicial system, even if confined to arguing them out by strict analogy. But when such cases arose, clearly outside the realm of prior decisions and bearing larger issues by implication, judges should beware. They might be presented "with certain analogies on one side and other analogies on the other." But it was crucial to remember:

> that what really is before us is a conflict between two social desires, each of which seeks to extend its dominion over the case, and which cannot both have their way. The social question is which desire is strongest at the point of conflict. The judicial one may be narrower, because one or the other desire may have been expressed in previous decisions to such an extent that logic requires us to assume it to preponderate in the one before us. But if that be clearly so, the case is not a doubtful one. Where there is doubt the simple tool of logic does not suffice, and even if it is disguised and unconscious the judges are called on to exercise the sovereign prerogative of choice.[94]

Holmes stopped short of recommending that the courts eschew such cases altogether, but he did warn against deciding in such a manner as to preclude nonjudicial mechanisms from working out conflicting social interests. Fourteen years later, after having served eleven years on the Supreme Court, he made his position clearer and more explicit in a speech to the Harvard Law School Association of New York:

---

[92] Holmes, "Law in Science and Science in Law," *Collected Works*, 3:415.
[93] Holmes, "Law in Science and Science in Law," *Collected Works*, 3:418.
[94] Holmes, "Law in Science and Science in Law," *Collected Works*, 3:418–19.

It cannot be helped, it is as it should be, that the law is behind the times. I told a labor leader once that what they asked was favor, and if a decision was against them they called it wicked. The same might be said of their opponents. It means that the law is growing. As law embodies beliefs that have translated themselves into action, while there still is doubt, while opposite convictions still keep a battle front against each other, the time for law has not come; the notion destined to prevail is not yet entitled to the field. It is a misfortune if a judge reads his conscious or unconscious sympathy with one side or the other prematurely into the law, and forgets that what seem to him to be first principles are believed by half his fellow men to be wrong.[95]

By the year 1913, when he said this, Holmes had come to spend much of his time waving a red flag when the Court was drawn into moral and political questions. Popular discontent with the Court was, as Holmes described it to his audience, "palpable." The public saw the Court as a "tool of the money power," and thought the Court had "usurped" the right to declare an act of Congress unconstitutional; "I get letters, not always anonymous, intimating that we are corrupt."[96]

Although the *laissez faire* approach to due process found in the *Lochner* decision lost favor, the Court did not adopt Holmes's canons of restraint. Due process jurisdiction would grow in new directions. With few exceptions, legal scholarship would largely overlook pragmatic methodology and its implications. Learned Hand, who studied philosophy as a Harvard undergraduate during the era of William James, Josiah Royce, and George Santayana, was to draw on pragmatism in resisting the tendency to regard the Bill of Rights as a set of judicial principles. Felix Frankfurter's efforts to restrain the Court from expanding due process willy-nilly into civil liberties cases would be roundly rejected by the Court's majority at mid-century.[97] Both men were as heavily influenced by Holmes as were any scholars or judges during this century. But their tradition of judicial restraint, bringing to constitutional jurisprudence canons of method drawn from the common law, has apparently expired.

CONSERVATISM, LIBERALISM, AND CLS

In place of the tradition of judicial restraint that emerged from the writings of Holmes a century ago, current conservative scholarship has urged

---

[95] Holmes, "Law and the Court," *Collected Works*, 3:506–7.
[96] Holmes, "Law and the Court," *Collected Works*, 3:505.
[97] *See generally* J. Lash, *From the Diaries of Felix Frankfurter* (1975), 78, which explains, in part, Frankfurter's view that, in civil liberties cases, "the legislative judgment had to be respected even if the Court might have reached a different conclusion."

adherence to the "original understanding" surrounding the adoption of the Constitution.[98] There are several troubling questions that this position fails to put to rest. First, and most often noted, the phrase fails to provide any specific guidance for the original controversies that most often plague the Court and its critics in the late-twentieth century. The founders could not anticipate the social and technological framework of modern society. What was the original understanding with regard to the constitutionality of televising a notorious criminal trial, an issue in which the guarantees of fair trial and free press conflict?

More important, the conservative approach accepts the very assumption of liberal judicial philosophy with which it seems most uneasy: the pivotal role of judges. In attempting to provide a "conservative" answer to the question posed by liberal jurisprudence, it fails to address problems inherent in the question. The question is: How are judges to give meaning to the sweeping language of constitutional guarantees? Even if the answer is "original under-standing," it accepts two aspects of the liberal solution that troubled Holmes: the notions that the Constitution contains one clear principle from which the new case can be resolved, and that it can be found and applied by subjective inquiry, albeit according to a presumptively restrictive formula. Even if the answer to the question is one acceptable to conservatives, it will neverthe-less be rooted in a subjective interpretation of the meaning "inherent" in the Constitution and, hence, will have a presumption of being final and incapable of subsequent judicial or legislative reconsideration.

Moreover, the position fails to deal adequately with the fact that, even under a strict reading, conflicting principles seem to be inherent in the "original understanding" itself, even regarding matters addressed with rela-tive specificity. A leading defender of the concept of original understanding, Robert H. Bork, suggests as much in discussing the Warren Court's deci-sion in *Brown v. Board of Education*,[99] which he supports.[100] The fourteenth amendment guarantee of equal protection had been interpreted in *Plessy v. Ferguson*[101] to mandate no more than separate, equal facilities for blacks. The social circumstances at the time of the amendment's adoption argue that separate-but-equal was closer to the original understanding. But Bork observes, "By 1954, when *Brown* came up for decision, it had been apparent for some time that segregation rarely if ever produced equality." Hence, Bork

---

[98] *E.g.*, R. Bork, *The Tempting of America: The Political Seduction of the Law* 6–11 (1990); Monaghan, "Stare Decisis and Constitutional Adjudication," *Columbia Law Review* 88 (1988): 723, 723–39; Scalia, "Originalism: The Lesser Evil," 57 *U. Cincinnati Law Review* (1989): 849, 852–65.

[99] 347 U.S. 483 (1954).

[100] Bork, *Tempting of America*, 74–83.

[101] 163 U.S. 537 (1896).

reads into the original understanding an ongoing obligation to "produce the equality the Constitution promised."[102]

The Court's realistic choice, therefore, was either to abandon the quest for equality by allowing segregation or to forbid segregation in order to achieve equality. There was no third choice. *Either choice would violate one aspect of the original understanding, but there was no possibility of avoiding that.*[103]

---

[102] Bork, *Tempting of America,* 82.

[103] Bork, *Tempting of America,* 82 (emphasis added). The overwhelming consensus favoring the Court's reversal of *Plessy v. Ferguson* in *Brown v. Board of Education* suggests the question of how the *Brown* Court, had it consisted of "Holmsean pragmatists" (as characterized in this chapter), might have justified reversing *Plessy.* This question is highlighted by the fact that legal pragmatism places considerable reliance on custom and precedent to inform the content of constitutional law, and *Plessy* was a precedent that conformed to a widely accepted practice, *i.e.,* racial segregation. There has been a tendency, especially since Herbert Wechsler's Oliver Wendell Holmes Lecture (April 7, 1959), "Toward Neutral Principles of Constitutional Law," *Harvard Law Review* 73 (1959): 1, to assume that only an overriding "principle" would be sufficient to trump the precedent and overrule *Plessy.*

The better answer may be to focus instead on the facts. A pragmatic judge is open not only to declaring prior lines of precedent inapplicable to a new case, but also to reversal of prior precedent in the face of compelling circumstances. The decision in *Plessy* was grounded in the conclusion that enforced racial separation was consistent with "equal protection of the laws." *Plessy,* 163 U.S. at 548. Evidence was amassed in *Brown* that it was not. Indeed, it is not the "principle" advanced in *Brown* that gains its authority over *Plessy* by dry logical analysis, but the overwhelming weight of evidence, consisting of every relevant instance in which enforced racial separation was demonstrably unequal. *Brown v. Board of Education,* 347 U.S. 483, 493–95 (1954).

The originalist approach advanced by Bork plainly accepts this, but attempts to dress the argument to suit its overall agenda. In the text under discussion, Bork writes, "By 1954, when *Brown* came up for decision, it had been apparent for some time that segregation rarely if ever produced equality." Bork, *supra* note 124, at 82. This is a concession that *Plessy* was really overruled on the facts as they applied to the plain words of the fourteenth amendment, not merely by reaching back into the mist of historic minds and intentions.

All this is not to suggest that discussion of principle and policy are utterly without standing in judicial analysis. Holmes allowed as much in *Privilege, Malice, and Intent,* in which the thrust of his argument appears to be that, in "hard" cases, wherein the judges are without clear precedent and are inclined to appeal to policy, they should do so openly and not shroud policy considerations in principles so general that no one would object to them. Holmes, "Privilege, Malice, and Intent," *Collected Works,* 3:380. At times, Holmes made comments suggesting that he favored utilitarianism as a broad approach to legal policy; yet the thrust of his early scholarship was to undermine John Austin's attempt to construct a utilitarian positivist legal theory. *See* Kellogg, "Holmes, Pragmatism, and the Deconstruction of Utilitarianism," *Transactions of the Charles S Peirce Soc'y* 23, 99, 102–6. From the outset, pragmatism has been opposed to foundationalism in the sense that there must exist one comprehensive and final explanation-yet it recognized the value of generalizations based on efforts at comprehensive explanation. A useful comment regarding the pragmatic approach to reasoning, and applicable to this question, is Peirce's statement that

[p]hilosophy ought . . . to trust rather to the multitude and variety of its arguments than to the conclusiveness of any one. Its reasoning should not form a chain which is no stronger

Because the Constitution does not provide much specific guidance for modern controversies, Bork is obliged to leave some play in the method whereby judges apply original understanding. Thus, even if all members of the bar and the judiciary agreed with Bork's thesis, there would still be considerable liberty to argue either side of an urgent controversy from opposing principle. Bork describes the method as follows:

> In short, all that a judge committed to original understanding requires is that the text, structure, and history of the Constitution provide him not with a conclusion but with a major premise. That major premise is a principle or stated value that the ratifiers wanted to protect against hostile legislation or executive action. The judge must then see whether that principle or value is threatened by the statute or action challenged in the case before him. The answer to that question provides his minor premise, and the conclusion follows.[104]

As CLS writers have demonstrated, it is possible to argue for any outcome by choosing among the opposing general principles in authoritative material and showing that one or another principle is "threatened by the statute or action challenged."[105] It seems clear that this method is subject to the same abuses that Holmes perceived in *Vegelahn* and *Lochner*, and that it would still permit the Supreme Court excessive license to override either common law or legislation on final constitutional grounds.

Careful scrutiny of documents and events clarifying the Constitution's original meaning is an important element of the judicial role, but it cannot be elevated, or "privileged," without meeting criticisms similar to those CLS has made of other doctrinal approaches. In an important sense, the popular formula for conservative jurisprudence is rooted in the liberal tradition and fails to provide an alternative to it. It is, accordingly, equally vulnerable to all of the criticisms that CLS makes of liberal legal theory generally, as a review of those criticisms will demonstrate.

The nub of the issue lies, as one defender of liberalism has shown, in the CLS "challenge to a principle central to liberal legal thought—the rule of law."[106] Although CLS writings diverge on important matters, "[t]he central contention

---

than its weakest link, but a cable whose fibers may be ever so slender, provided they are sufficiently numerous and intimately connected. Peirce, "Some Consequences of Four Incapacities," *Collected Papers* (Cambridge, MA: Belknap Press, 1978), 5:157.

I am grateful to Mark Tushnet for bringing this issue to my attention.

[104] Bork, *Tempting of America*, 162–63.
[105] Bork, *Tempting of America*, 163.
[106] Altman, *Critical Legal Studies*, 9–10.

of CLS is that rule of law is a myth."[107] The meaning of "rule of law" in this context is not one of which the antonym is disrespect for the law. Rather, it means, as will be seen, an approach to legal and political theory placing primary reliance on law and legal institutions defining what is just and right.

As noted in the previous chapter, there are three main prongs to the CLS attack. The first encompasses the claim that the rule of law is not possible in a society espousing a liberal view of individual freedom. The latter implies a "pluralism of fundamentally incompatible moral and political viewpoints," infecting modes of order as well as conflict.[108] The existence of presumptively pure *legal* reasoning autonomous from political and ethical choice, is impossible.[109] Originalists have essentially ignored this charge as directed at liberal legal theory, but would presumably take refuge from it, just as liberals do, by appealing to principles inherent in the Constitution.

Pragmatism's response is to emphasize that the "pluralism of fundamentally incompatible moral and political views"[110] is by nature reflected in the fabric of law, by reason of its reflection of the fabric of life. Judging is nevertheless possible, if done by close analogy and case-specific decisions and not by arbitrary selection from the diverse body of "principles" that can be inferred from authoritative legal materials. This position can only be defended under the assumption that law and legal institutions do not comprehensively define what is just and right—a position that originalists, especially given their near-absolute deference to legislation, have failed to articulate.[111]

---

[107] Altman, *Critical Legal Studies,* 10.
[108] Altman, *Critical Legal Studies,* 13.
[109] Altman, *Critical Legal Studies,* 13–14.
[110] Altman, *Critical Legal Studies,* 13.
[111] This position would appear to be implied in the views expressed by Thayer, Hand, and Frankfurter, quoted above. All three urge constitutional restraint in situations where strong arguments may exist that constitutional standards are violated, in order to promote broader responsibility for the protection of those standards than that strictly given to the legal process. They take this position whether or not the legislative process appears likely to remedy the presumptive violation. This is most clearly evident in Frankfurter's dissent in *West Virginia State Board of Education v. Barnette,* involving a state-enforced mandatory flag salute law that Frankfurter openly disagreed with, while maintaining nevertheless that "much which should offend a free-spirited society is constitutional." 319 U.S. 624, 670 (1943) (Frankfurter, J., dissenting). In effect, all three men clearly suggested that some degree of judicially tolerable dissonance between "the just and right" and reality may be necessary to a constitutional democracy, even where it is not clear that the situation will be corrected legislatively.
    This position violates the "rule of law" element of liberal legal theory. It does not necessarily deny that law and legal processes are an important part of society's quest for justice, it rather denies that they are necessarily definitive. The implication is that what people actually think and do, apart from the law and the existing body of "legal" issues, is an important part of that quest and, ultimately, of the definition of justice. Indeed, Thayer, Hand, and Frankfurter say, in effect, that certain elements of right and justice, clearly guaranteed by the Constitution itself, cannot be guaranteed by enforcement, and that even a judicial system wholly constituted of perfect judges, all with the hypothetical powers of Dworkin's Hercules, could not produce a society meeting the Constitution's ideals. This is because the judges' efforts would undermine a key element: the internal commitment of the people,

The second prong involves the claim that "the legal doctrines of contemporary liberal states are riddled by contradictions."[112] Every legal principle is opposed by another, in every factual context. Judges covertly rely on moral and political considerations in deciding upon which of the incompatible legal norms they will base their decisions. As one CLS writer puts it, "traditional legal theory requires a relatively large amount of determinacy as a fundamental premise of the rule of law. Our legal system, however, has never satisfied this goal."[113]

Originalists are also critical of judges for relying on moral and political considerations and maintain that this can be avoided through consensus regarding the Constitution's original meaning. Pragmatism denies that such a consensus is possible. It concedes that legal and constitutional authorities contain contradictory moral and political principles, when interpreted or expressed as such. This is precisely why judges should not readily rely on moral and political principles even when drawn from authoritative sources. The primary source of determinacy in law is found not primarily within the ethical and moral principles judges may espouse in their decisions, but mainly within settled lines of fact-specific precedent.

The third prong attacks the notion that law is even "capable of constraining the exercise of social and political power."[114] Law is an artifact, a human

---

nurtured through their own continuing responsibility for maintaining those ideals without sole reliance on litigation.

The position must be squared with those instances in which Thayer, Hand, and Frankfurter have accepted the necessity of judicial intervention under the Constitution. How, for example, would Frankfurter explain his vote for constitutional reversal of *Plessy v. Ferguson* in *Brown v. Board of Education* in light of his extreme advocacy of restraint in *West Virginia State Board of Education v. Barnette?* None of the three have elaborately addressed this question, beyond the sort of warning found in the passage from Thayer quoted at length by Frankfurter in *Barnette:*

the exercise of [judicial review], even when unavoidable, is always attended with a serious evil, namely, that the correction of legislative mistakes comes from the outside, and the people thus lose the political experience, and the moral education and stimulus that come from fighting the question out in the ordinary way, and correcting their own errors.

Barnette, 668 (Frankfurter, J., dissenting, quoting Thayer, *John Marshall,* 104–10). Therefore, they "owe to the country no greater or clearer duty than that of keeping their hands of these acts wherever it is possible to do it (*Barnette,* 670)."

Although their position on the rule-of-law issue was not fully elaborated, it serves to distinguish the approach of Holmes, Thayer, Hand, and Frankfurter from that of Friedrich A. Hayek, noted for his praise of the common law and repudiation of socialism and state planning. Hayek, *Law, Legislation and Liberty,* 94–123. Unlike the position implicit in legal pragmatism, Hayek resoundingly endorsed the principle of the rule of law and attacked socialist economic policies for being inconsistent with it. Hayek, *The Road To Serfdom,* 72–87 (1944); *see* Altman, *supra* note 133, at 28 (placing Hayek solidly within the tradition of liberal legal theory).

[112] Altman, *Critical Legal Studies,* 14.

[113] Singer, "The Player and the Cards," 13.

[114] Altman, *Critical Legal Studies,* 16.

creation; to regard it as an independent force controlling those who have created and sustained it is akin to fetishism or superstition. While liberal jurisprudence has come to accept the assumption that law, and indeed the notion of "society," are human artifacts rather than expressions of an underlying natural order, "[n]o one," says the CLS theorist Roberto Unger, "has ever taken the idea of society as artifact to the hilt."[115]

The essence of this third claim is that, if legal language has any settled core of meaning, the interpretations required to decide cases are inescapably tied to individual moral and political beliefs. Our law does have an objective structure, but it derives from a particular, temporal, and inadequate or incomplete ethical perspective. As Unger has said:

> The nation, at the Lycurgan moment of its history, had opted for a particular type of society: a commitment to a democratic republic and to a market system as a necessary part of that republic. The people might have chosen some other type of social organization. But in choosing this one, in choosing it for example over an aristocratic and corporatist polity on the old-European model, they also chose the legally defined institutional structure that went along with it.[116]

The liberal response to this is essentially that the choice of our form of polity and law was a philosophically justifiable one and can be rationally defended in terms of legal theory. With this position under fire, liberalism reduces the essence of the rule of law to the protection of the broadest individual freedoms possible through the requirements of fair notice and the legal accountability of established authority to a pre-existing system of authoritative norms.[117] This requires a differentiation between law and politics, such that the political realm is kept distinct as one in which competing conceptions of the good and right are accommodated through the democratic process, while the realm of law is restricted to interpreting and applying those accommodations.[118]

Originalist conservatism appears to adopt essentially the same strategy. Liberalism's catalogue of fundamental freedoms and the precise requirements of notice and accountability may be amended somewhat by an originalist, but the answer to Unger would be the same: Within the original understanding of the Constitution is a set of maxims sufficient to justify the rule of law. Law and legal institutions may be fraught with controversial indeterminacies, but they can

---

[115] Unger, *Social Theory: Its Situation and Its Task,* 1.
[116] Unger, *The Critical Legal Studies Movement,* 5.
[117] *See* Altman, *Critical Legal Studies,* 57–103.
[118] Altman, *Critical Legal Studies,* 79–90.

and should be resolved by resort to the law's authoritative materials. In essence, those problems are legal problems, and they can be resolved by the "law."

The pragmatic position, on the other hand, does not require legal theory to provide a rationale for the choice of institutional structure. If the choice was a sound one, it most likely was not made by legal philosophers or even just lawyers. Instead, it was made in uncountable incremental steps by actors in every realm of social life. The choices made may have, to some degree, become embedded in the common law by a process of successive approximation, in which strictly "legal" institutions did not impose a "legal" rationale on the choices. The process must permit a controlling role for nonlegal choices, albeit one in which the choices become reflected in sufficiently determinate language to be applied consistently language that will unavoidably take on a life of its own, but not intolerably so, if kept faithful to the concrete circumstances it was designed to address.

The primary obligation of legal institutions is one of facilitating, and not obstructing, nonlegal means of addressing the indeterminacies of social life-including those involving the just and right. This is true also of the Constitution, which for Learned Hand was to be regarded as an historical compromise, not a set of durable principles or a resource from which to strengthen or modify the morals of society. As Holmes said in his *Lochner* dissent, "a constitution . . . is made for people of fundamentally differing views."[119] Hence, it is altogether natural that the Constitution should tolerate, reflect, or even incorporate, conflicting principles.

CONCLUSION

Amidst such misgivings as those expressed by CLS about law and conventional liberal doctrine, one might expect a strain of concern over the degree of involvement of courts and lawyers in American life. However, CLS is too committed to legal activism, by law journal article if not by lawsuit, and seeks to expand the freedom of lawyers to make political arguments. CLS takes the position that the prevailing rationales for judicial restraint are simply part of the body of opposing principles that serve the interests of those in power; they should be abandoned in order to enfranchise the legal arguments of the powerless.

Meanwhile, conservative scholars have been surprisingly silent on the breach between liberalism and CLS and have failed to exploit the discredit it may cast on legal activism generally. This is owing in substantial part to the fact that current conservatives draw their leading formula from liberal methodology. In proposing guidance in constitutional cases from the document's

---

[119] *Lochner v. New York*, 198 U.S. 45, 75–76 (1905) (Holmes, J., dissenting).

original understanding, these conservatives have become enmeshed in the twentieth-century debate over solving the false problem of "legal indeterminacy." In doing so, they not only run afoul of the impossibility of such a task in constitutional law, they also fail to address the parallel claims made by CLS with regard to indeterminacy in common as well as constitutional law.

This is why the originalist position wavers between conceding some limited room for constitutional review and showing an almost absolutist deference to the presumptively more democratic institutions of representative democracy. Original understanding gains a large part of its rhetorical force from denunciations of the "countermajoritarianism" of Supreme Court review of legislation. Yet, it maintains that the Court may nevertheless review legislation under such constitutional language as may be strictly construed, and decide those cases according to more conservatively defined "constitutional principles."

The pragmatic position is able to maintain a strong position of legislative deference without having to assume that the answers to constitutional cases lie within the Constitution and its original understanding. Embodied in the document are guarantees that cannot be interpreted or applied without regard to the content and method of the common law. Properly understood, the common law is not countermajoritarian in content or in method.[120] But it can become so, and so can constitutional jurisprudence, through reliance on the casuistic mechanisms that conventional legal theory has invented to deal with "legal indeterminacy." Legal indeterminacy has become the touchstone of twentieth-century jurisprudence. The latter fails to recognize that indeterminacy lies not in law but in life, and that there are means other than law alone for dealing with it.

To return to the complaint of CLS scholar Allan Hutchinson, with which this paper began, the debasement of the democratic ideal through the "opium" of philosophical reflection is not a necessary condition of the legal enterprise. We need not be saddled with it forever. It derives rather from a massive misappropriation by lawyers and legal scholars of the intellectual framework that

---

[120] Some response is required to a comment by Jennifer Nedelsky, discussing the legacy of the Federalist/Anti-Federalist arguments over the vision of fledgling government in the United States. Nedelsky's comment challenges what may appear here to be a presumption that custom, and the supposedly pre-existing social choices informing legal decisions, are inherently more democratic than the alternative of an "activist" judiciary:

> We can be confident that customs reflect the consent of the people only if we believe that all the people had equal access to the shaping of those customs. We know, of course, that the contrary is almost always true. In no society in which the common law has developed have we reason to believe that all people's voices were, over time, equally heard, attended to, and assimilated in the accumulated customs of "the people." Why then should we have faith that "custom" is anything other than the preferred norms of those groups with sufficient power to shape that "custom" and that the common law is not merely the interpretation of those preferred norms by even more rarefied groups of judges?

they inherited from centuries of common-law experience, and from the success of the institutional arrangements and guarantees welded by the framers of the Constitution. It has been supported in this capture by the tendency of intellectuals as a class to think according to overarching formulae, giving rise to the notion that the legal enterprise requires a threshold of transcendental uniformity and certainty in order to claim legitimacy.

CLS scholars have accepted this assumption, so solidly is it entrenched within the modern legal tradition. Rather than supporting CLS, pragmatism undermines the CLS challenge to the legitimacy of legal decisions by reducing critical theory to a set of objections to current theory and practice. These may require reform, even radical reform, but they do not argue for increasing the political role of lawyers and the legal priesthood, or expanding any further their already pervasive influence in our lives.

Nedelsky, "Democracy, Justice, and the Multiplicity of Voices: Alternatives to the Federalist Vision," *Northwestern University. Law Review* 84 (1989): 232, 244–45. Nedelsky also states, later in the same article:

> We should not abandon the core of the Federalist insight that democratic values alone will not ensure just or legitimate government. The question is whether we should accept their further judgment that *limits* on democracy—both structural constraints on the political efficacy of some, and formal, judicially enforced limits on democratic outcomes—are the best means for giving effect to that insight. I think we should take seriously the notion that fuller democracy can bring with it not more, but less of the inherent problem of the potential for the abuse of collective power. While such a notion suggests that we should rely far less on limits than our current system does, it does not mean that we have to abandon all conceptions of the virtue of limits, even judicially enforced limits. But the political thought and scholarship of recent decades requires us to rethink the meaning of law, democracy, and judicial limits as tools of justice.

Id. at 246–47 (footnote omitted) (emphasis in original).

Neither of Nedelsky's comments is inconsistent with the pragmatic position. The latter might suggest that the rethinking of democracy she calls for should address the issue of how "custom" is developed and how it becomes reflected in judicial decisions. But the pragmatic position would deny that we need to rethink *whether* it is a key element in the framing of judicial law. CLS, however, takes a general position that would imply in this context that the legal process itself is responsible for redressing the nondemocratic formation and residue of custom. Legal pragmatism would suggest that this is equally the responsibility of all citizens, not just lawyers. I am grateful to Mark Tushnet for pointing out this issue.

Chapter 9

Legal Indeterminacy and the Hard Case

Ronald Dworkin and Critical Legal Studies both focus on the so-called "background elements" of the legal system—the principles and policies that lie behind the rules and texts that positivists emphasize. Dworkin has long claimed that recourse to the background affords a necessary and sufficient resource to support legal decisions in cases where the foreground is disputed or indeterminate. According to CLS (taken as a general approach), the background is so riven with contradiction as to be capable of supporting any result, and thus inadequate for definitive recourse.

In *Critical Legal Studies: A Liberal Critique*, Andrew Altman noted the lack of sustained dialogue between Ronald Dworkin, as a representative of the liberal tradition in jurisprudence, and CLS. He decried the fact that "liberal theorists and their CLS critics have been highly dismissive of one another's work." Two decades later, Jeremy Waldron made a similar observation in his essay "Did Dworkin Ever Answer the Crits?" He questioned whether Dworkin's vision of law as integrity in *Law's Empire* can overcome the CLS argument that opposing principles suffuse community and argued that Dworkin's theory demands a robust constructive role for judges that is undermined by the CLS position.[1]

In *Law's Empire* Dworkin claimed that judges must strive in hard cases to instantiate a "community of principle" in a society that CLS contends is

---

[1] Waldron, Jeremy. 2009. "Did Dworkin Ever Answer the Crits?" in Scott Hershovitz (ed.), *Exploring Law's Empire: The Jurisprudence of Ronald Dworkin* (Oxford: Oxford Scholarship Online, 2009). For their helpful comments on earlier drafts, I would like to thank Jeffrey Brand-Ballard, Michele Friend, Joshua Miller, and Eric Saidel of the George Washington University Department of Philosophy, as well as Claudio Michelon, Haris Psarras, Francisco Saffie, Findlay Stark, Neil Walker, and other members of the University of Edinburgh Legal Theory Group.

always already riven with conflict. In *Justice for Hedgehogs*,[2] while barely mentioning CLS, Dworkin advances a unitary view of interpretation against forms of skepticism regarding the very existence of such a community of principle that CLS writers vigorously defended. The divide between Dworkin and CLS is highly abstract. This chapter seeks to illuminate the problem through a reexamination of legal uncertainty. In his essay "Did Dworkin Ever Answer the Crits?" Enlarging Waldron's critique, this chapter contends that the underlying issue is the nature of legal uncertainty itself.

Both CLS and Dworkin view uncertainty as an algorithmic positioning beyond what Waldron terms a contemporaneous "foreground" of clear rules and texts. This synchronic view has crystallized in the wake of H. L. A. Hart's *The Concept of Law*. It ignores the positioning of cases in a diachronic relation to ongoing legal disputes and social problems, where principled resolution may be premature, in an early stage of a controversial situation, pending further experience. Judges, as their interpretive role in such cases is variably shared with the community at large, should properly exercise minimalist restraint in the exploratory stage of ongoing controversies.

Along with their univocal view of hard cases, CLS and Dworkin privilege a judge-oriented individualist epistemology of legal principles, as Dworkin's mythical super-judge "Hercules" exemplifies: the realm of principles is knowable only (if at all) by the idealized rational judge. This chapter defends a restrained and participatory, or socialized, epistemology for legal principles, leaving space when appropriate for input from outside the adjudicatory system. When a new case bears an evident relationship to a broader and continuing controversy, the time for principled decision may not be ripe.

This highlights a distinct form of uncertainty that has, nevertheless, been commonly perceived as "legal indeterminacy." The perception of indeterminacy in this category of cases derives from the appearance of equal balance among competing interpretations, characteristic of unsettled classification of an emergent form or class of dispute. When the judicial role in such a case is viewed in relation to an emergent or unsettled problem, the perception of intractable difficulty can and should be seen not as a radical indeterminacy, but as representing a stage of inquiry into developing perceptions of underlying conditions.

This vantage point recognizes a danger implicit in any generalized approval of judicial "recourse to principle": the distorting influence of ideology and subjectivity in the judicial application of moral principles. Premature recourse to principle (and indeed of constitutional principle) may foreclose fact-based inquiry in unsettled controversies. As Cass Sunstein has noted, this cautionary observation applies even to final constitutional courts of appeal. I

---

[2] Cambridge, MA: Belknap Press, 2011.

begin by examining the arguments in Waldron's 2009 paper supporting the thesis that Dworkin did not fully "answer the crits." This involves the debate over whether the "background" is sufficient to resolve legal disputes through judicial recourse to principle.

Waldron observes that CLS skepticism obliged Dworkin to move toward a robust constructive role for judges. For Waldron, this dispute highlights the relation of background principles and policies to the commitments of the community at large. After clarifying this, I turn to analyzing legal difficulty within the putative "foreground," and to the analytical perception of indeterminacy in "hard cases," tracing the notion of legal indeterminacy as it has been influenced by the arguments of legal realists, H. L. A. Hart and legal positivists, CLS, and Dworkin. In doing so, I contend that the perception of "principled resolution" in the famous cases of *Riggs v. Palmer* and *Henningsen v. Bloomfield Motors*, rather than supporting a constant option for recourse to principles in hard cases, is actually consistent with a restrained approach—with the diachronic theory rather than the synchronic one of both CLS and Dworkin.

The diachronic view undermines any universalized theory of immediate interpretive resolution by appeal to morals, principles or values—and equally undermines universalizing the "impossibility" critique of CLS. Indeed, it raises the question of what actual cases truly require of appellate judges.

WALDRON ON DWORKIN AND CLS

In "Did Dworkin Ever Answer the Crits?" Jeremy Waldron explores the nature of adjudication in "hard" or "doubtful" cases, where primary recourse to relevant rules, cases and texts reveals no clear answer. The question then arises whether there exists a coherent secondary resource for judges within the body of legal doctrine. Evaluating logical coherence in legal doctrine and its sources, Waldron examines, *inter alia*, writings of Duncan Kennedy and Roberto Unger as exemplifying the "internal skepticism" of Critical Legal Studies. He compares this to Ronald Dworkin's position in *Law's Empire*, characterizing it as "descriptive optimism."[3]

In his essay, part of a 2009 volume on Dworkin's writings, Waldron considers the adequacy of Dworkin's answer to internal skepticism. Noting that "CLS was never particularly interested in Dworkin, nor he in them," Waldron notes nevertheless that both CLS and Dworkin share a common interest in and focus upon what Waldron terms the "background elements" of the legal

---

[3] Waldron, "Did Dworkin Ever Answer the Crits," 155.

system—the "principles and policies that lie behind the rules and texts that legal positivists emphasize." The background is viewed as distinct from the set of primary sources to which lawyers and judges naturally turn at the first instance. Waldron notes that Critical Legal Studies, taken as a movement, shares many key assumptions with Dworkin. While differing on the relative determinacy of a "foreground," it nevertheless accepts the idea of a background and of the contribution of background principles and policies to legal argument and decision. It accepts the status of this background as law, and agrees that it is at least as important for jurisprudence as Dworkin claims.

CLS is less sympathetic to the positivist emphasis on the foreground, while insisting that the background is indeterminate and adjudication cannot escape judicial subjectivism. The two share a synchronic model of legal difficulty that ignores the relation of immediate perceptions of indeterminacy to yet unsettled problems. Waldron notes that what the two approaches say about the background is very different. Dworkin has claimed since 1967, in his initial challenge to H. L. A. Hart's defense of the positivist separation of law and morals, that recourse to the background, in particular to certain principles that bear a "moral" character, affords a necessary resource for legal decisions in cases in which the foreground is disputed or indeterminate. The background is, moreover, a sufficient resource for finding the right answer to any hard case. CLS writers have persistently claimed that the background is so riven with contradiction as to be capable of supporting any result in close cases, an internal skepticism that views the background as inadequate for Dworkin's form of recourse.

Dworkin's descriptive optimism holds that the background elements of a legal system like that of the United States are capable of bearing the heavy weight of determinate argument that Dworkin assigns to it in his theory of law. Waldron contends that the comparison with CLS forces us to confront the question of how judges actually accomplish this—how do they choose from among the disparate body of principles and policies that are arguably embedded in legal texts and precedents.[4]

First, Waldron observes that in order to fully answer the CLS critique, Dworkin must place considerable emphasis on what can only be regarded as the "constructive" side of his argument. Instead of saying that the legal background is plainly coherent, Dworkin, given the force of CLS arguments that it is plainly incoherent, has to claim that it is capable of being made coherent at the hands of a sufficiently resourceful interpreter. But, Waldron says, "the response cannot rest there. Dworkin's constructivism might license an ingenious and versatile manipulation of existing legal materials: we take the parts of the (often contradictory) background that we like or approve, and

---

[4] Waldron, "Did Dworkin Ever Answer the Crits," 159f.

we use them to add some sort of doctrinal credibility to the positions we are aiming at."[5]

Such manipulation is precisely what CLS has claimed to be an open invitation to subjective preference. Therefore, argues Waldron, Dworkin's conception requires a further justification, one that Dworkin took pains to furnish in *Law's Empire.* That justification is that the background materials to which judges appeal keeps faith with "the network of mutual commitments that makes us the community we are."

Only by appealing to a larger common or social vision can Dworkin reject the arguments of a pure pragmatist, who will otherwise deny that we should bother with the background at all, once the foreground has been shown to be indeterminate, but simply make a case directly for whatever is likely to promote the social good. To rebut the pragmatist position—which Dworkin acknowledges has to be rebutted to make room for his conception of law as integrity—it is not enough to show that we can make something coherent and attractive out of the legal background.

The Dworkinian advocate has to show that we must attempt to make something "coherent and attractive out of the legal background."[6] Hence, Dworkin makes an extended argument in *Laws Empire,* advancing the notion that the goal of the judicial role is to keep faith with a "community of principle." However, Waldron claims that this response to the pragmatist does not truly address the core of the CLS position as most strongly articulated by leading CLS writers. The more Dworkin insists on reaching creatively into the background to keep faith with the community of principle, the more he must confront or ignore arguments that the background is riven with inconsistency.

In Waldron's words, "the constructivism that Dworkin appeals to, in order to evade the CLS critique, succeeds (if it does) only at the cost of cutting loose of the idea that the community is in some sense already committed to a coherent and principled position which the Dworkinian lawyer has a responsibility to unearth."[7] In this insight, Waldron connects legal difficulty to the

---

[5] Waldron, "Did Dworkin Ever Answer the Crits," 156.

[6] Waldron, "Did Dworkin Ever Answer the Crits," 156.

[7] Waldron notes that much of CLS criticism of Dworkin is superficial—that his jurisprudence is "elitist," and insufficiently concerned with "the deprived and disadvantaged in society." But there is at least one line of attack to which Dworkin has been obliged to respond. Roberto Unger and Duncan Kennedy have pressed the notion that the background has no single author, its diverse perspectives deriving from continuing conflict throughout the law's history. The opposing principles found in the background are not just rival tendencies, but incompatible visions or theories of what we owe to others and the collective life of our society. They already comprise a "weighing and ranking" of diverse values. "It is futile to imagine that moral and practical conflict will yield to analysis in terms of higher level concepts." Dworkin's response to such claims is that the assertion of an array of decisions riddled with contradictions is itself already an "interpretation" of the background materials. This response plays a major role in his recent contribution to the now-broadened debate in *Justice for Hedgehogs.*

broader issue of community experience. The constructive task in jurisprudence, highlighted here by Waldron, bears an important relation to still emergent patterns yet unexpressed in the formalities of legal language. Examples
may be readily drawn from the literature; notably, Edward Levi observes this
phenomenon (highly relevant, as will be seen, to *Henningsen v. Bloomfield
Motors*) in his 1949 *Introduction to Legal Reasoning* as does Grant Gilmore
in *Death of Contract*.[8]

Waldron's essay sheds light on a conventionally accepted model of legal
uncertainty, shared by Dworkin and CLS and seen univocally as outside
a determinate foreground. He has highlighted the constructive nature of
recourse to the background, and the problem of subjectivity in judicial appeal
to general principle. We should question the notion of legal uncertainty and
ask whether basic assumptions are made that create the very dilemma that
seems unresolvable.

THE PERCEPTION OF INDETERMINACY
IN LEGAL REALISM, HART, AND CLS

The argument in favor of a diachronic model of legal uncertainty, suggested
above, requires revising, if not actually reversing, certain perceptions that have
hardened since the influence of H. L. A. Hart on conceptual jurisprudence. The
contemporary picture of the "hard case," lying outside a foreground of determinate legal authorities, should be understood in the context of Hart's unique
place in twentieth-century jurisprudence. In confining legal indeterminacy to
the "interstices" between verbal meanings, Hart also made it synchronic with
existing legal texts—thus outside a contemporaneous foreground.

Conventional discourse holds that an uncritical "formalism" prevalent in
the nineteenth century was shaken by legal realist attacks on unexamined
assumptions of legal determinacy. Legal realism was itself a diverse movement, with various authors addressing the nature of judicial objectivity, judicial behavior, and the nature of legal resources. As Andrew Altman observed
in 1986, legal realist criticisms of formalist legal determinacy were lumped
together and characterized as "excesses" by Hart in writings including *The
Concept of Law*.[9]

Waldron offers that the Dworkinian advocate has the burden of proof to show how lawyers and judges
actually do achieve the goal of integrity. They must pick and choose among the contradictory materials, and discard the rest. But this highlights the danger of granting a license to unelected lifetime
judges to justify their subjective preferences on "moral" grounds.

[8] Edward Levi, *Introduction to Legal Reasoning*, 1949; Grant Gilmore, *Death of Contract* (Columbus, OH: Ohio State University Press, 1974).

[9] Altman, "Legal Realism," 206.

In his comments on legal realism, Hart conceded that there was a significant amount of indeterminacy in the law, but argued that it necessarily occupied a peripheral zone. The law could be conceptualized as a system of rules, and there are some cases in which the rules do not clearly specify the correct legal outcome. This is due to the ineliminable open texture of not just legal but natural language (for which Hart drew on Friedrich Waismann[10]). All general terms have both a core of meaning and a "penumbra," or a range in which it is unclear and irresolvably controversial as to whether the term applies to a specific case.

For Hart, this penumbral range was considerably smaller than the extension of the core. Hart used as an example the term "vehicle," as in a prohibition of "vehicles in the park;" baby-strollers would fall harmlessly into the "penumbra." For Hart ,the nature of law's indeterminacy is limited to a periphery outside a system of rules that provides specific outcomes in most cases. But Hart gave little attention to showing that this was a full and fair account of the realist critique. Thus were the contentions of realism "domesticated," persuading many writers that followed Hart that its claims had been "transcended."[11]

Given the prevalence of this attitude, it is not surprising that Dworkin gave little attention to the legal realists. Whereas CLS would later emphasize a "global" indeterminacy of a background riven with norms and principles in contradiction, the realists focused on a "local" uncertainty, the immediate ambiguity of fact and alternative rules in the context of individual cases. As Altman documented in 1986, the realist perception of difficulty was far deeper and more pervasive than Hart's characterization.

First, realist analysis perceived a "cluster" of rules relevant to the decision in any litigated case. In any single case there were two or more potential points of doubt due to rule vagueness, rather than a single point deriving from the open texture of language. Second, many realists rejected the distinction between holding and dictum. While the "holding" referred to the essential grounds of a decision, the "dicta" putatively covered nonessential commentary that might include points of law not treated as basic to the outcome. The actual line suggested by this distinction was virtually impossible to identify, and hence for practical purposes vague and shifting. Thus, judges writing subsequent opinions were not bound by any original perception of what was essential.[12]

---

[10] Friedrich Waismann, *The Principles of Linguistic Philosophy* (London: Macmillan, 1965).

[11] Altman, "Legal Realism."

[12] Altman, "Legal Realism," 208–9. Hart conceded that "there is no single method of determining the rule for which a given authoritative precedent is an authority," but he added that "Notwithstanding this, in the vast majority of decided cases, there is very little doubt. The head-note is usually correct enough." Hart, *The Concept of Law*, 131. On the realist analysis, the headnote states only one of a number of rules that could constitute the holding. Hart conceded that judges narrow and widen precedents such that there is no uniquely correct formulation of a rule extracted from cases, but he claimed "general agreement" on the outcome. The realist response to this would be that there are

While focusing on forms of doubt and difficulty, legal realism did not universally adopt the radical indeterminacy of CLS. In ignoring the diversity of realist writings on legal uncertainty, Hart and others have failed to appreciate a line of realist, or perhaps post-legal realist, literature that identifies one form of uncertainty related to inquiry over time, admirably illuminated by Edward Levi. This form of intractability occurs when competing lines of precedent are applied to novel forms of experience. As will be shown below, the dispute is thus viewed not simply from the standpoint of a judge in one case, but in the nature of its relation to an ongoing class of cases—for example, plaintiffs injured by a "dangerous instrumentality," covered by a signed limited warranty, parties to an "impossible" contract, and so on.

From the perspective of logical space between lines of authority over time, rather than occupying interstitial textual space in one definitive moment, we may picture a new case that is not "outside" a discrete set of rules or body of legal doctrine, but arguably "inside" yet drawn in competing directions, equally pulled toward two (or more) established lines of precedent—for example, whether an exploding coffee urn or a defective automobile is a dangerous instrumentality, or whether the promise of a gift is sufficient consideration for an enforceable contract.[13]

Hart's influence and Dworkin's subsequent challenge solidified the dominance of a foreground/background model that Waldron highlighted in 2009.[14] This model privileges the individual inquirer and ignores the ongoing process of negotiated classification by multiple inquirers. A novel case may at first appear indeterminate in the context of prior precedent. As it recurs, it is recognized as a new situation, compared and defined, and eventually clarified in relation to prior patterns of decision. The next section examines this process and the role of judges, principles, and community in what Waldron correctly highlights as a "constructive," albeit tentative and experimental, enterprise.

THE PERCEPTION OF INDETERMINACY IN THE CONTEXT OF CLASSIFICATION

Waldron's essay suggests that there may be no resolution at the abstract level of the disagreement between CLS and Dworkin. Given the background of the

---

still competing rules to choose from, and it does not follow that the law determines the outcome. Altman, "Legal Realism," 210.

[13] Gilmore, *Death of Contract*, 19.

[14] After Hart "domesticated" the realist indeterminacy thesis, essentially deflating its insistence on the perception of opposing rules (which Hart did not fully address), his thesis left ample room for Ronald Dworkin's arguments for principle-based adjudication. This was not new to jurisprudence; the realist rejection of formalism left room for a similar synchronic argument in Herbert Wechsler's "principle balancing"; Dworkin might be viewed as heir to Wechsler's search for "neutral" principles." (See Altman, "Legal Realism," 212f.)

post-Hart model of uncertainty, we may look instead to the nature of legal uncertainty itself. Edward Levi's classic essay on the history of "dangerous instrumentalities" portrays the social construction of a legal principle, and it also shows how tentative and experimental is the process, often drawn out over a period of many years, indeed going back over a century in the case of liability for injury from an object of imminent danger, eventually applied to the automobile.

Levi's is a lengthy and complex narrative. To simplify the analysis, I will adapt a historical example,[15] as a necessary precursor to reevaluating Dworkin's argument regarding *Riggs*, the case of the murderous legatee, and *Henningsen*, the case of the limited automobile warranty. Imagine a new common law jurisdiction with minimal codes or regulations. Cases arise that involve abutting landowners, some of whom prefer open spaces, and others privacy. Many of the latter favor walls and structures close to their boundary, and because there are no zoning or building codes they are limited only by their wills and desires. Lawsuits are brought by abutting plaintiffs claiming violation of their natural right to light and air by these neighbors' boundary walls and structures. Jury trials are granted, and the wall-builders counter-claim their right to free enjoyment of private property.

Many of the cases are submitted to the jury, and some are bench-tried by district and superior court judges. They are decided entirely on their particular facts, and this is reflected in the court documents, local press, and judicial opinions. Some cases involve high walls and structures, others low ones, some wood, others stone, some are aesthetically pleasing, others ugly, and so on. The majority of the litigants appear satisfied with the results of the *de novo* trials, but some find the results unsatisfactory and appeal to the regional Supreme Court. That Court reviews the initial judgments for procedural regularity, to assure itself that the facts supported the decision. Thus, if the trial court found that there was no substantial blockage of light and air, and the decision so holds, the judgment is upheld; and vice versa.

Certain claims are ruled irrelevant, such as whether the structure is wood or stone, nice or ugly. Eventually, the lawyers specializing in boundary cases make arguments drawn from the growing record. Predictably, the lawyers focus on the height of the wall and the distance from the common boundary, citing these dimensions in the cases that support their clients. Meanwhile, landowners engaged in new construction, aware of the developing court

---

[15] My example is based on an 1866 English case, *Beadel v. Perry*, first cited by Holmes in his edition of Kent's Commentaries on American Law and later developed in "The Theory of Torts" where his lifelong reference to judges "drawing lines" between opposing precedents in hard cases appears to originate. See Kellogg, *Holmes, Legal Theory, and Judicial Restraint*, 32.

decisions, adjust their expectations and refrain from building without agreement to certain heights generally deemed excessive near property lines.

Reviewing the cases over time, the lawyers, and eventually trial judges,
conclude that there is a critical relationship reflected in the pattern of judgments: walls that exceed a certain ratio of height to the distance to the
boundary are increasingly found to violate the abutting landowner's right to
light and air. This leads to a rule of law. After several years of considering
various other factors, the Supreme Court eventually rules en banc, with an
opinion in the major (hypothetical) case of *Feather v. Stone,* that a particular
ratio of height and distance "respects the fundamental right of a property
owner's freedom to prosper and enjoy his own land, while protecting that
of his neighbor's access to the beauty and breezes." Henceforth the ratio is
a "safe harbor," and any wall built within it is legal. With this noted (and
appropriately "principled") decision, the controversial boundary-wall dispute
is considered resolved.

As this suggests, at the initial stage of litigation of a new class of cases,
there is a climate we may call indeterminacy. Use and enjoyment of private
property implies two opposing rights, access to light and air and freedom of
use. Being utterly general and at first without bodies of precedent, the two
rights secured jurisdiction in the boundary-wall cases but gave no specific
guidance. The early lawsuits were decided on the basis of particular facts; on
what appeared fair to the triers of fact, whether jury or judge. Two bodies of
precedent grew, one upholding and the other overturning walls and structures.
These cases were relatively easy, such as where a high wall is built without
agreement right against the adjoining property's edge.

But some cases were painfully close, the dimensions close to a yet-emerging
consensus. The cases closely balanced on the facts are always the hardest to
decide. By this I note that facts may appear in balance between two opposing
"rights" as well as of lines of decision, with no judicial rule (or legislation)—
yet—to evaluate them. By the time *Feather v. Stone* (where the facts seemed
perfectly balanced) reached the high court, there was an appearance of both
local and global indeterminacy; local because the lawyers could cite the
opposing bodies of precedent allowing and removing structures, and global
because they could argue equally from the opposing global rights of free
enjoyment of private property and the preservation of environmental values.

To the individual judges, the close case may have seemed indeterminate.
For the judicial system, it was a stage of inquiry, the resolution dependent
on many factors leading to the eventual governing legal principle, where the
eventual legal "line" is drawn. As Levi recounts in *Introduction to Legal
Reasoning*, this has included adjusted practices and public perceptions, translated by counsel into legal arguments for and against the prospect of liability. Such is the actual process of "construction" highlighted by Waldron's

critique of Dworkin. It is not the mythical judge Hercules who must find the answer. Juries and judges import prevalent notions of fairness, practice, and technology from the parties engaged in the very disputes that create the appearance of indeterminacy. Construction takes place within a context of concern for basic values that seem in conflict. Yet the perceived conflict of basic values does not undermine or delegitimize the law. Conflicting values may seem "incommensurable" in the broadest sense, yet they may be commensurated in application.

How does this differ from the *Riggs* and *Henningsen* cases? The boundary-wall cases implicate an ongoing class of disputes over time, which the testator-murder in *Riggs* does not. *Riggs v Palmer* involved what might be regarded as a famously unusual situation. The testator, Francis Palmer, had left small legacies to his two daughters and a life estate to his wife, with the remainder (the principal legacy) to his teenage grandson Elmer Riggs. The latter, then living with his grandfather and aware that the bequest was under reconsideration, poisoned his own grandfather to retain and effectuate the bequest.

After first examining the legislative history of the will statute and determining that it was not determinative, the court used the fourfold formulation "No one shall be permitted to profit by his own fraud, or to take advantage of his own wrong, or to found any claim upon his own iniquity, or to acquire property by his own crime," describing its propositions as "maxims of the common law." The court also cited a line of authority for an opposing "principle"—the U.S. Supreme Court decision in *New York Mutual Life Insurance Company v. Armstrong* (117 U. S. 591). There it was held that the person who procured a policy upon the life of another, payable at his death, and then murdered the assured to make the policy payable, could not recover.

Riggs is not strictly a case outside the foreground; the line of *Mutual* could be extended to wills. But unlike insurance fraud, testator murder is rare. It has not presented the courts with an ongoing problem, like the boundary walls, like injuries from a "dangerous instrumentality." How would it look if the facts of *Riggs* were in equilibrium between two opposing lines of authority? Assume for illustration that the same case arose, but under a will providing "I recognize that my beloved grandson Elmer was orphaned at the age of 3 and obliged to grow up in desperate circumstances, and despite his mercurial nature and proclivity toward troubles with the law, I leave him the sum of $500 to help with the costs of rehabilitative education." In this instance, the settled law of wills would likely prevail. Elmer is still guilty of seeking to profit from his own wrong, Dworkin's principle still applies, but the case would go the other way.

Now consider facts that occupy the middle ground—in a society replete with bad characters poisoning their benefactors. In the hardest cases, the bequests are higher than $500, the language only vaguely recognizing badness of character. *Riggs* itself, on the facts alone, was an easy case. *Henningsen v Bloomfield Motors*, decided in 1960, also played a key part in Dworkin's argument. There, principled generalization arose from a history of factually balanced uncertainty. In his 1967 challenge to Hart, reprinted in *Taking Rights Seriously*, Dworkin removed Henningsen from its history; he records that the case decided "the important question of whether (or how much) an automobile manufacturer may limit his liability in case the automobile is defective.

Plaintiff Henningsen had bought a car and signed a contract which said that the manufacturer's liability for defects was limited to 'making good' defective parts." Henningsen argued that "the manufacturer ought not to be protected by this limitation" but "was not able to point to any statute, or to any established rule of law, that prevented the manufacturer from standing on the contract. The court nevertheless agreed with Henningsen." This account supported Dworkin's claim that the case was decided according to the principle "that the courts will not permit themselves to be used as instruments of inequity and injustice."

But Dworkin omits that it was a jury that at first "agreed with Henningsen." The case was appealed on a jury verdict of liability for the manufacturer. On appeal, the two issues were whether the express warranty was controlling, and whether an implied warranty existed beyond the express provisions. Addressing the implied warranty first, the appellate court said "we hold that under modern marketing conditions, when a manufacturer puts a new automobile in the stream of trade and promotes its purchase by the public, an implied warranty that it is reasonably suitable for use as such accompanies it into the hands of the ultimate purchaser. Absence of agency between the manufacturer and the dealer who makes the ultimate sale is immaterial."

This key issue, of liability for injury from a defective automobile to a remote plaintiff, is precisely the one that, according to Levi, took a century to resolve in the famous opinion of Judge Cardozo in *MacPherson v. Buick*, 217 N.Y. 382, 111 N.E. 1050 (1916). As Levi explains, "the mechanism of legal reasoning should not be concealed by its pretense."[16] Tracing the

---

[16] "The pretense is: that the law is a system of known rules applied by a judge; the pretense has long been under attack. In an important sense legal rules are never clear, and, if a rule had to be clear before it could be imposed, society would be impossible. The mechanism accepts the differences of view and ambiguities of words. It provides for the participation of the community in resolving the ambiguity by providing a forum for the discussion of policy in the gap of ambiguity. . . . The mechanism is indispensable to peace in the community." Levi, *Introduction*, 1 (footnote omitted). Levi notes that "change in the rules is the indispensable dynamic quality of law. It occurs because the scope of rule of law, and therefore its meaning, depends upon a determination of what facts will be considered similar to those present when the rule was first announced. The finding of similarity or difference is the key step in the legal process." (2) The existence of some facts in common

history back to *Dixon v. Bell* in 1816, Levi identifies three phases. In the first, the courts recognize the need for a common approach to recovery by a party injured by an object not acquired directly from the manufacturer—the loaded gun in *Dixon*. In the second, a plausible classification is tried out, the concept of an object "inherently dangerous," pronounced in *Longmeid v. Holliday* (1857).[17]

These cases begin with mislabeled poison and end with a defective automobile. As in the hypothetical boundary decisions, a line must be drawn including some cases (the poison) and excluding others (a defective lamp, a pre-automotive carriage). "During this time also," notes Levi, "there is the inevitable attempt to soar above the cases and to find some great overall rule" (Judge Brett's principle of "duty of ordinary care" in *Heaven v. Pender*, 1883). This Herculean effort is bypassed by later experience. In the third phase, the concept of inherently dangerous is abandoned in favor of the notion of imminent danger.[18]

The rule is pronounced in *MacPherson v. Buick* by Judge Cardozo as follows: "If the nature of a thing is such that it is reasonably certain to place life and limb in peril, when negligently made, it is then a thing of danger. . . . [But] there must be a knowledge of a danger not merely possible but probable." All this is missing from Dworkin's account. The law already held the automobile to account, regardless of its relation to the seller. The real struggle was over after MacPherson, though it took 100 years.[19]

---

brings into play the general rule. If this is really reasoning, then by common standards, thought of in terms of closed systems, it is imperfect unless some overall rule has announced that this common and ascertainable similarity is to be decisive. But no such fixed prior rule exists. . . . Therefore, it appears that the kind of reasoning involved in the legal process is one in which the classification changes as the classification is made (3).

[17] Levi, *Introduction*, 10–20.

[18] As Levi describes the process, reasoning by example shows the decisive role which the common ideas of the society and the distinctions made by experts can have in shaping the law. The movement of common or expert concepts into the law may be followed. The concept is suggested in arguing difference or similarity in a brief, but wins no approval from the court. The idea achieves standing in the society. It is suggested again to a court. The court this time reinterprets the prior case and in doing so adopts the rejected idea. In subsequent cases, the idea is given further definition and is tied to other ideas which have been accepted by courts. It is now no longer the idea which was commonly held in the society. It becomes modified in subsequent cases. Ideas first rejected but which gradually have won acceptance now push what has become a legal category out of the system or convert it into something which may be its opposite. The process is one in which the ideas of the community and of the social sciences, whether correct or not, as they win acceptance in the community, control legal decisions. Erroneous ideas, of course, have played an enormous part in shaping the law. An idea, adopted by the court, is in a superior position to influence conduct and opinion in the community; judges, after all, are rulers. And the adoption of an idea by a court reflects the power structure of the community. But reasoning by example will operate to change the idea after it has been adopted. Levi, *Introduction*, 5–6.

[19] Levi describes the common law as a "moving classification system" that "requires the presentation of competing examples." In doing this, the litigants "have participated in the law making. . . . They are bound by something they helped to make. Moreover, the examples or analogies urged by the

Both CLS and Dworkin have failed to appreciate that distinct forms of legal difficulty have varied theoretical implications for judicial recourse to general principles. Both privilege a judge-oriented individualist epistemology of legal principles (as Dworkin's mythical judge "Hercules" exemplifies). The view offered here rejects the univocal conception of a "hard case" as outside a determinate foreground. Legal uncertainty may be related to developing but yet unresolved aspects of an underlying problem. This paper defends a restrained and participatory, or socialized, epistemology for legal principles, leaving space when appropriate for input from outside the adjudicatory system. This approach recognizes the need for adjustments of belief and conduct to resolve ongoing community conflicts. Rather than appealing to antecedent general principles in all hard cases, judges properly exercise minimalist restraint in the earlier stages of ongoing controversies. I hope to have clarified a perspective that recognizes a danger implicit in any generalized approval of judicial "recourse to principle." Repeatedly voiced by Holmes, it is the influence of ideology and subjectivity in the judicial application of moral principles.

---

parties bring into the law the common ideas of the society. The ideas have their day in court, and they will have their day again. This is what makes the hearing fair, rather than any idea that the judge is completely impartial, for of course he cannot be completely so." He points out that there is "an additional requirement which compels the process to be this way. Not only do new situations arise, but in addition peoples' wants change. The categories used in the legal process must be left ambiguous in order to permit the infusion of new ideas." Levi, *Introduction,* 4–5.

Chapter 10

The Abuse of Principle
Robert Alexy's Jurisprudence

It has become a commonplace in contemporary analytical jurisprudence that the so-called "doubtful" or "hard" case, not resolved by any clear legal authority, is either legally indeterminate or can be resolved only by judicial recourse to principles.[1] My thesis in this chapter is that there is an aspect of the "doubtful case" that militates strongly against recourse to principle. When viewed as representative of an early stage in the resolution of similar cases, perhaps the very first of a continuing class of disputes, then (especially in controversial cases of broad import) judicial recourse to principles may lead to an improvident choice of reasons, and in any event violates fundamental democratic values.

This diachronic view of case classification argues for early judicial minimalism or particularism, or narrowly reasoned decision-making. Principles incorporate moral views, which vary and conflict from judge to judge even as they vary and conflict in the society at large. New cases brought before the courts often implicate emerging controversies in society. At an early stage of a new controversy, legal claims may not be fully representative of all considerations relevant to their resolution, and public as well as expert attitudes have yet to form.

Therefore, judges should limit argument from principle and define decisions narrowly for two reasons: 1) principled resolution should await judicial exposure to sufficient cases to explore all considerations, and 2) public debate among legal and non-legal scholars as well as citizens should be permitted to play a role in the development of practical reasoning surrounding the broader controversy, as well as the transformation of practices relevant to it.

---

[1] Robert Alexy, *The Argument from Injustice: A Reply to Legal Positivism*, L. Bonnie and Stanley L. Paulson (trans.) (Oxford: Clarendon Press, 2002), 169–70.

OPEN AREA AND THE DOUBTFUL CASE

The notion that judges should appeal to principle in doubtful cases comes from the notion of the law having an "open texture"[2] or an "open area" as described by Robert Alexy.[3] Of special significance are the vagaries of legal language, the possibility of norm conflicts, the absence of a norm on which to base a decision, and, in certain cases, the possibility of making a decision even contrary to the literal reading of a norm. One can speak here of an 'open area' of the positive law, which may be more or less broad, but which exists in every legal system.

A case that falls within the open area shall be called the 'doubtful case.'[4] Alexy notes that the classical positivist position is that "since only the positive law is law, the judge must decide in the open area, that is, in all doubtful cases, on the basis of non-legal or extra-legal standards. Accordingly, he is empowered by the positive law to create new law essentially as a legislator does, on the basis of extra-legal standards." Alexy favors a non-positivist view, that law includes principles, and therefore all doubtful cases may be resolved by appeal to principle.

Alexy in the above passage recognizes four different types of doubt or uncertainty: vagaries of legal language, norm conflicts, absence of a controlling norm, or even the possibility of a case in which the facts run contrary to a literal reading of the relevant norm. This chapter will focus in particular on the middle two categories, absence or conflict of controlling norms. In the first of these two categories, absence of a controlling norm, this may involve a case that fits nowhere because of the comprehensive novelty of circumstance, having been utterly unanticipated by the existing system of statute and prior decision.

The case could be an anomaly, of a type never to be seen again. Or it could be what the common law has traditionally called a "case of first impression," which can mean the first of a new type, the result of innovation in business or technology, yet unregulated by statute, or even the result of an emergent social controversy over a human right such as equality or privacy. In such a case, the argument against principal is that (1) the particular dispute between two parties may be less than fully representative of the "principles" that may in due course be recognized as applicable, and (2) the activities surrounding the controversy or innovation are still in a state of transition toward an eventual reconciliation of conflicting purposes, such that legal principles should not yet be formulated and fixed.

---

[2] Hart, *Concept of Law*, 120.
[3] Alexy, *Argument from Injustice*, 69–70.
[4] Alexy, *Argument from Injustice*, 69.

Principles in the law derive strength from prior particularized decisions. In their formulation, the first function of courts is to conduct what has been called a process of classification: The initial formulation of legal precepts, whether in the sense of "rules" ("(rule-) principles") or of principles proper, involves essentially a process of classification of instances for similar treatment. So does the process of refinement which then sets limits to a precept, extends the precept, or subjects it to some clustering of sub-precepts.[5]

Alexy has addressed the reason for the necessity of this process, reinforcing the need for classification: The basic reason for following precedents is the principle of universalizability, the requirement that we treat like cases alike, which lies behind justice as a formal quality. This immediately reveals one of the decisive difficulties of following precedent: no two cases are ever completely identical. It is always possible to find a difference. The actual problem thus shifts to one of determining which differences are relevant.[6] In many doubtful cases, this classification process cannot be done immediately by synchronic analysis, where the courts have insufficient or unrepresentative exposure to the conditions relevant to formulating a rule by practical reasoning.

We can conceive of new cases arising from technological innovations in digital communication, medicine and biology, the growth and diversity of governmental and non-governmental institutions, changing population demographics, and the prolongation of life expectancy despite states of illness, pain, and morbidity. Difficult questions arise, like When does life begin and end? What is personal autonomy and invasion of privacy? When is medical treatment criminally responsible for the death of a suffering and morbid patient? Arguments from principle are often framed in such terms as "Is there a right to die?" In cases raising doubtful questions of legal rights and duties in a newly controversial area, it is generally the case that practices affecting those rights are unsettled and inchoate, and opinions regarding appropriate practices are unsettled as well.

Legal claims, and legal outcomes, may in fact serve to focus on relevant practices and, over time, to encourage their refinement and transformation. In early litigation it is not necessary or typical for preliminary legal outcomes to prescribe practices. It is characteristic that they focus attention on them. The varying practices involving particular drugs and precautions, specific legal permissions, and designated medical and administrative procedures are

---

[5] Julius Stone, *Precedent and Law: Dynamics of Common Law Growth* (Sydney and Melbourne: Butterworths, 1985), 269.

[6] Alexy, *A Theory of Legal Argumentation: the Theory of Rational Discourse as Theory of Legal Justification*. Neil MacCormick (trans.) (Cambridge, MA and Oxford: Oxford University Press, 1989), 275.

influenced by the attention focused by litigation. Meanwhile, opinions and attitudes are affected by the nature of the very cases made public through litigation.

A voluminous literature of educated and expert opinion is part of the opinion-making process. Public and expert opinion affects, and is affected by, the refinement of practices. In effect, there is a feedback loop in which, as the name suggests, information about the result of an action is sent back to the input of the system, transforming the very nature of language about and understanding of the system. Argument from rights and principles reflects moral opinion concerning practices. Argument from a "right to die" is least effectively advocated when there exists little information concerning relevant circumstances of medically assisted suicide. The phrase was barely familiar before the recent transformation of medical care and longevity. It is most effectively advocated when fully understood, and when specific precautions have been taken to address the general arguments surrounding it.

Similarly, judicial decisions at an early phase are typically fact-specific. Before the transformation, the phrase "right to die" evoked individual suicide; medical assistance in drastic instances was obliged to overcome traditional attitudes. According to Alexy the analytical model supposes that all doubtful cases should have been decided according to principle. Cass Sunstein in *One Case at a Time: Judicial Minimalism on the Supreme Court* has characterized the "right to die" as a "new dilemma," and applauds the fact that the US Supreme Court has yet refrained from a broadly defined resolution: It is particularly important that the issue of physician assisted suicide is facing not neglect or indifference but intense discussion in many states. It is far too early for courts to preempt those processes of discussion, certainly if we consider the fact that there is no systematic barrier to a fair hearing from any affected group.[7]

Despite appearances, the Court's current doctrines reflect this point.[8] Narrowly reasoned decisions have focused attention on the development and refinement of practices. Principles that reflected traditional attitudes would have failed to contribute useful practical reasoning to the feedback loop, and would have truncated the "intense discussions" favored by Sunstein. (I should note that state and local legislation is part of this feedback, representing democratic participation even while not finally resolving the constitutional issues.)

Does this mean that the doubtful area is not "open" in the sense in which Alexy has described it? I have suggested that if this area is open, it is not univocally open, with all openness of a uniform quality, since different legal

---

[7] Sunstein, *One Case at a Time*, 76–116.
[8] Sunstein, *One Case at a Time*, 77.

controversies are in different stages of classification and resolution at any one time. Thus, at the very least, different degrees of generality of reasoning are appropriate for different stages of judicial inquiry.

Moreover, when the open area is viewed in the context of other influences in the feedback loop, it is not purely an open area in the law alone, but it is open also with regard to extra-legal opinion, practices, and understanding. The analytical model of immediate reference to principles in all doubtful cases is inconsistent with the project of judicial classification, and it ignores the operation of a feedback loop influenced by non-legal knowledge and opinion. It assumes that legal principles are already available for reference, whereas their form and language are ultimately dependent on the path through which the larger controversy is understood and resolved.

CONFLICT OF PRINCIPLES AND "BALANCING"

Alexy writes that principles, as optimizing rather than definitive commands, must be balanced by a judge in a case where they conflict. [T]he argument from principles is based on the distinction between rules and principles. Rules are norms that, upon satisfaction of the conditions specified therein, prescribe a definitive legal consequence, that is, upon satisfaction of certain conditions, they definitively command, forbid, or permit something, or definitively confer power to some end or another. For simplicity's sake, they may be called 'definitive commands'. The characteristic form of their application is subsumption.

By contrast, principles are optimizing commands. As such, they are norms commanding that something be realized to the greatest possible extent relative to the factual and legal possibilities at hand. This means that principles can be realized to varying degrees and that the commanded extent of their realization is dependent on not only factual potential but also legal potential. The legal possibilities for realizing a principle, besides being determined by rules, are essentially determined by competing principles, implying that principles can be balanced against one another. The characteristic form for applying principles is the balancing of one against the other (2002: 70). Alexy follows both Dworkin (1977) and Hart (1994, Postscript) in the view that where rules run out, judges appeal to principle. But, he appears more skeptical than Dworkin that principles are dispositive regarding outcome.[9]

How can a judge resolve a case by balancing? We may view the controversy over medically assisted death as one in which two powerful norms

---

[9] Alexy, *Argument from Injustice*; Dworkin, *Taking Rights Seriously*; and Hart, *Concept of Law*, Postscript.

conflict, the right of autonomy and privacy versus the prohibition against homicide. The metaphor of a balance suggests that cases of medically assisted death arrive somewhere along a scale of varying distance from one extreme or the other. Where medical assistance is minimal, like prescribing a drug that is used in violation of medical instruction, autonomy wins. If the patient is unsure or confused and improper medical intervention results in death, the prohibition of homicide wins.

Alexy recognizes that what may appear to be judicial balancing is subject to competing interpretations, and he has addressed the question: A criterion for whether or not the judge appeals to principles for support is whether or not he undertakes to strike a balance. The following proposition seems to be true: in undertaking to strike a balance, one necessarily appeals to principles for support. For it is necessary to strike a balance precisely when there are competing reasons, each of which is by itself a good reason for a decision and only fails to lead directly to a definitive decision because of the other reason, calling for another decision; reasons like this are either principles or supported by principles.[10] Principles, it would appear from this passage, are to be identified as a relevant norm that a judge gives as a reason that is not definitive. In his article "On the Structure of Legal Principles," Alexy specifies that, in a particular case of the collision of principles (for example whether a trial may proceed where the accused is in danger of stroke or heart failure), "the court solves the problem by determining a conditional priority of one of the colliding principles over the other with respect to the circumstances of the case."[11] In the foregoing account of the formation of legal principles regarding medically assisted death, context is critical. Context is also time-variant, and it is changing with attitudes, practices, and technology.

Strictly speaking, competing principles are not in collision but in transformation; traditional ones are inapplicable due to the novelty of circumstances, and a new principle must be found by experimental engagement of the law with the relevant community. Neither the metaphor of a scale, nor the inference of balancing from the appearance of indefinite reasons, accurately portrays what takes place as judges draw on facts to decide cases. Balancing is a static metaphor, in which *a priori* principles are available by immediate reference and operate through immediate balancing. To draw on these as generals in a novel case is an abuse of argument from principle. When new data is forthcoming, through the constant but contingent flow of cases, framing and reframing the arguments on which legal principles are based, principles must be seen as yet undetermined, and the process must leave ample room for extra-legal input and influence in the path of reformulation.

---

[10] Alexy, *Argument from Injustice*, 72.
[11] Alexy, *Argument from Injustice*, 296.

CONCLUSION

Can the balancing analogy be reconciled with this account of legal principles? Can the analytical argument from principle be broadened to include the interaction between legal argument and decision with the developing extra-legal context? The issue depends upon whether the analytical model can be adapted to incorporate a time-sensitive and two-way interactive process.

Analytical jurisprudence has been dominated by the question whether law is separate from morals: The central problem in the debate surrounding the concept of law is the relationship of law and morality. Notwithstanding a discussion that reaches back more than two millennia, there remain two basic, competing positions—the positivistic and the non-positivistic.[12] This has contributed a powerful conceptual and linguistic bias to analytical legal theory in favor of a concept of law with a definitive boundary—whether that boundary includes morals or not.

The search for an intrinsic relation has led to the intensive focus on specification of the a priori conceptual contents of law. This in turn has obscured the interaction of legal principles with society at large, their path-dependency, and their time-contingency. Analytical method is committed by its conceptual-linguistic tradition to analysis and specification of legal boundary and content. The analytical model cannot be adapted to incorporate a time-sensitive and two-way interactive process because to do so would require not merely breaking down but dismantling and abandoning all static conceptual partitions. No account of weighing or balancing principles by a boundary-and-content analysis of specific considerations can assimilate the fundamental role of interactive experience in formulating legal principles.[13]

Analytical jurisprudence since Thomas Hobbes has drawn on a model of law as autonomous, exogenous, acting on and controlling society. The alternative model suggested here is endogenous, embedded, reflecting and modifying society as part of a broader process of social ordering.[14] The alternative model implies a view of rights and principles under constructivist rather than deontological assumptions, associated with a communitarian perspective,[15] emphasizing the accumulation by society of self-knowledge in its adjustment to new experience.

---

[12] Alexy, *Argument from Injustice*, 3.
[13] I claim that no interpretation of Alexy's account of proportional balancing and his factors of appropriateness and necessity is consistent with the gradual interactive process explicated here, and that to restate the argument sufficiently to incorporate it would require abandoning the analytical model. However, the theory of principles in the law has a long and complex history, as does the competition between analytical and historical jurisprudence. I am reminded by comments of Claudio Michelon, Francisco Saffie, and Neil Walker that it would be unwise to suggest that there exists an unbridgeable gap between them.
[14] Postema, *Bentham and the Common Law Tradition*, 314.
[15] Sandel, *Liberalism and the Limits of Justice*, 135.

Part IV

THE FUTURE OF LEGAL PRAGMATISM

Where does legal pragmatism lead, and what is its value to the world? The preceding chapters have emphasized its value as a ground opposing ideology and subjectivity in the courts, against the human tendency, identified 350 years ago by Francis Bacon, to over-rely on previously settled "axioms," while avoiding confrontation with what Holmes called the "difficulty and responsibility" of addressing novel legal problems in their emergent complexity. The primary value of legal pragmatism, in this account, is a revival and rehabilitation of the inductive Baconian empirical tradition. Holmes saw law as a critical component of the human solution of social problems, maintaining order and avoiding violence through the engagement of "many minds" in the resolution of disputes and the convergence of opposing precedents.

This interpretation of legal pragmatism is particularly valuable in light of the dramatic growth of legal jurisdiction over new controversies in the United States through the due process clause of the United States Constitution. With the Bill of Rights acting as a virtual net, collecting an increasing diversity of controversies, Holmes's pragmatism is uniquely designed to keep the judicial role as separate as possible from that of the legislative and executive branches. Litigation may sort out problems piecemeal, but it should not be invited to impose overall solutions axiomatically and prematurely.

There is a broader dimension to this when we consider the *international* growth of constitutional adjudication. Over twenty-five years ago, Tate and Vallinder wrote in *The Global Expansion of Judicial Power* (1995):

> In Europe, French and German legislators and executives now routinely alter policies in response to, or in anticipation of, the pronouncements of constitutional courts. In Latin America and Africa, courts are—or will be—important participants in ongoing efforts to protect new or fragile democracies from the

threats of military intervention, ethnic conflict, and revolution. This global expansion of judicial power, or "judicialization of politics," is accompanied by quasi-judicial procedures. For better or worse, the judicialization of politics has become one of the most significant trends of the end of the millennium.

This development has been accompanied by references to "pragmatism" as a case-specific consequentialism, thereby giving international constitutionalism a "functionalist" cast. But this comes at a cost: if legal pragmatism is viewed as primarily instrumental rather than exploratory, closer to Posner than to Holmes, it is placing constitutional courts more directly in confrontation with policymakers, putting judges at odds with legislators and administrators in their role as ultimate problem solvers, subjecting judges to political criticism, and potentially undermining popular faith in a politically neutral judiciary.

Holmes's restrained view of the judicial role provides a foundation for greater cooperation in a republic of divided powers, as well as broad non-judicial participation in the working out of solutions, thereby reducing the political dimension of judicial activity. It also, as noted, yields a unitary theory of legal logic, replacing the dualism of formalism and realism. These are advantages that I have tried to illuminate in the preceding chapters of Parts I through III.

A question that was asked at the outset is: How does legal pragmatism illuminate pragmatism in general? Fallibilism, for Joseph Margolis, is "the true nerve of Peirce's entire output," but the literature, he writes, is "remarkably slack—baffled, really—for all the attention it's received through the 150 years in which Peirce's grand output has been dissected." This is not the place to address that literature. Rather, we should examine the ground of Holmes's inductive logic, focusing on the social dimension of the continuum of logical inquiry, and how it may inform theories of ethics and normative knowledge.

The core meaning of fallibilism is fundamentally incompatible with the dominant analytical position that the law "runs out," that valid legal authority has a boundary beyond which present legal knowledge does not reach, thus creating the tension between formalism and realism, the "dream" and the "nightmare," the strict separation of law and morals, and Ronald Dworkin's adroit argument that judges should resort to moral principles when they perceive a lacuna in the written law. Holmes's social induction raises challenging new questions regarding pragmatism in general, as it bears on ethical theory and practice. The term "fallibilism" alone may be insufficient to uncover these questions, such as regarding the sources of falsification and how they are addressed.

The final chapter explores new territory. Chapter 11 examines social induction as a further advance on the prior, but little recognized or understood, association of pragmatism with the sociology of knowledge, with law as a source of normative knowledge.

Chapter 11

American Pragmatism and European Social Theory

TOWARD A SOCIOLOGY OF LEGAL KNOWLEDGE

The founder of sociology of knowledge was Karl Mannheim. He defined it as follows in 1933:

> The principal thesis of the sociology of knowledge is that there are modes of thought which cannot be adequately understood as long as their social origins are obscured. . . . It is not men in general who think, or even isolated individuals who do the thinking, but men in groups who have developed a particular style of thought in an endless series of responses to certain typical situations characterizing their common problem. . . . Men living in groups do not merely coexist physically as discrete individuals. They do not confront the world from the abstract levels of a contemplating mind as such, nor do they do so exclusively as solitary beings. On the contrary they act with and against one another in diversely organized groups, and while doing so they think with and against each other.[1]

In this chapter, I compare Holmes's developmental theory, set forth in early essays and *The Common Law*, with the European sociologists Scheler and Emile Durkheim. Unlike Durkheim, Holmes did not hold that categories of thought reflect features of group organization and social solidarity. The nature and modes of legal classification emerge against a historical background from resolution of conflicts among disparate interests. Holmes's model is more skeptical of progress than Scheler's but accepts a role for meliorative intelligence in revising embedded habits and paradigms.

---

[1] Mannheim, *Ideology and Utopia*, 2–4.

Kenneth Stikkers has illuminated the convergence between Max Scheler's phenomenological sociology and a central theme of nineteenth-century American pragmatism: their joint break from both Platonic and Aristotelian philosophy through the insight that knowledge neither precedes our experience of things (ideae ante res), as in Platonic idealism, nor follows from experience in an empirical correspondence with an objective world, the Aristotelian model (ideae post res). Scheler followed American pragmatism's insight that knowledge resides in concrete human acts (ideae cum rebus), where it becomes functionalized. Chicago pragmatists, in turn, recognized the importance of Scheler's pioneering statement of the "sociology of knowledge," and its commonality with pragmatism's emphasis on community inquiry.[2]

Two features stand out in the functional model that are hidden by the classical Platonic and Aristotelean approaches: the dynamic and changing nature of knowledge and its products, and their intimate connection with human conduct and experience. Both of these are obscured by synchronic tendencies of analytical theory, and have been brought to light within specific realms of inquiry, as in contemporary science studies, where a burgeoning but controversial "sociology of scientific knowledge" has emerged in the wake of Kuhn's *Structure of Scientific Revolutions.*[3]

Stikkers recounts the influence of the pragmatist William James on the German scholars Wilhelm Jerusalem and Max Scheler, and notes that Charles Peirce had already suggested, prior to Dilthey and Durkheim and without any apparent benefit from the insights of Marx, that the forms of human knowing are fundamentally forms of social life, without reducing the latter to the forms of economic life. This radically naturalist insight became central to early writings in the sociology of knowledge and has influenced post-Kuhnian science studies.

What about law, if indeed it can be seen as another form of community inquiry? Given the convergence of American pragmatism and this strain of European social theory, it should not be surprising to find something comparable to a sociology of legal knowledge in the work of pragmatism's classical legal theorist, Oliver Wendell Holmes Jr. Pragmatism grew out of the Metaphysical Club, and it is well known that half of the original members of the Metaphysical Club were lawyers. Bruce Kuklick and others have recounted the common influences on all the members of the Club such that we might expect parallels in the conception of law.[4]

---

[2] Kenneth Stikkers, "Dialogue Between Pragmatism and Constructivism in Historical Perspective," in L. Hickman, S. Neubert, and K. Reich (eds.), *John Dewey Between Pragmatism and Constructivism* (New York, NY: Fordham University Press, 2009), 80–82.

[3] See generally Barnes et al., *Scientific Knowledge.*

[4] Bruce Kuklick, *The Rise of American Philosophy* (New Haven, CT: Yale University Press, 1977).

THE UNLIKELY COMPARISON OF
HOLMES AND DURKHEIM

In 1899, two years before the publication of Emile Durkheim and Marcel Mauss's *Primitive Classification*, Oliver Wendell Holmes Jr. made the following comment in an address later published as "Law in Science and Science in Law":

> It is perfectly proper to regard and study the law simply as a great anthropological document. It is proper to resort to it to discover what ideals of society have been strong enough to reach that final form of expression, or what have been the changes in dominant ideals from century to century. It is proper to study it as an exercise in the morphology and transformation of human ideas.[5]

This extraordinary passage, emphasizing "morphology" over the dominance of fixed analytical and conceptual theories of law, reflects research twenty-five years earlier, in the period 1873–1876, when Holmes turned from an earlier influential version of analytical jurisprudence (the *Lectures in Jurisprudence* of John Austin) to writings on legal history, anthropology and primitive culture, to consolidate a theory of legal transformation. In an 1876 essay "Primitive Notions in Modern Law,"[6] Holmes observed that many of the rights and duties recognized in Anglo-American law were "survivals" of "the primitive notion, that liability attached directly to the thing doing the damage."

Moreover, "the various considerations of policy which are not infrequently supposed to have established these doctrines, have, in fact, been invented at a later period to account for what was already there—a process familiar to all students of history." He would go on to apply this insight to an account of case-by-case "growth" of legal liability, eventually extending it to all areas of law. Thereafter, he drew on this transformational scheme for insights into developing legal doctrine throughout his influential judicial career.[7]

In comparison, Durkheim and Mauss asked, in *Primitive Classification*, the more general question, "[W]hat leads men to classify?" For them it seemed that the answer lay in the most rudimentary forms of organization in the development of society. They concluded that "[T]he first logical categories were social categories; the first classes of things were classes of men, into which these things were integrated. It was because men were grouped, and thought of themselves in the form of groups, that in their ideas they grouped other things,

---

[5] Holmes, "Law in Science and Science in Law," *Collected Works*, 3:407.
[6] Holmes, "Primitive Notions in Modern Law," *Collected Works*, 3:4.
[7] Holmes, "Primitive Notions in Modern Law," *Collected Works*, 3:5; Kellogg, *Holmes, Legal Theory and Judicial Restraint*, 118–56.

and in the beginning the two modes of grouping were merged to the point of being indistinct." "Thus the history of scientific classification is, in the last analysis, the history of the stages by which this element of social affectivity has progressively weakened, leaving more and more room for the reflective thought of individuals. But it is not the case that these remote influences which we have just studied have ceased to be felt today. They have left behind them an effect which survives and which is always present; in it is the very cadre of all classification, it is the ensemble of mental habits by virtue of which we conceive things and facts in the form of co-ordinated or hierarchized groups."[8]

While for the past century the intellectual legacies of Holmes and Durkheim have occupied separate academic worlds, both drew a similar demarcation between what they saw as a primitive "affective" stage of civilization and a modern "rational" stage, while insisting on the continuing influence of the former upon the latter, itself incrementally transformed by increasingly "reflective" intelligence. Thus, there are common elements in both: transformational change with surviving vestigial elements, suffusing logical method and undermining logical essentialism, the bedrock of analytical thinking. For both, a community- or society-focused historical process is at the root of the existence and management of ordered conceptions. For both also, the ongoing role of classification in human intelligence is a fundamental concern.

The main difference is that Durkheim and Mauss set out to discover the origins of human classification in general, finding them in social structure and the evolving nature of solidarity, while Holmes's interest was drawn to its operation in Anglo-American law. In that sense, Holmes began his study of legal classification *in medias res*, focusing on his own nineteenth-century context. Having in 1869 taken over the editorship and revision of the principal American legal encyclopedia, *Kent's Commentaries on American Law*, he equipped himself to compare the varieties of developing legal doctrine with the recent and influential analytical system of John Austin's *Lectures in Jurisprudence*, published in London in 1861.

The *Lectures* first came to his attention as he left Harvard College to join the Union Army at the onset of the American Civil War. His focus on Austin continued after returning to Cambridge in 1864, where he attended Harvard Law School, engaged in philosophical discussions with his peers, became the editor of *Kent's Commentaries*, and wrote critical and formative essays for the American Law Review. By 1876–1877, he had been drawn into the examination of legal history and early culture and institutions, "to prove the historical truth of a general result, arrived at analytically . . . five years ago."[9] That result

---

[8] Emile Durkheim and Marcel Mauss. *Primitive Classification* (Chicago, IL: University of Chicago Press, 1963), 82–83, 88.

[9] Holmes, "Primitive Notions in Modern Law," *Collected Works*, 3:21.

involved a reconsideration of the Austinian project of universal classification and it is intimately connected with his famous opening line in *The Common Law*: "the life of the law has not been logic, it has been experience." This turning point is fundamental to understanding his thought and career.

From introductory courses on jurisprudence, American law students are still familiar with Austin's famous command definition of law. Less familiar is the detailed character of Austin's *Lectures*, embodying an attempt to establish a universal arrangement of law, which he outlined as a system of rights. Holmes first explored this thesis by advancing an alternative system based on the concept of duty. An intensive comparison of categories with cases, extending over several years, eventually led to rejection both of Austin's command definition and his logical arrangement of law as a system of rights, and indeed of any universal analytical scheme. This highlighted the question—prompted by his observations of the continuing influence of historical anomalies—of how the ordered hierarchies of legal classification and their manifestation in a structured system are arrived at. Looking at the process of change within the existing system, and in the context of a course taught to Harvard undergraduates, Holmes characterized his own definition of law as "prediction" of judicial decisions.[10]

After his general study of classification with Mauss, Durkheim would later move more specifically to law. In *The Division of Labor in Society* (1933), he hypothesized an evolution of diminishing reliance on criminal in favor of civil forms of legal liability and procedure, and interpreted this as supporting the thesis of transformation from "mechanical" to "organic" social solidarity. Durkheim now distinguished criminal and civil liability as reflecting distinct forms of social solidarity. Holmes, immersed in the case-law of his revision of *Kent's Commentaries*, would instead bring the two forms together in a uniform theory of criminal and civil liability.

Holmes would characterize historical change (he avoided the term "evolution") as having universally transformed standards of legal liability from "moral" to "external," intending by these terms to highlight the gradual de-emphasis of an element of subjective blame rooted in primitive revenge. Equally important, he saw the actual process of transformation—and here lies his insight into the cumulative mechanism of legal classification—rooted in the response of legal institutions to ongoing social conflict. It would inform both his thought and later judicial practice.

The legal sociologist Roger Cotterrell has illuminated the continuing influence of Durkheim on socio-legal studies and social theory in general.[11] We might compare this to the relative lack of influence, or even interest, in

---

[10] Holmes, "Book Notice," *Collected Works*, 1:295.
[11] Roger Cotterrell, *Emile Durkheim: Justice, Morality and Politics* (Farnham: Ashgate, 2010).

Holmes's transformational theory. Over the years since his death Holmes has rarely been mentioned among accounts of socio-legal theory or legal sociology. He is missing from Peter Stein's overview of *Theories of Legal Evolution: the Story of an Idea* , as well as from Alan Watson's *The Evolution of Law* and Norbert Rouland's, *Legal Anthropology*. While his theory of liability qualifies as a contribution to legal anthropology, it is not recognized as such.

This has obscured the contemporary relevance of Holmes's 1899 comment on the law as "a great anthropological document," worthy of study "as an exercise in the morphology and transformation of human ideas." The remark suggests that, with Durkheim, he saw the development of law as illuminating basic moral concerns. His recognition of a deep influence of conflict, and the survivals of a primitive past, puts a somewhat darker cast on the prospects of society than the visions of his contemporaries Peirce and James. While he is considerably less optimistic than Durkheim about reform, he came to recognize a place for meliorative intelligence in the common law that would gain favorable interest from John Dewey.[12]

You may see elements of a Darwinized Hegel in Holmes's approach to rulemaking, influenced perhaps by another member of the Club (and his only admitted mentor) Chauncey Wright, who in 1873 published an influential essay "The Evolution of Self-Consciousness," written at the encouragement of no less than Charles Darwin himself. Holmes appears to have absorbed Wright's attitude, and he took it in a different direction, toward the development of legal intelligence, as part of a socialized ordering process. And now we can sense what he implied in defining law as prediction of what courts will do. Law is not an already-set system of rules with a preexisting answer for every new case. It is a constantly developing system of classification, influenced by multiple communities of inquiry.

Do rules of law still emerge from meandering patterns of individual judgments, as Holmes suggested 140 years ago, or is everything handled by legislation and administrative rulemaking? How about a new problem like assisted suicide? This class of dispute started out as a series of criminal prosecutions of doctors for murder, until the opposing claim of patient autonomy got some traction, from constitutional language, applied to changing medical circumstances. The problem soon found its way to the appellate courts. In *One Case at a Time: Judicial Minimalism on the Supreme Court* (1999) Cass Sunstein cautioned the same thing as Holmes did in 1870: it is often premature to lay down a sweeping general rule. Ultimately, we may need legislation, but even that cannot come too soon, before the exploratory stage, which includes a

---

[12] John Dewey, *Experience and Nature* (New York, NY: Dover 1956), 417–18.

process of feedback and adjustment from non-lawyers. Legislation is itself a stage in the process of inquiry.[13]

An implication of this is to qualify the classical model of democratic social choice, famously criticized by Kenneth Arrow. Social choice through law is ongoing outside the electoral cycle, for good or ill, in the process of conflict resolution, influenced by feedback from relevant communities. As with assisted suicide, each successive decision may respond to feedback from diverse communities of interest, including medical, legal, and academic professionals, senior citizens, lobbying groups, and so on. Decisions are also influenced by social adjustment and the adoption of new practices, from medical procedures to living wills.

What are the key elements here? 1. We are looking at legal cases not singly, as raising an isolated question of existing law against a synchronic analytical background, but as stages of inquiry into social problems, and against a diachronic background. 2. Notwithstanding the role of "great judges," the guiding intelligence is not individual but social—hence it implies a socialized epistemology of legal rules and concepts. 3. Inquiry itself is generated not solely by pure dispassionate analysis, but also by the urgency of conflict and the need for resolution; the legal "conversation" is messier than any ideal model of dialogue. 4. Inquiry takes place in a context of preexisting generals to which legal institutions look back even while plotting new cases in relation to them. 5. The judicial role of comparing and contrasting can be viewed as an incremental and cumulative line-drawing, influenced by many factors over time. 6. Judges are members of a community of inquiry, but acting within a network of other communities, both expert and lay. 7. The interaction between disparate communities operates during the line-drawing process as a "feedback loop" from judicial decisions to their effects, which feeds new experience into the judicial system.

CONTEMPORARY SCIENCE STUDIES

These elements outline a view of law, albeit one drawn from Anglo-American experience, as both a process of social inquiry and a specialized system of classification. A comparable view of the development of natural science has become increasingly evident since the appearance in 1962 of Thomas Kuhn's

---

[13] Sunstein, *One Case at a Time*. Statutes too are the work of many minds, in elected bodies. Diverse circumstances are explored all at once, in legislative committees, instead of seriatim through litigation. Unclear circumstances remain, to be addressed in a case-specific manner by the judiciary, if not through legislative amendment. See, e.g., Roscoe Pound, *The Spirit of the Common Law* (Boston, MA: Beacon Press, 1921), 174; Edward H. Levi, *An Introduction to Legal Reasoning* (Chicago, IL: Chicago University Press, 1949), 27.

Structure of Scientific Revolutions—although Ludwik Fleck's *Genesis and Development of a Scientific Fact* had already offered such a view in 1935. In their book *Scientific Knowledge: A Sociological Analysis* (1996), leading representatives of the "Edinburgh School" of science studies outline an approach to contemporary science as another specialized, moving system of classification.[14] Scientific research responds to social problems; its major figures draw more heavily on research traditions than on brilliant insights; it often involves conflicts among separate research traditions, and seemingly incommensurable principles, like the notions of particle versus flux in electricity; experiments can be seen as exercises in classification; and scientific theorists are members of a professional community of inquiry, acting within a network of other communities, both expert and lay.

These observations concerning common law method, comparing early writings of Holmes with themes of Emile Durkheim, and touching on recent studies of science, may seem far afield from Max Scheler's wide-ranging interests and speculations. Nevertheless, they may be useful in filling out the notion of "functionalized knowledge," which characterized both classical pragmatism and Scheler's phenomenological sociology. It is in the exploration and comparison of concrete studies in disparate fields that any promise of a unified sociology of knowledge may lie.[15]

What precisely does it mean to speak of a sociology of knowledge, and hence of a sociology of legal knowledge? The phrase has a different emphasis from the much discussed sociology of law or (more generally) of "sociolegal" studies. Whereas the latter generally refer to diverse social science perspectives directed to the subject of law, whether as institution, system, practice, or history,[16] the former would appear directed more toward the social component of the knowledge element, cognate with a similar study of knowledge in general. While the literature of socio-legal studies is vast and

---

[14] Barnes et al., *Scientific Knowledge*, 46–80.

[15] Hasok Chang, *Is Water H₂O: Evidence, Realism and Pluralism* (Dordrecht: Springer, 2012), 15: "[P]hilosophical analyses of science have been unduly limited by the common habit of viewing science as a collection of propositions, focusing on the truth value of those propositions and the logical relationships between them. The premier subject of discussion in philosophy of science has been theories as organized bodies of propositions. This has led to the neglect of experimentation and other non-verbal and non-propositional dimensions of science in philosophical analyses. Many historians, sociologists and philosophers have pointed out this problem, but so far no clear alternative philosophical framework has been agreed-upon to provide a language for fuller analyses of scientific practice. A serious study of scientific practice must be concerned with what it is that we actually *do* in scientific work. This requires a change of focus from propositions to actions . . . all scientific work, including pure theorizing, consists of actions—physical, mental, and "paper-and-pencil" operations . . . all verbal descriptions we make of scientific work must be put into propositions, but we must avoid the mistake of only paying attention to the propositional aspects of the scientific actions.

[16] Michael Freeman, *Law and Sociology: Current Legal Issues*, vol. 8 (Oxford: Oxford University Press, 2006).

much of it relevant to this topic, there is surprisingly little specific discussion of a sociology of legal knowledge.[17]

There is, however, a considerable literature on the general sociology of knowledge. While its first formulations are Scheler's, its main influence may be owed to Karl Mannheim, in particular his *Ideology and Utopia* (1929), which was translated into English in 1936 and found its way into American university curricula.[18] Scheler's work on the subject, in particular his essay "Probleme einer Soziologie des Wissens," or "Problems of a Sociology of Knowledge," was not translated until 1980, by Manfred A. Frings. Both of these works in German were pioneering ventures into the subject, and both were highly speculative, especially compared to Holmes, who of course did not consider his own research to be within any such field, as it had not yet been defined.

That speculative nature caused problems of understanding on both sides of the Atlantic, which remain today. Critics interpreted both Scheler and Mannheim as advancing a radical form of deflationary anti-foundationalism, reducing all thought to its social origins, regardless of a constraining world. Mannheim had cautiously defined the field as follows: "The principle thesis of the sociology of knowledge is that there are modes of thought which cannot be adequately understood as long as their social origins are obscured." In fairness to him, the relevance of social origins made but a modest demand on the already developing naturalism of western philosophy, already begun with Hume, Kant, and Hegel.[19]

In the years following World War I, Western philosophy sought a renewal of secure and even triumphant foundations in its turn toward rigorous reductive analysis. Analytical philosophy came to dominate American academia even as strains of "postmodernism" seeped in from Continental sources. The late resurgence of pragmatism in this context transformed the environment. Drawing on W.V. Quine and Donald Davidson, Richard Rorty made pragmatism fashionable among analytical philosophers, welcoming rigorous analysis into themes explored by James and Dewey, reconciling them with postmodern anti-foundationalism. The early emphasis on fallibilism, with its tentative, social, and experimental aspects, has been downplayed. Pragmatism's post-Rorty renewal has scattered it in several directions, such that discussion of a historic mission or essential insight may be impossible.

---

[17] While there are texts that may bear on the subject, the phrase itself is rarely used. See e.g. Duncan Kennedy, "A Semiotics of Legal Argument," in *Academy of European Law*, Collected Courses of the Academy of European Law (ed.) (Netherlands: Kluwer Academic Publishers, 1994), vol. III, Book 2, 309, 322; Mariana Valverde, *Law's Dream of a Common Knowledge* (Princeton, NJ: Princeton University Press, 2003).

[18] Mannheim, *Ideology and Utopia*, 2.

[19] Stikkers, "Dialogue Between Pragmatism and Constructivism," 67.

The widest gulf would seem to be that between the analytical neopragmatism now carried forward by Robert Brandom and others influenced by Rorty, and the historicist, fallibilist tradition emergent from Peirce, James, and Dewey, the non-analytical strain that influenced Scheler. This essay brings Holmes under that retrospective umbrella, and points toward a connection with recent empirical and historical studies in the sociology of scientific knowledge.

For this purpose, Kenneth Stikkers's account of the early association of Scheler with American pragmatism, in the published proceedings of a conference on pragmatism and constructivism, is a welcome contribution. Stikkers had previously published an introduction to Frings's translation in 1980 of Scheler's "Probleme einer Soziologie des Wissens." There, Scheler outlines its relation to a range of topics, including science, religion, politics, international relations, and other speculative themes of his phenomenological sociology.[20] Writings of the early pragmatists provided Scheler with an important resource for his systematic understanding of the post-war period of crisis and its global relevance. He credited pragmatism with disclosing the fundamental practical basis of knowledge and offering the first genuinely novel alternative to rationalist and empiricist epistemologies.[21] Citing James, knowledge for Scheler was a function of the dynamic human creative interaction with the world; ideas do not merely report or mirror reality, but emerge within practical human engagement and in doing so transform the world.

In his opening to *Problems of a Sociology of Knowledge*, Scheler summarized the overall context:

> The following studies have a limited goal. They are an attempt to point out the unity of a sociology of knowledge as a part of the sociology of culture, and

---

[20] Kenneth Stikkers, "Introduction," in *Max Scheler, Problems of a Sociology of Knowledge*, M. A. Frings (trans.) (London: Routledge & Kegan Paul, 1980). Scheler's account bore a social orientation distinct from Husserl's eidetic phenomenology, and incorporated Scheler's intense focus on the nature and operation of shared societal values, a concern heightened by the traumatic state of Europe following the First World War and the widespread sense of cultural and intellectual crisis. Scheler's world view was informed by a sense of ideas and values worked out through conflict. He was and remains a respected visionary; Heidegger called him "the strongest philosophical force in Germany, nay, in all Europe." Stikkers, "Introduction," 3.

[21] William James, "Pragmatism," in *The Works of William James*, Frederick H. Burkhardt, et al. (ed.) (Cambridge, MA: Harvard University Press, 1975), 104–6. Through a correspondence with Wilhelm Jerusalem, the writings of William James had been introduced to Scheler in 1910. In 1908, Jerusalem published a German translation of James's *Pragmatism*, and the first mention of "sociology of knowledge" in English is apparently found in a letter from Jerusalem urging James to supplement his psychological account of cognition with a thoroughgoing sociology, and proposing to send him an essay on "Soziologie des Erkenntinis." The essay came to the attention of Scheler, who republished it in 1921 and introduced pragmatism to Germany in an essay entitled "Erkenntnis und Arbeit," published in 1926. Scheler's criticisms of pragmatism suggest either that he misunderstood original sources, or relied excessively on secondary ones. His mention of arbeit or "work" in the title reflects the popular notion of pragmatism as "what works." Stikkers, "Dialogue Between Pragmatism and Constructivism," 71–75.

above all to develop systematically the problems of such a science. . . . They attempt to bring about some systematic unity in the rhapsodic and disordered mass of problems at hand, some of which have already been taken up in detail by science and others only half met or barely suspected, problems posed by the fundamental fact of the social nature of knowledge and of its preservation and transmission, its methodical expansion and progress.

He went on to include within this outline "the relationship of the sociology of knowledge to the theory of the origin and validity of knowledge (epistemology and logic), to the genetic and psychological studies of knowledge as it evolves from brutes to man, from child to adult, from primitive to civilized man, from stage to stage within mature cultures," to "the positive history of various kinds of knowledge."[22]

Holmes, drawing on a common perspective with the early pragmatists, had already cast light on the social nature of legal inquiry, the origin of liability in revenge, and its genesis and transformation in evolving from "brutes to man." Scheler's postwar interest in the role of conflict in the emergence of values is shared in Holmes's 1899 comment, calling law a resource "to discover what ideals of society have been strong enough to reach that final form of expression, or what have been the changes in dominant ideals from century to century." While Scheler is clearly a more speculative thinker, Holmes, as a veteran of an earlier bloody conflict, came to share similar concerns from a particularist and historical focus. Having rejected a strictly analytical approach to law before writing his major work, which led directly to his judicial career, he would anticipate Scheler's focus on transformation in his 1899 comment that law provided "an exercise in the morphology and transformation of human ideas."[23]

I advance an approach toward a sociology of legal knowledge that brings the subject into a coherent relation with a general sociology of knowledge, as well as with recent studies in the sociology of scientific knowledge. In this final chapter, I have compared Holmes's evolutionary theory, set forth in *The Common Law*, with Durkheim and Scheler. Unlike Durkheim, Holmes does not hold that categories of thought reflect features of group organization and social solidarity. The nature and modes of legal classification primarily emerge against a historical background from resolution of conflicts among habitualized conduct of groups and interests, eventually giving rise to rules and principles, embodied not in pure language but also, necessarily, in general patterns of conduct. It is more particularist than Scheler, rooted in conflict resolution as informing a discrete form of dialogue. While deeply skeptical of

---

[22] Scheler, *Problems of a Sociology of Knowledge*, 33.
[23] Holmes, "Law in Science and Science in Law," *Collected Works*, 3:407.

progress, Holmes's model allows a role for emergent meliorative intelligence in revising vestigial habits and overcoming established paradigms.

Transformation is a key theme to which I have alluded throughout this chapter. Transformation is the element in human experience to which both Holmes and Durkheim looked in their studies of law. It is the attribute of human experience, which, to sheer analysis of concepts and language, however rigorous, remains obscured. It is an aspect of philosophy and social theory that continues to influence the traditions of pragmatism and the sociology of knowledge, even while both have made it an essential focus of their own self-understanding; that is, the two traditions have seen their own guiding perspectives reflexively, as themselves subject to transformative experience.

Bibliography

Alexy, Robert. 1989. *A Theory of Legal Argumentation: The Theory of Rational Discourse as Theory of Legal Justification*. Trans. Neil MacCormick. Cambridge, MA and Oxford: Oxford University Press.

———. 2000. "On the Structure of Legal Principles." *Ratio Juris*, vol. 13, no. 3 (September), 294–305.

———. 1989. *The Argument from Injustice*. Trans. L. Bonnie & Stanley L. Paulson. Oxford: Clarendon Press.

Altman, Andrew. 1986. "Legal Realism, Critical Legal Studies, and Dworkin." *Philosophy and Public Affairs*, vol. 15, no. 3, 205–235.

———. 1990. *Critical Legal Studies: A Liberal Critique*. Princeton, NJ: Princeton University Press.

Austin, John. 1873 [1861]. *Lectures in Jurisprudence or the Philosophy or the Philosophy of Positive Law*, 3d ed. London: John Murray.

Bacon, Francis. 1994. *Novum Organum*. Trans. Peter Urbach. Chicago, IL: Open Court.

Barnes, Barry, David Bloor & John Henry. 1996. *Scientific Knowledge: A Sociological Analysis*. Chicago, IL: Chicago University Press.

Bentham, Jeremy. (1948) [1823]. *An Introduction to the Principles of Morals and Legislation*. Oxford: Oxford University Press.

Bernstein, Richard. 1987. "One Step Forward, Two Steps Backward: Richard Rorty on Liberal Democracy and Philosophy." *Political Theory*, vol. 15, 538.

Bernstein, R., ed. 1960. *On Experience, Nature, and Freedom*. Indianapolis, IN: Bobbs-Merrill Co.

Bork, Robert. 1990. *The Tempting of America: The Political Seduction of the Law*. New York, NY: The Free Press.

Bowen, Francis. 1864. *A Treatise on Logic*. Cambridge, MA: Sever & Francis.

Brandom, Robert. 2008. *Between Saying and Doing: Towards an Analytic Pragmatism*. Oxford: Oxford University Press, 2008.

————. 2011. *Perspectives on Pragmatism: Classical, Recent, and Contemporary.* Cambridge, MA and London: Harvard University Press.

Cairns, John. 2003. "Legal Theory." In *Cambridge Companion to the Scottish Enlightenment.* Cambridge: Cambridge University Press.

Calabresi, Guido. 1982. *A Common Law for the Age of Statutes.* Cambridge, MA: Harvard University Press.

Chang, Hasok. 2012. *Is Water H$_2$O: Evidence, Realism and Pluralism.* Dordrecht: Springer.

Cotterrell, Roger. 2010. *Emile Durkheim: Justice, Morality and Politics.* Farnham: Ashgate.

Dewey, John. 1938. *Logic: the Theory of Inquiry.* New York, NY: Henry Holt & Co.

————. 1956. *Experience and Nature.* New York, NY: Dover.

————. 1988. *Later Works,* vol. 14. Carbondale, IL: Southern Illinois University Press.

Durkheim, Emile. 1933. *The Division of Labor in Society.* New York, NY and London: The Free Press.

———— & Marcel Mauss. 1963. *Primitive Classification.* Chicago, IL: University of Chicago Press.

Dworkin, Ronald. 1977. *Taking Rights Seriously.* Cambridge, MA: Harvard University Press.

————. 1986. *Law's Empire.* Cambridge, MA and London: The Belknap Press.

————. 2006. *Justice in Robes.* Cambridge, MA: Belknap Press.

————. 2011. *Justice for Hedgehogs.* Cambridge, MA and London: The Belknap Press.

Edmond, Gary and David Mercer. 1998. "Representing the Sociology of Scientific Knowledge and Law." *Science Communication,* vol. 19, no. 4, 307–327.

Endicott, Timothy A. O. 2000. *Vagueness in Law.* Oxford: Oxford University Press.

Fisch, Max. 1984. "Introduction." In *Writings of Charles S. Peirce: A Chronological Edition,* 1867–1871, vol. 2. Indiana University Press.

————. 1942. "Justice Holmes, The Prediction Theory of Law, and Pragmatism." *Journal of Philosophy,* vol. 39, 85.

————. 1964. "Was there a Metaphysical Club in Cambridge?" In *Studies in the Philosophy of Charles Sanders Peirce.* Amherst, MA: U. Massachusetts Press.

Flower, Elizabeth & Murray Murphey. 1977. *A History of Philosophy in America.* New York, NY: Capricorn.

Freeman, Michael. 2006. *Law and Sociology: Current Legal Issues,* vol. 8. Oxford: Oxford University Press.

Freund, Paul. 1968. *On Law and Justice.* Cambridge, MA: Harvard University Press.

Fuller, Steve. 2002. *Social Epistemology.* Bloomington, IN and Indianapolis, IN: Indiana University Press.

Garrett, Don. 2015. *Hume.* London and New York, NY: Routledge.

Gilmore, Grant. 1974. *The Death of Contract.* Columbus, OH: Ohio State University Press.

Goodman, Nelson. 1972. "Seven Strictures on Similarity." In *Problems and Prospects*. New York, NY and Indianapolis, IN: Bobbs-Merrill.

Graham, Hubbs & Douglas Lind, eds. 2014. *Pragmatism Law and Language*. New York, NY and London: Routledge.

Grey, Thomas C. 1989. "Holmes and Legal Pragmatism." *Stanford Law Review*, vol. 41, 787.

———. 1984. "The Constitution as Scripture," *Stanford Law Review* I, vol. 37, 5.

———. 2003. *Judicial Review and Legal Pragmatism*. Wake Forest Law Review Association.

Haack, Susan. 1978. *Philosophy of Logics*. Cambridge: Cambridge University Press.

Haakonssen, Knud. 1981. *The Science of a Legislator: The Natural Jurisprudence of David Hume and Adam Smith*. Cambridge University Press.

Habermas, Jurgen. 1996. *Between Facts and Norms: Contributions to a Discourse Theory of Law and Democracy*. Trans. William Rehg. Cambridge, MA: MIT Press.

Hale, Sir Matthew. 1921. "Reflections by the Lord Chiefe Justice Hale on Mr. Hobbes his Dialogue of the Lawe, Printed in William Holdsworth." In *A History of English Law*. London: Methuen, 1956, 499–513.

Hacking, Ian. 1983. *Representing and Intervening*. Cambridge: Cambridge University Press.

Hand, Learned. 1959. "The Spirit of Liberty." In *The Spirit of Liberty: Papers and Addresses of Learned Hand*. New York, NY: Vintage Books, 193.

Hantzis, Catherin Wells. 1988. "Legal Innovation Within the Wider Intellectual Tradition: The Pragmatism of Oliver Wendell Holmes, Jr." *Northwestern University Law Review*, vol. 82, 541.

Hart, H. L. A. 1958. "Positivism and the Separation of Law and Morals." *Harvard Law Review*, vol. 71, 593, 607.

Hart, H. L. A. 1994. *The Concept of Law*. Oxford: Clarendon Press.

Hayek, Friedrich. 1973. *Law, Legislation and Liberty*. Chicago, IL: University of Chicago Press.

Herget, James E. 1990. *American Jurisprudence 1870–1970*. Houston, TX: Rice University Press.

Herschel, John. 1840. "Whewell on Inductive Sciences, Review of the *History* and the *Philosophy*." *Quarterly Review*, vol. 68, [1841], 177–238.

Hesse, Mary. 1974. *The Structure of Scientific Inference*. London: Macmillan.

Holmes, Oliver Wendell, Jr. 1995. *The Collected Works of Justice Holmes: Complete Public Writings and Selected Opinions of Oliver Wendell Holmes*. Edited by Sheldon M. Novick. Chicago, IL and London: University of Chicago Press.

———. 1881. *The Common Law*. Boston, MA: Little Brown and Co.

Howe, Mark deW. 1957. *Justice Oliver Wendell Holmes: The Shaping Years 1841–1870*. Cambridge, MA: Harvard University Press.

———. 1961. *Holmes-Pollock Letters*. Cambridge, MA: Harvard University Press.

———, ed. 1962. *The Occasional Speeches of Justice Oliver Wendell Holmes*. Cambridge, MA: Harvard University Press.

Hume, David. 1896. *A Treatise of Human Nature*. Oxford: Clarendon Press.

Hutchinson, Allan. 1989. "The Three 'Rs': Reading/Rorty/Radically." *Harvard Law Review*, vol. 103, 555.

James, William. 1975. "Pragmatism." In *The Works of William James*. Edited by Frederick H. Burkhardt, et al. Cambridge, MA: Harvard University Press.

———. 1912. *A Pluralistic Universe*. London: Longmans, Green & Co.

Kellogg, Frederic R. 2018. *Oliver Wendell Holmes Jr. and Legal Logic*. Chicago, IL and London: Chicago University Press.

———. 2007. *Oliver Wendell Holmes Jr., Legal Theory, and Judicial Restraint*. Cambridge University Press.

———. 2011. "The Abuse of Principle: Analytical Philosophy and the Doubtful Case." *Archiv fur Rechts und Sozialphilosophie*, vol. 97, 218.

———. 1984. *The Formative Essays of Justice Holmes: The Making of an American Legal Philosophy*. Westport, CT and London: Greenwood Press.

———. 2004. "Holistic Pragmatism and Law: Morton White on Justice Oliver Wendell Holmes, with Reply by White, Holmes and Hart on Prediction and Legal Obligation." *Transactions of the Charles S. Peirce Society*, vol. 60 (Fall), 559, 569.

———. 2016. "The Snake and the Roundabout: Ethical Particularism and the Patterns of Normative Induction." *Duc in Altum Cadernos de Direito*, vol. 8, no. 16, 19.

———. 1992. "Who Owns Pragmatism?" *Journal of Speculative Philosophy*, vol. 6, 67–80.

———. 1987. "Holmes, Pragmatism, and the Deconstruction of Utilitarianism." *Transactions of the Charles S Peirce Soc'y*, vol. 23, 99, 107–109.

Kennedy, Duncan. 1994. "A Semiotics of Legal Argument." In *Academy of European Law*, Edited by Collected Courses of the Academy of European Law, vol. III, Book 2, 309. Netherlands: Kluwer Academic Publishers.

———. 1982. "Legal Education as Training for Hierarchy." In *The Politics of Law: A Progressive Critique*, Edited by D. Kairys. New York, NY: Pantheon, 47.

———. 1983. "The Political Significance of the Structure of the Law School Curriculum." *Seton Hall Law Review*, vol. 14, no. 1, 15.

Kent, Charles A. 1889. "University of Michigan Celebration Marking the Centennial of the Constitution." In *Constitutional History of the United States as Seen in the Development of American Law*. Michigan University, 333.

Kornbluth, Hilary. 1996. *Inductive Inference and its Natural Ground: An Essay in Naturalistic Epistemology*. Cambridge, MA and London: MIT Press.

Kuhn, Thomas. 1962. *The Structure of Scientific Revolutions*. Chicago, IL: Chicago University Press.

Kuklick, Bruce. 1977. *The Rise of American Philosophy*. New Haven, CT: Yale University Press.

LaPiana, W. P. 1990. "Victorian from Beacon Hill: Oliver Wendell Holmes's Early Legal Scholarship." *Columbia Law Review*, vol. 90, no. 809, 811–812.

Leiter, Brian. 1995. "Legal Indeterminacy." *Legal Theory*, vol. 1, 481–492.

Levi, Edward H. 1949. *An Introduction to Legal Reasoning*. Chicago, IL and London: Chicago University Press.

Little, Eleanor. 1954. "The Early Reading of Justice Oliver Wendell Holmes." *Harvard Library Bulletin*, vol. 8, 163.

Lyons, David. 1999. "Open Texture and the Possibility of Legal Interpretation." *Legal Philosophy*, vol. 18, no. 3, 297–309.

MacCormick, Neil. 1978. *Legal Reasoning and Legal Theory*. Oxford: Clarendon Press.

———. 2008. *Practical Reason in Law and Morality*. Oxford: Oxford University Press.

Manicas, Peter. 1971. *Logic as Philosophy*. New York, NY: Reinhold.

Mannheim, Karl. 1936. *Ideology and Utopia*. Trans. L. Wirth & E. Shils. New York, NY: Harcourt, Inc.

Margolis, Joseph. 2010. *Pragmatism's Advantage*. Stanford, CA: Stanford University Press.

———. 2012. *Pragmatism Ascendent*. Stanford, CA: Stanford University Press.

Mensch, Elizabeth. 1982. "The History of Mainstream Legal Thought." In *The Politics of Law: A Progressive Critique*. Edited by D. Kairys. Basic Books.

Mill, John Sturat. 1872 [1843]. *A System of Logic, Ratiocinative and Inductive*. London: Longmans, Green, Reader & Dyer.

Misak, Cheryl. 2013. *The American Pragmatists*. Oxford: Oxford University Press.

Monaghan, Henry. 1988. "Stare Decisis and Constitutional Adjudication." *Columbia Law Review*, vol. 88, 723.

Murphey, Murray. 2005. *C. I. Lewis: The Last Great Pragmatist*. Albany, NY: State University of New York Press.

Nagel, Thomas. 1986. *The View From Nowhere*. New York, NY and Oxford: Oxford University Press.

Nedelsky, Jennifer. 1989. "Democracy, Justice, and the Multiplicity of Voices: Alternatives to the Federalist Vision." *Northwestern University Law Review*, vol. 84, 232.

Okrent, Mark. 1988. *Heidegger's Pragmatism: Understanding, Being, and the Critique of Metaphysics*. Ithaca, NY: Cornell University Press.

Peirce, Charles. 1982. *Writings of Charles S. Peirce: A Chronological Edition, 1857–1866*. Bloomington, IN: Indiana University Press.

Pohlman, H. L. 1984. *Justice Oliver Wendell Holmes and Utilitarian Jurisprudence*. Cambridge, MA and London: Harvard University Press.

Posner, Richard. 2003. *Law, Pragmatism, and Democracy*. Cambridge, MA and London: Harvard University Press.

Postema, Gerald J. 1986. *Bentham and the Common Law Tradition*. Oxford: Clarendon Press.

Pound, Roscoe. 1921. *The Spirit of the Common Law*. Boston, MA: Beacon Press.

Putnam, Hilary. 1971. *Philosophy of Logic*. New York, NY: Harper & Row.

———. 1981. *Reason Truth and History*. Cambridge University Press.

Quine, W. V. 1970. *Philosophy of Logic*. Cambridge, MA: Harvard University Press.

———. 1976. *The Ways of Paradox and Other Essays*. Cambridge, MA: Harvard University Press.

———. 1966. *Elements of Logic*. Cambridge, MA: Harvard University Press.

———. 1960. *Word and Object*. Cambridge, MA: Harvard University Press, 125–128.

Rawls, John. 1955. "Two Concepts of Rules." *Philosophical Review*, vol. 64, no. 1, 3–32.

Rorty, Richard. 1979. *Philosophy and the Mirror of Nature*. Princeton, NJ: Princeton University Press.

———. 1982. *Consequences of Pragmatism*. Minneapolis, MN: University of Minnesota Press.

———. 1999. *Philosophy and Social Hope*. New York, NY: Penguin Books.

———. 1990. "The Banality of Pragmatism and the Poetry of Justice." *Southern California Law Review*, vol. 63, 1811–1819.

———. 1989. *Contingency, Irony and Solidarity*. Cambridge: Cambridge University Press.

———. 1987. "Thugs and Theorists: A Reply to Bernstein." *Political Theory*, vol. 15, 564.

Rouland, Norbert. 1994. *Legal Anthropology*. London: Athlone Press.

Russell, Bertrand. 1914. "Logic as the Essence of Philosophy." In *Our Knowledge of the External World*. London: Allen & Unwin, 33.

———. 1912. *Problems of Philosophy*. New York, NY: Henry Holt & Co.

Ryan, Frank X., Brian Butler & James Good, eds. 2019. *The Real Metaphysical Club*. Albany, NY: SUNY Press.

Sandel, Michael. 1982. *Liberalism and the Limits of Justice*. Cambridge: Cambridge University Press.

Scalia, Antonin. 1989. "Originalism: The Lesser Evil." *University of Cincinnati Law Review*, vol. 57, 849, 852–865.

Schauer, Frederick. 1991. *Playing by the Rules: a Philosophical Examination of Rule-Based Decision-Making in Law and Life*. Oxford: Clarendon Press.

Scheler, Max. 1980. *Problems of a Sociology of Knowledge*. Trans. M. A. Frings. London: Routledge & Kegan Paul.

Sellars, Wilfrid. 1962. "Philosophy and the Scientific Image of Man." In *Frontiers of Science and Philosophy*. Edited by Robert Colodny. Pittsburgh, PA: University of Pittsburgh Press.

Shapin, Steven & Simon Schaffer. 1985. *Leviathan and the Air-Pump: Hobbes, Boyle, and the Experimental Life*. Princeton University Press.

Singer, Joseph. 1984. "The Player and the Cards; Nihilism and Legal Theory." *The Yale Law Journal*, vol. 94, 13.

Skrupskelis, Ignas K. & Elizabeth M. Berkeley, eds. *Correspondence of William James*. Charlottesville, VA: University of Virginia Press.

Sleeper, Ralph. 1986. *The Necessity of Pragmatism: John Dewey's Conception of Philosophy*. Yale University Press.

———. 1993. "The Pragmatics of Deconstruction and the End of Metaphysics." In *Philosophy and the Reconstruction of Culture*. Edited by John J. Stuhr. Albany, NY: SUNY Press.

Snyder, Laura J. 2006. *Reforming Philosophy: A Victorian Debate on Science and Society*. Chicago, IL and London: Chicago University Press.

———. 2011. *The Philosophical Breakfast Club*. New York, NY: Broadway Books.

Solum, Lawrence B. 1987. "On the Indeterminacy Crisis: Critiquing Critical Dogma." *University of Chicago Law Review*, vol. 54, 462.

Stein, Peter. 1980. *Legal Evolution: The Story of an Idea*. Cambridge: Cambridge University Press.

Stikkers, Kenneth. 1980. "Introduction." In *Max Scheler, Problems of a Sociology of Knowledge*. Trans. M. A. Frings. London: Routledge & Kegan Paul.

———. 2009. "Dialogue Between Pragmatism and Constructivism in Historical Perspective." In *John Dewey Between Pragmatism and Constructivism*. Edited by L. Hickman, S. Neubert & K. Reich. New York, NY: Fordham University Press.

Stone, Julius. 1985. *Precedent and Law: Dynamics of Common Law Growth*. Sydney: Butterworths.

Strauss, David A. 1996, "Common Law Constitutional Interpretation." *University of Chicago Law Review*, vol. 63, 877–935.

Summers, Robert. 1982. *Instrumentalism and American Legal Theory*. Ithaca, NY: Cornell University Press.

Sunstein, Cass R. 1999. *One Case at a Time: Judicial Minimalism on the Supreme Court*. Cambridge, MA and London: Harvard University Press.

Tate, C. Neal & Torbjorn Vallinder. 1995. *The Global Expansion of Judicial Power*. New York, NY & London: NYU Press.

Tamanaha, Brian. 2014. *Beyond the Formalist-Realist Divide*. Chicago, IL: Chicago University Press.

Thayer, James B. 1893. "The Origin and Scope of the American Doctrine of Constitutional Law." *Harvard Law Review*, vol. 7, no. 129, 155–156.

Tushnet, Mark. 1988. *Red, White, and Blue: A Critical Analysis of Constitutional Law*. Cambridge, MA: Harvard University Press.

———. 1984. "Critical Legal Studies and Constitutional Law: An Essay in Deconstruction." *Stanford Law Review*, vol. 26, 625.

Unger, Roberto M. 1983. *The Critical Legal Studies Movement*. Cambridge, MA: Harvard University Press.

———. 1975. *Knowledge and Politics*. New York, NY: Macmillan.

———. 1987. *False Necessity: Anti-Necessitarian Social Theory in the Service of Radical Democracy*. Cambridge: Cambridge University Press.

———. 1976. *Law in Modern Society: Toward a Criticism of Social Theory*. New York, NY: The Free Press.

———. 1987. *Social Theory: Its Situation and Its Task*. Cambridge: Cambridge University Press.

Valverde, Mariana. 2003. *Law's Dream of a Common Knowledge*. Princeton, NJ: Princeton University Press.

Voparil, Christopher. 2011. "Rorty and Brandom: Pragmatism and the Ontological Priority of the Social." *Pragmatism Today*, vol. 2, no. 1, 133.

Waismann, Frederick. 1965. *The Principles of Linguistic Philosophy*. London: Macmillan.

Waldron, Jeremy. 2009. "Did Dworkin Ever Answer the Crits?" In *Exploring Law's Empire: The Jurisprudence of Ronald Dworkin*. Edited by Scott Hershovitz. Oxford: Oxford Scholarship Online.

Watson, Alan. 1985. *The Evolution of Law*. Baltimore, MD: Johns Hopkins University Press.

Wechsler, Herbert. 1959. "Toward Neutral Principles of Constitutional Law." *Harvard Law Review*, vol. 73, 1.

Westbrook, Robert B. 1991. *John Dewey and American Democracy* Ithaca, NY: Cornell University Press.

Whewell, William. 1837. *The History of the Inductive Sciences, from the Earliest to the Present Time*, 3 vols. London: John W. Parker.

———. 1847. *The Philosophy of the Inductive Sciences, Founded upon Their History*, 2 vols. London: John W. Parker.

White, G. Edward. 1972. "From Sociological Jurisprudence to Realism: Jurisprudence and Social Change in Early Twentieth-Century America." *Virginia Law Review*, vol. 58, 999–1028.

———. 1986. "From Realism to Critical Legal Studies: A Truncated Intellectual History." *Southwestern Law Journal*, vol. 40, 819–843.

Williamson, Timothy. 1994. *Vagueness*. London and New York, NY: Routledge.

Wiener, Philip. 1949. *Evolution and the Founders of Pragmatism*. Cambridge, MA: Harvard University Press.

Wood, Gordon. 1972. *Creation of the American Republic*. New York, NY: Norton & Co.

Wright, Chauncey. 1873. "The Evolution of Self-Consciousness." *North American Review*, vol. 116, 245–310.

———. 1865. "The Origins of Modern Science." In *The Philosophical Writings of Chauncey Wright: Representative Selections*. Edited by Edward H. Madden. New York, NY: The Liberal Arts Press, 1958, 3–10.

Index

About the Author

Frederic R. Kellogg was born in Boston, Mass., in 1942. He graduated from Harvard College in 1964 and Harvard Law School in 1968, and studied social theory at the Harvard Graduate School of Arts and Sciences under Talcott Parsons in 1968. He received the LLM in 1978 and SJD in 1983 from George Washington University. Kellogg was a state and federal prosecutor and served on the staff of US Attorney General Elliot Richardson. He resigned with the Attorney General in 1973 in the "Saturday Night Massacre," after Richardson refused an order from President Richard Nixon to fire Special Watergate Prosecutor Archibald Cox. Kellogg practiced as a criminal defense and public interest and civil rights lawyer and served in the 1980s as General Counsel of the National Endowment for the Arts. He has published four books on Justice Oliver Wendell Holmes, Jr. Kellogg taught jurisprudence as a Fulbright Scholar in Poland (1996) and Brazil (2008), and was a MacCormick Fellow at the University of Edinburgh in 2009. He is currently a Visiting Professor at the Federal University of Pernambuco in Recife, Brazil.

Kellogg was awarded an honorary doctorate in 2002 from Bridgewater State University in Bridgewater, Massachusetts.

CPSIA information can be obtained
at www.ICGtesting.com
Printed in the USA
LVHW101915290822
726885LV00003B/137